Social policy 1830–1914

Birth of Modern Britain series

General editors:

A. E. Dyson
Senior Lecturer in English Literature,
University of East Anglia

and

R. T. Shannon
Reader in English History,
University of East Anglia

Titles in the series:

Nonconformity in the nineteenth century
edited by David M. Thompson

Class and conflict in nineteenth-century England 1815–1850
edited by Patricia Hollis

The idea of the city in nineteenth-century Britain
edited by B. I. Coleman

The universities in the nineteenth century
edited by Michael Sanderson

Education and democracy
edited by A. E. Dyson and Julian Lovelock

Social policy 1830–1914
Individualism, collectivism and the origins of the Welfare State

Edited by
Eric J. Evans
Department of History
University of Lancaster

Routledge & Kegan Paul

London, Henley and Boston

First published in 1978
by Routledge & Kegan Paul Ltd
39 Store Street,
London WC1E 7DD,
Broadway House
Newtown Road,
Henley-on-Thames,
Oxon RG9 1EN and
9 Park Street,
Boston, Mass. 02108, USA
Set in Bembo by
Computacomp (UK) Ltd
Fort William, Scotland
and printed in Great Britain by
Redwood Burn Ltd, Trowbridge & Esher
© Eric J. Evans 1978

British Library Cataloguing in Publication Data

Social Policy, 1830–1914. – (Birth of modern
Britain series).
1. Great Britain – Social policy – History – Sources
I. Series.   II. Evans, Eric John
300'941   HN385   77–30330

ISBN 0 7100 8613 X
      0 7100 8626 1   Pbk

General editors' preface

The series is concerned to make the central issues and topics of the recent past 'live', in both senses of that word. We hope to appeal to students of history and literature equally, since each has much to offer, and learn from, the other. The volume editors are encouraged to select documents from the widest range of sources, and to convey the 'feel' of particular controversies when passion ran high. One problem for the modern student is hindsight: often, we fall back on over-simplified versions of history – Whig or Marxist, progressive or conservative – because we fail to imagine events as they were. We hope here to re-create situations through the passions and commitments of participants and contemporary commentators, before the outcome was known. In this way, students are encouraged to avoid both over-simplified judgments and that dull sense that whatever happened was inevitable which can so devitalize our understanding of any period's history, or its art.

We believe that this treatment of the recent past, bringing out of the sense of immediacy and conflict, is also the soundest basis for understanding the modern world. Increasingly, we realize that continuity is more striking than discontinuity: nothing could be more naive than a claim for 'modernity' which assumes that the past is 'irrelevant' or dead. It was during the age of Arnold and Gladstone, Disraeli and Tennyson, Darwin and Chamberlain that our most distinctive modern problems defined themselves – the growth of great cities and technology; the battle between individualism and collectivism; the coming of democracy, with all its implications for education, class, vocation and the ordinary expectations of living; the revolutions in travel and communication; the shifting relationships between individuals and the state. Many of the major ideas that shape our world were also born: and in the ferment of day-to-day crises and perplexities, prophetic and widely-ranging hopes and fears, we see the birth of modern Britain, the emergence of our world of today. Volume editors have been encouraged in their selection of material from contemporary sources to illuminate that density and complexity of things which is the essence of 'reality'.

In this volume Dr Evans explores what he rightly describes as the 'prime historical question of the nineteenth century': why the State adopted an increasingly interventionist stance towards society and the economy. Dr Evans's general interpretation of this process has, we believe, two great and very welcome merits. First, while accepting the reality of a 'laissez-faire' ethos influencing public life in the period up to about 1870, he stresses the countervailing existence, not least among the people most conspicuously responsible for that influence, of a most practical awareness of the problems of and the proper limits to the doctrine's application. Second, he resists the temptation to over-estimate the extent to which notions of State intervention had developed before the First World War. The result is a most judicious and finely poised reassessment of perhaps the most important and certainly the most conspicuous aspect of the birth of modern Britain.

For suggestions for further reading, see the introductions to each group of documents.

Contents

Acknowledgments

The debt which I owe to the many scholars whose specialist studies in nineteenth-century social policy have made this general collection possible will be immediately apparent to every reader. The brief bibliographies at the end of the introduction to each section must serve as inadequate thanks to most of these. In addition, many of the ideas for the organization and arrangement of the book came to me when pondering discussions and tutorials with Lancaster undergraduate and postgraduate students over the past six years. Among many, I must mention Tony Coles who has shared his extensive knowledge of the workings of social policy in Cumberland freely with me. Formal discussion and casual conversation alike with friends in the history department have stimulated my thoughts. In particular, Harold Perkin has offered valuable encouragement and advice throughout; Stephen Constantine, who has shared with me the teaching of the course which acted as a focus for my ideas, often clarified my thoughts or suggested alternative approaches. I am grateful, also, to the University of Lancaster for allowing me two terms' sabbatical leave in 1975–6, part of which was used to draw together the threads and impose some kind of order on a mass of disparate material.

I am indebted to the staffs of the many libraries and record offices visited during the preparation of this collection for prompt and efficient production of books and manuscripts. I am especially grateful to the staff of the Manchester Central Library, where much of the groundwork was done, for unfailing courtesy in the face of heavy demands.

I am fortunate, too, in the secretarial assistance I have received. Diana Dodd typed early drafts of parts of the volume with great care; Marian Jackson's assistance during the awkward later stages of editing, checking and collating has been quite invaluable and I owe her much. My wife, Christine, has shown her usual tolerance to my eccentricities when deadlines approached. This is the more appreciated since the nocturnal clacking of a typewriter offers but discordant accompaniment for her violin. I should be grateful, too, to our small children for remaining asleep during the combined onslaught.

All the above have smoothed the way and prevented much error. For that which remains I am entirely responsible.

Transcriptions of Crown-copyright records in the Public Record Office appear by permission of the Controller of H.M. Stationery Office. I am grateful to the British Library Board for permission to quote from material by Sir Charles Trevelyan and Sir Stafford Northcote. I am grateful also to the following for permission to quote from documents in their possession: the County Archivist, Cumbria County Council (material previously in the custody of the former municipal borough councils of Whitehaven and Workington), the Archivist-in-Charge at the Cumbria Record Office, Kendal (Guardians' Report on Milnthorpe Workhouse), the Archivist of Durham County Council (Diocesan inspector's report on Church Schools, Report on Sanitary Conditions in Whickham urban district and Medical Officer of Health reports for County Durham), the Archivist of Lancashire County Council (records deposited by the former Chorley borough council), the Archivist of Leeds City Council (records of the Leeds School Board), the Archivist of Leicestershire County Council (General Report on secondary schools in Leicester), the Librarian, Sheffield University Library (Mundella papers). I am grateful to Sir William Gladstone for permission to quote from *Joseph Chamberlain and the Tariff Reform Campaign*.

Hornby   E.J.E.
October 1977

Introduction

I

The history of British social policy between 1830 and 1914 is a history of
changing attitudes to the role of the State in regulating, guiding and, in a
limited sense, controlling the destinies of its people. As such it is of central
importance in understanding the predominance of government in the
1970s when more than half of the nation's wage and salary bill is met by
rate- and tax-payers. This being so, it is surprising that the subject has
until recently been rather neglected. Perhaps it is because its study lends
itself to the proliferation of unhelpful and confusing 'isms'; possibly
administrative, political, social and economic historians have kept too
rigidly to their own patches and hindered the emergence of a unified view.
At all events, too many students regard the subject as 'difficult' and, given
the chance, skip it altogether in search of topics from the essay list between
Peel and the Parliament Act which seem to reveal themselves more readily.
This is a shame, since it leaves them ill-prepared to consider arguably the
prime historical question of the nineteenth century: why did the State
adopt increasingly interventionist positions in society and the economy? I
hope that the ensuing collection of documents and attendant commentary
will provide some of the raw material from which that question may be
answered.

I have chosen to divide the book into three sections, the titles of which
indicate that I believe that the growth of government shows an emphasis
on certain themes at certain times. Since this is controversial, and in
particular since it conflicts with the simplified organic model which
suggests that government, like Topsy, 'just growed', I had better state at
the outset that I do not believe these themes to be mutually exclusive.
Though I believe, in a qualified sense, that there was an age of *laissez-faire*
between *c.* 1830 and *c.* 1870, it does not mean that important and
influential people, like Gladstone, stopped believing in the last quarter of
the nineteenth century that people did best when they were left to manage

their own affairs. Nor do I believe, though I have said that collectivism became 'viable' between *c.* 1870 and *c.* 1895, that the State began to dominate people's lives in this period. In fact, the State remained extremely reluctant to tell people what to do, and was only just coming to terms with the need to instruct them what they should not do. Similarly, though I believe that there were indeed 'birth pangs of welfarism' between *c.* 1895 and 1914, it does not follow that these were the critical years which witnessed the emergence of the Welfare State. Initiatives which we can now see as crucial were taken, in feeding school children, in providing pensions for the aged and in compulsory insurance against sickness, but the emergence of a Welfare State was by no means inevitable by 1914. Further battles had to be waged and no one should underestimate the importance of the scars left by the long years of inter-war depression, particularly in the north of England, south Wales and central Scotland.

I am aware, in short, that the categorizations I have chosen may seem schematic. Certainly they require qualification in order that violence may not be done to the complexity of the historical process which changes men's minds and makes them receptive to concepts which were anathema to their fathers. My justification is that historians must needs generalize and extrapolate if they are to bring order from the chaos of otherwise random historical facts. I stick by mine only because they seem to me to impose a certain rationality on the many ramifications of social policy; it is for others to judge whether they are found a help or a hindrance.

II

I have said that I believe that there was an 'age of *laissez-faire*' in the middle of the nineteenth century. I also believe that, even in its heyday, *laissez-faire* was being 'tempered' by revelations about the seamier side of industrial Britain and by philosophers and writers who drew certain conclusions about these revelations. In any case, the *laissez-faire* concept has to be defined and qualified to be of any value. The classical economists, supposedly uncritical purveyors of *laissez-faire* ideas, knew well enough that the very term is misleading. J. R. McCulloch might be thought to have put it devastatingly enough in 1848 to deter incautious writers:[1]

> The principle of laissez-faire may be safely trusted to in some things but in many more it is wholly inapplicable; and to appeal to it on all occasions savours more of the policy of a parrot than of a statesman or a philosopher.

Laissez-faire defined as the complete absence of interference under all circumstances was never sensibly contemplated. Adam Smith did indeed believe that the free play of market forces promoted a natural harmony of interests which worked to the greater good of mankind but he envisaged an important residual role for the State quite apart from the provision of external security. David Ricardo, who took a much less sanguine view of the effects of competition while still maintaining that wages should be left to find their proper level in the free market, found room for State intervention in his chapter 'The Condition of the People' in *Principles of Political Economy and Taxation*. Similar examples of recognition that the State has an important role can be found in J.R. McCulloch, Nassau Senior, John Stuart Mill or any notable classical economist. Lionel Robbins, indeed, identified them in his lucid study *Theory of Economic Policy in English Political Economy* (1952). No one, after reading that work, can sensibly maintain that the classical economists believed in total *laissez-faire*. Their popularizers, a Harriet Martineau, say, or a Samuel Smiles, might seem to suggest that they did, but the economists themselves were both too cautious and too realistic.

Why, then, does this misleading label continue to stick more than twenty years after Robbins re-interpreted the economic scriptures and more than a generation after sober scholars began to reveal all in expert exegeses of the writings of Smith, Bentham, McCulloch *et al.* ? Why can so distinguished a historian as Eric Hobsbawm, for example, still assert in a widely used textbook that 'By the middle of the nineteenth century government policy in Britain came as near laissez-faire as has ever been practicable in a modern state' ?[2] It is not (at least not in this instance) that he needs to postulate doctrines of pure competition in order to identify and nail the baddies who ground the faces of the poor while preparing the way for the revelation of the internal contradictions of capitalism in the next generation. There is a less sinister, if more mundane, explanation. *Laissez-faire* did not mean the same thing to all men. The classical economists themselves dismissed the notion of what might be termed 'fundamentalist *laissez-faire*'—that the great clockmaker in the sky winds up economy and society together, sets them in motion, and sits benevolently back while the great organism ticks and whirrs harmoniously for ever in self-winding and ever-profitable motion. But does the collapse of this fanciful image vitiate the entire concept of *laissez-faire*? By no means. It remains possible to argue the viability of *laissez-faire* in those who believed that clock would require minor, if necessary, adjustments or it would not function properly, and might stop altogether. Or, abandoning the metaphor, a government which believed passionately in permitting individuals, institutions and enterprises to follow their own business unfettered, nevertheless accepted an ultimate responsibility to interfere in order to ensure the same freedom for others to pursue their interests in the same way. This responsibility derived more from Ricardo's view of the world of free competition than Smith's, but it was hardly the more interventionist for that. The intervention was grudging, minimal, and on offer only when a water-tight case in favour had been presented. Political economists and governments saw intervention as an evil, but they were realistic enough to concede that some evils were inevitable in order to avert the yet greater evils of monopoly, anarchy or the thousand other natural shocks which a totally unregulated economy was heir to.

The rejection of the *laissez-faire* of the lunatic asylum seems to me uncertain grounds for the rejection, properly defined, of an age of *laissez-faire*. In the middle of the nineteenth century, governments believed that State interference with, for example, wage or profit levels, hours of labour, or the autonomy of local administration was to be countenanced as a last resort only. They perforce rejected fundamentalist *laissez-faire*, but fully accepted the obligation to intervene only so far as was necessary to ensure the fairest and fullest operation of the free market economy.

Every undergraduate knows that the 1830s and 1840s saw very significant examples of State intervention. The poor laws were dismantled, and rationalized under central supervision. Factories were subject for the first time to government inspection. Chadwick and others revealed the close links between industrial squalor, disease and early death, and a general Board of Health was established to supervise the problem. The State began to make available moneys to advance the education of the lower orders of society. There are other examples, but these will suffice to show why some historians, notably David Roberts in *Victorian Origins of the Welfare State* (1960), saw this as the decisive period for the emergence of a collectivist State. Some contemporaries saw it in the same way. The young Herbert Spencer, in two philippics, *The Proper Sphere of Government* (1843) and *Social Statics* (1851), inveighed against the growth of government which, he believed, would produce first inefficiency and then tyranny. *The Times*, usually throughout its long and frequently undistinguished history an opponent of new ideas, denounced the Poor Law Commission in 1847 as 'novel and dangerous ... with the arm of a policeman, the tongue of a beadle, the bearing of a hangman, and the bowels of a gaoler'.

It is not sufficient, however, to infer from the obvious fact of government intervention the invalidity of the entire concept of *laissez-faire*. The nature and purpose of the interventions are critical. Between *c*. 1830 and certainly 1860, but probably 1870, governments intervened only in order, as they saw it, to regulate. At no point did they envisage the State having a positive role to play. Governments saw themselves as freeing the market to operate for the greater good of all, as Adam Smith had argued it would. During this period, also, the final trappings of a regulated, mercantilist economy were swept away. The corn laws were surrendered by the landed interest in 1846, opening the way for free trade in foodstuffs achieved in stages up to 1874. The seventeenth-century Navigation Acts, long evaded, followed in 1849, and colonial preference in the 1850s. The world was exposed to the full force of British trading competition. The irony was that Britain's early industrial revolution gave her in the 1850s and 1860s effectively not a free trade, but a monopolistic position, since she could decisively undercut competitors in most fields. This was hardly what Smith had in mind in 1776, but arguably only in this period did Britain actually benefit from her vaunted free trade position.

In foreign trade, *laissez-faire* was undoubtedly the order of the day. With the orotundities of Gladstonian free-trade rhetoric ringing in their ears, it is perhaps not surprising that some historians have suggested that governments before 1870 pursued consistently *laissez-faire* policies in economic matters, while abandoning them, however cautiously, in social policy. This is essentially the position of Arthur Taylor in his valuable general pamphlet *Laissez-faire and State Intervention in Nineteenth-Century Britain* (1972). There is some attraction in this. It does at least enable scholars to preserve the trappings of an age of *laissez-faire*, while shirking the knotty and ambivalent problem of social policy. On close examination, however, I do not believe that it stands up. First, there was intervention in economic affairs. Patent laws regulated the diffusion of new ideas; governments exercised large potential rights over railways after 1844; the Bank Act of 1858 and the Limited Liability Act of 1862 offered some protection to the innocent, or not so innocent, victims of *laissez-faire* trading. On a rather deeper level, this explanation assumes that the categories 'social' and 'economic' are mutually exclusive. This is not so. State intervention through an inspectorate in factories presumably interferes with a labour force essential to the economy at the same time as it protects children and women from the grosser forms of entrepreneurial exploitation. Also, by the 1860s, the State was dictating methods of production in one industry. The Alkali Act of 1863, passed at the behest of powerful property owners like the Earl of Derby, ensured that manufacturers of chemical soda should condense the hydrochloric acid gases which had been destroying vegetation and harming livestock in the vicinity of the factories. It would be unfair not to mention also, however, that some manufacturers had already realized that condensed hydrochloric acid was a marketable commodity. The ready availability of a profitable industrial by-product was a not inconsiderable factor in persuading the legislature that intervention could be countenanced.

In fact it seems neither possible nor necessary to divorce economic from social matters in order to maintain the viability of an age of *laissez-faire*. If we define *laissez-faire* as the belief that government intervention can achieve little positive good, and should be reserved to ensure the elimination of abuses which hinder the free market then I would argue that governments did pursue *laissez-faire* policies in both social and economic fields. The intervention itself was limited and diffident. Whatever the fears of *The Times*, the centralized poor law commissioners recoiled from the task of enforcing a national policy for poor relief. They were not permitted to compel Unions to erect workhouses, thus making impossible the abolition of outdoor relief — the *bête noire* of Edwin Chadwick and Nassau Senior. Parliament voted ever larger sums to Church schools after the initial £20,000 grant in 1833. By 1861 it was contributing £800,000. From 1839 it inspected the work of schools and teachers so supported; but in this period it recoiled from the obligation to provide State schools. British education was a partially State-supported private enterprise, heavily dependent, it is true, on the established Church; but the responsibilities of the State did not extend beyond ensuring that it got value for money. Schools which received no State aid could continue largely unmolested to provide superb education, or none.

Nor was the primacy of local interests seriously challenged by central government. It was not until the Public Health Act of 1872 that local authorities were compelled to appoint medical officers of health. The roll of honour of those cities which had not previously thought such an appointment necessary includes (to name only the largest) Sheffield, Newcastle and—nice irony—Joseph Chamberlain's Birmingham. In that year, 150 infants of every 1,000 died in England and Wales before reaching their first birthday. In some northern towns, almost 1 in 4 died. In 1842, the year of publication of Chadwick's famous *Sanitary Report*, the national figure had been 152. The overall death rate per 1,000 in 1842 had been 21·7. In 1872 it stood at 21·3. A generation of largely localized initiatives had precious little effect on the most sensitive indicator of all. After thirty years of more compulsory activity the rate in 1902 stood at 16·3.

The industrial revolution, while massively increasing economic growth, created social problems which could not remain unregulated. There was an implicit threat to the established order in an untamed and largely irreligious population freed from the fetters which operated more or less efficiently under the aegis of squire and parson in an eighteenth-century English village. Industrialization created its own imperatives, and some degree of intervention by the State was quite unavoidable. This intervention, however, was usually in a permissive or advisory capacity. Local authorities were told what they might do, rarely what they must. Individuals and institutions were encouraged to act, but only rarely did the State accept that it must take the lead if they would not. Above all, the nature of such intervention as was offered suggests that governments believed in the total efficacy only of the free market and self-help. State control diminished individual initiative, and could lead to progressive deterioration and ultimate collapse. As the health of the nation depended on the vigour of its commerce, any interference which put these at risk was to be avoided. The concept of an age of *laissez-faire* thus depends as much upon attitude as it does upon action. In part, this concept derives from the reverence with which the philosophy of self-help was received, and the almost equal helpings of obloquy and neglect accorded to those who could not or would not help themselves. In part it rests on the primacy of the commercial and entrepreneurial ethic. The world was deemed to lie open to those who could use their talents to make their way in the race of life. It was not part of the duties of the State to act as handicapper, or to provide the aid which would enable a larger proportion of the population to compete on equal terms. Indeed, since the winners were those who contributed most to Britain's industrial supremacy, there was every incentive to place as few obstacles in their way as possible.

By 1870, therefore, the role of government was still generally seen as safeguarding society against greater evils. Its task was not to promote good in its own right. The political economists, inspectors and civil servants had not yet moved beyond this essentially negative view of State intervention. Their reports provided only an ever-growing set of instances in which the State should taken an interest to meet the exigencies of the moment. Emphatically, these were not designed to undermine the principle of *laissez-faire*. It is not that governments did nothing; it is that, given the facts as they stood revealed by a formidable army of fact-grubbers in government offices, statistical societies and elsewhere, they still did so little. For this reason, I find it difficult to accept Dr Kitson Clark's view: 'I do not myself think the conception of a "period of *laissez-faire*" is helpful.'[3] Suitably qualified, I think it both helpful and important in understanding mid-Victorian society.

It is useful at this point to consider Harold Perkin's valuable seven-stage model of development of collectivism.[4] The thrust of his argument is different from mine, but the model may be used to indicate the extent to which the State was interfering in a period I have suggested can be described as one of *laissez-faire*. As we shall see, three of his stages were common before 1870, two more were available in a specialized and restricted sense. The other two were not provided.

The first stage involved intervention to prevent nuisances or dangers—in factories, mines and elsewhere. The preferred interventionist method, by Benthamites like Chadwick and Senior, and adapted by others was the State inspectorate. This form of intervention usually resulted in the State's establishing a larger supervisory bureaucracy than was originally envisaged, as inspectors found out more and suggested amending legislation to close previously unsuspected loopholes. Second, the State insisted on certain conditions: for example, children employed in textile mills being provided with at least two hours' education each working day. In the third stage, the State provided financial support for preferred, though privately provided, enterprises. The grants for education in Church schools from 1833 are the best example of this. In education, also, the State moved rapidly to the fourth stage: direct State provision of a necessary service to the majority of the population. The 1870 Education Act was designed to fill the gaps in voluntary provision. Compulsory education was not laid down until 1880, and not made free until 1891. The fifth stage—public provision of a given service to the entire population—was provided in a restricted sense by local authorities who made street lighting and perhaps gas lamps available via the public purse. The logical development of such provisions—Chamberlainite gas and water socialism—however, properly awaits the last quarter of the nineteenth century. The sixth stage is State monopoly of essential services. The Post Office was a State monopoly, but one dating back to the seventeenth century, and the age of mercantilism. By the end of the nineteenth century, the State controlled telegraph and telephone services. The full weight of State monopoly in other forms of communication, fuel and power and rail transport, of course, was reserved for the twentieth century. The final stage, 'clause four socialism' we might call it, nationalization of the means of production, distribution and exchange, was neither in prospect nor contemplated in 1870. Even by 1900, the socialist thrust, dominated as it was by middle-class Fabians, had been much more in terms of stages five and six—municipal socialism and limited State monopolies—than in terms of nationalizing viable private industries.

Perkin uses his model to suggest not an antithesis but a continuum between individualism and collectivism. At one level, this comes close to MacDonagh's famous organic model of government growth—that nineteenth-century government grew naturally under the ineluctable pressure of facts. The strength of Perkin's argument, it seems to me, lies in the early stages of his model. Individualism (or *laissez-faire*) and these forms of collectivism, if such they be, could and did happily co-exist. They were positively desired by political economists and the more active civil servants of the period. But these stages—inspection, limited conditions and a certain financial support—are perfectly compatible with an overall supremacy of *laissez-faire*. They act as subordinate areas of collective interference, necessary to preserve the viability of *laissez-faire*.

As Perkin himself notes, stages four to seven, and particularly stage seven, represent much bigger steps than stages one to three. He draws attention to this very point in order to debunk Dicey's alarmist and unhistorical notion that any collectivist initiative inevitably leads by stages to socialist perdition. In fact, there was little travel beyond stage three until the last quarter of the nineteenth century, and almost none to stage seven even then, except in the restricted sense of land nationalization, which ironically was to prove in the twentieth century the most unyielding and intractable nationalization problem of all. The final three stages of the Perkin model postulate State intervention of a kind incompatible with an age of *laissez-faire*. The State necessarily and properly provides services, justified on their own level and integral to the efficient performance of the economy. At the very point before 1870 where the State's role transfers from an essentially negative, ring-holding function to a positive one, its adherents are far fewer and the State's interventions minimal. In this sense, though Perkin sees individualism versus collectivism as a false antithesis, it seems proper to look for the advent of an age of collectivism between 1870 and 1914.

One relevant indicator of the restricted nature of government intervention is State expenditure on interventionist activity. Horace Mann pointed out in 1869 that estimates for the civil service establishment had risen from £3·7m in 1848 to £11·8m in 1858 and £15·2m in 1868.[5] This growth, however, was hardly as dramatic as these figures suggest at first sight. In 1869 the government's gross expenditure totalled £75·5m. Of this a mere £1·59m (2·1 per cent) was spent on salaries and other running costs of public departments. £13,000 sufficed for the public health department, £12,500 for the factory inspectorate, £10,500 for the inspectorate of mines, £3,300 for the alkali works inspectorate, £2,400 for that of prisons and, somewhat surprisingly in such paltry company, £2,000 for the inspectorate of lime juice. There was little in these figures to suggest the onward march of a rampant and uncontrollable bureaucracy such as that *The Times* or observers like J. Toulmin Smith suggested had come into being.[6]

In truth, what might be called 'interventionist expenditure' formed a tiny fraction of government outgoings. In 1869, a year of peace, £26·9m was spent on the army and navy, while only £3·92 (5·19 per cent of the total) was spent on works and buildings, expenses of public departments, education, art and science combined. The implication of these figures is clear enough. Expenditure on what might in the widest sense be called health and welfare schemes was still overwhelmingly left to local and individual initiatives. The central government did not impose a heavy burden on the tax-payer for these services. It was in fact still in 1870 able to adhere to Gladstonian principles of finance—low total expenditure, and as small a proportion of government income as possible to be provided by direct taxation. In 1869, income tax was levied at 6d in the £ (itself quite a high rate for the time—3d, 4d and 5d was more common) and brought in no more than 12·15 per cent of the total government income of £70·8m. Customs and excise, by contrast, provided 60·8 per cent. Expenditure on interventionist or quasi-welfare schemes disturbed this pattern not at all.

III

If 'an age of *laissez-faire*' is accepted as appropriate to the period *c*. 1830–*c*.1870, it is necessary to inquire how governments came to accept an increasingly interventionist position at the end of the nineteenth century.

There is no tidy answer to the question. Those who argue for an organic or self-generated pattern of government growth can place a deal of evidence on their side. Without entering an essentially sterile debate, it seems clear that the process by which government inspectors and civil services were led to propose ever-increasing State intervention affected both those who had drunk deep from the pools of Benthamite philosophy and those who had not. But it was in public health, which attracted both Benthamites and non-Benthamites to its service, that this process first crossed the critical borderline from permission to compulsion. In this area the savage imperatives of squalid conditions and immensely high mortality required the most drastic solutions.

Sir John Simon, as Medical Officer of the committee of the Privy Council on Health, reported in 1865 that the fruits of his experience had led him to submit 'that the time has arrived when it ought not to be discretional in a place whether that place shall be kept filthy or not.... The language of the law besides making it a *power*, should name it also a *duty* to proceed for the removal of nuisances to which attention is drawn.' The sequel was the Sanitary Act of 1866. Undoubtedly helped by the panic created by the cholera outbreak of 1865–6, Simon was able to persuade first a Whig then a minority Tory government of the desirability of imposing uniform powers and responsibilities on local health authorities. As the *Lancet* observed, 'The pith of this enactment consists in the *compulsory powers* which it creates.' Further feedback was necessary in the light of experience, but the 1875 Public Health Act which eventually resulted, and which is the better remembered of the two enactments, enshrined no new principle. The 1866 Act had dictated that, if necessary, the parsimony and recalcitrance of local rate-payers must be overborne by wider and greater interests. It was the central tenet of Simon's faith, and it opened the way to a redefinition of the role of the State *vis-à-vis* its citizens.

The principle of compulsion was quickly extended into another area of public health—vaccination. Free, public schemes for vaccination against smallpox, operated through local Boards of Guardians, had been available since 1841. Because of the dilatoriness of many Boards and the undeniable taint of pauperism which accompanied vaccination applications in some areas, however, the system was very far from universal, and in the middle of the nineteenth century, deaths from smallpox usually exceeded 5,000 per annum. Once more, the officials of the Medical Department pressed for greater powers to ensure uniformity of treatment. By the 1867 Vaccination Act—another of Simon's works—all children up to the age of fourteen became liable for vaccination. Boards of Guardians were permitted to appoint vaccination officials who could enforce vaccination in the area of their jurisdiction on pain of fines or even imprisonment. The final link in the chain of compulsion was forged in 1871 when the appointment of a salaried vaccination officer became obligatory on all Boards of Guardians. He could check all cases, and prosecute defaulting parents. From 1871 to 1898, Britain became a country of compulsory vaccination, and the scourge of smallpox was all but eliminated.

By the beginning of the 1870s, then, a decisive breach in the dyke of individual self-reliance and local self-government had been made. This is not to say, however, that it automatically ended the age of *laissez-faire* and bid welcome to an age of collectivism. It was one thing to admit that the State should compel minimum standards of public health, quite another to argue that it was the State's task to ensure minimum standards of maintenance for people in old age, provide adequate housing to replace the disease-ridden and overcrowded slums which littered large cities, educate the youth of the nation in State schools, or provide the means of support for temporarily unemployed workers. In the public health case, the limitations place on individual freedom were at worst ambivalent. In these others, State initiatives would inevitably impede or supersede private enterprise and the free play of market forces. In addition, they posited a role for the State as provider of positive good rather than as preventer of greater evil. Acceptance that any or all of these duties were the legitimate concern of the State surely vitiated the *laissez-faire* ideal as we have defined it. Yet each of them was seriously debated in the period 1870–1914 and in all of them developments took place which involved an extension of State responsibilities which would have been inconceivable in the mid-nineteenth century.

The operation of 'feedback', important though it was in extending State responsibilities, was by no means the only route by which the compulsory borderline could be crossed. In the last quarter of the nineteenth century, the massive pillars which had supported *laissez-faire* were severely shaken by economic and social crises and they began to crumble. As they did so, the too-easy assumptions which had supported the pillars were radically questioned and were seen to be largely untenable. Chief among these assumptions were: first, that the competitive ethic produced only losers whose failings were their own responsibility, and thus the duty of society to rectify only in a charitable or moral sense; second, that this ethic was the philosopher's stone which automatically guaranteed continued and ever-increasing prosperity; and third, that the government's role comprised nothing more than ensuring the availability of conditions of perfect competition.

The spate of first-hand studies of poverty between 1870 and 1901 did much to dislodge the notion that lack of means presupposed moral failings. Ironically, it was the Charity Organization Society which brought the scale of the problem to light in the 1870s. Under the able but inflexible Secretaryship of C. S. Loch, it was imbued with a strong sense both of moral purpose and of its own superiority, and it developed a fairly sophisticated system of case-work which pointed strongly—though its protagonists were unwilling to follow the directions—towards the inadequacy of private benefaction, however well organized. Quantification emerged in the next decade with Charles Booth's famous and pioneer *Life and Labour of the People in London*. His fieldwork in the East End first appeared in the *Journal of the Royal Statistical Society* in 1887 and it revealed that no fewer than 35 per cent of the population there, from those with small but inadequate regular earnings down to those whom Booth called 'the lowest class of occasional labourers', lived 'in poverty, or even in want'. Booth's findings were more or less confirmed by Seebohm Rowntree's study of York (1901), which revealed that 28 per cent of his survey fell below his standard of income necessary for the maintenance of physical health. Together, these surveys had a major influence in changing the direction of social policy. The efficacy of the old poor law, localized, in many places inefficient, and everywhere well-hated by the recipients of its doles, was called into question. In particular, it was felt necessary to separate the honest but impecunious from the idle, the profligate and those whom the Victorians liked to call 'the dangerous classes'. In itself this involved a clear recognition that the old conjunction of want with moral failings would no longer do.

Perhaps the greatest factor in the decline of *laissez-faire* was what historians used to call 'The Great Depression'. It is not necessary here to enter the debate about the nature of the Great Depression. Its relevance lies not in whether there was one, which is dubious, but whether contemporaries felt there was one, which is certain. Victorian businessmen were alarmed by the fairly rapid fall in prices, and decline in the rate of growth at the end of the nineteenth century. Above all, there was universal concern over the slump in profitability. Overseas competition was cutting into British markets previously considered safe. The success of E. E. Williams's *Made in Germany* (1896), which concentrated on British inability to meet the challenge of the newer industrial nations, was symbolic of a general unease. We may see the situation, as Professor McCloskey does,[7] as the inevitable consequence of competition in industrial society when other nations with greater natural resources caught up with Britain; and, particularly in the climate of the mid-1970s, we may wonder what the fuss was all about. We should not, however, underestimate the soul-searching it occasioned the Victorian middle class. In particular it had a dampening effect on free-trade philosophy. The easy equation of abolishing tariffs and increasing profits was coming unstuck. After all, Germany and the USA, Britain's keenest competitors, had never established the same degree of free trade. *Laissez-faire* was not to be overturned in an instant, of course. The old slogans retained their emotive power, as Joseph Chamberlain and the Tories were to find in the election of 1906, but the purity of the concept was greatly sullied by the experience of the last quarter of the nineteenth century.

The revelation that *laissez-faire* was no automatic guarantee of economic prosperity had implications for the role of the State. Perhaps, after all, governments could do more than just hold the economic ring. When the case was sufficiently strong governments might intervene; and the 1880s produced large numbers of strong cases in the fields of poverty and unemployment during a period of grave economic uncertainty. The economist Alfred Marshall, no revolutionary agitator, talking in his *Principles of Economics* of the dangers of unrestrained economic freedom, and D. G. Ritchie, the Oxford philosopher, spelled out the implications for State intervention in 1891 by looking at the problem from the viewpoint of the waste generated by *laissez-faire*.[8]

From the 1880s also, political leaders were indicating a new role for the State. Joseph Chamberlain's Radical Programme of 1885 promised State intervention on a wide front and redistributive taxation to pay for the welfare reforms deemed necessary 'to remove the excessive inequalities in the social condition of the people'. The 'eternal laws of supply and demand' and 'the sanctity of every private right in property' were castigated in a speech in Warrington the same year as 'the convenient cant of selfish wealth'. Politicians of other persuasions were anxious not to be left behind. The Marquis of Salisbury had prudently noted in 1884 that 'there are no absolute truths or principles in politics',[9] and the Conservative Party pursued policies of pragmatic intervention in the 1880s and 1890s in land reform, in enabling free elementary education to come about and in securing compulsory compensation for accidents sustained by employees at work. W. E. Gladstone grudgingly acknowledged in 1889 that 'there are things which the Government ought to do and does not do.'[10]

Of course, the potentially massive forces of the State were not girded for action at the end of the century purely because of economic crisis, nor yet because of the persuasive powers of empirical social scientists with a formidable dossier of case studies of the casualties of the free-enterprise system. Politicians were not unaware of the need to appease a mass electorate from which Peel and Palmerston were shielded. Once the genie is out of the bottle, political parties do not like to be outbid in auctions on what the State, properly controlled, can achieve for the people. It is not clear, however, that this new electorate was much swayed by promises of social reform and the extent to which a more democratic electorate forced collectivism upon essentially reluctant politicians can be exaggerated. It is also argued that orthodox politicians adopted more interventionist postures from the 1880s to head off the challenge of socialism. There may be something in this, though British socialism seems to have been disproportionately attractive to middle-class intellectuals, and the Fabians hardly offered a fundamental challenge to the *status quo*. Nevertheless their didactic influence should not be ignored.

IV

Between 1895 and 1914 the functions of the State continued to grow.
Many of the ideas germinating in the minds of progressive politicians in
the 1880s and 1890s came to fruit during the Liberal Government of
1905–14. A non-contributory old-age pensions scheme was begun in
January 1909. Care of children, the lifeblood of the nation, was vastly
improved by the provision of school meals, by regular medical inspection,
and by the 'Children's Charter' of 1908. Lloyd George introduced a
controversial and wide-ranging compulsory insurance scheme against
both sickness and unemployment. The sickness scheme involved limited
free medical treatment for the head of the family and more access to
hospitals. Conditions of work were also brought under stricter treatment.
Workers in the 'sweated' trades—tailoring, lace-making and the like—
predominantly women, were protected by legislation enabling minimum
wages to be paid. The miners won a similar concession in 1912, though
plans for a national minimum fell on deaf ears. Labour exchanges were
instituted in 1909 to facilitate movement of labour and prevent
unnecessary unemployment. Perhaps most far-reaching of all, the Liberals
committed themselves to paying for many of these reforms by
redistributive taxation. The principle that the rich should help to provide
the necessities of the poor by compulsory deductions ran counter to every
tenet of Gladstonian Liberalism, and Lloyd George persuaded his party to
face the most serious constitutional crisis of the century in defence of it.
The role of the State was thus much more positive, and its range of social
responsibilities far wider, in 1914 than in 1895. In 1891 government
expenditure on education, science, salaries and other administrative costs
of public departments amounted to 5s. 3d. per head of the population. In the
next twenty years, it more than doubled to 10s. 11d. Most of this increase
was accounted for by provision and administration of social welfare
schemes.[11]

It is unwise, however, to see such developments as the natural sequel to
events in the 1880s. The Edwardian era was not at all the period of cosy
and affluent gentility so often characterized by nostalgic autobiographers
and producers of long-running television soap-operas. It was a period of
strife, crisis and tension. Many changes in the role of the State are
responses to that crisis, not deeply matured plans receiving natural
majority assent in course of time. The 'national efficiency' crisis,
precipitated by the standard of recruits for the Boer War, persuaded the
Inter-Departmental Committee on Physical Deterioration to recommend,

and the government to enact, measures designed to improve the national stock by providing greater care for children. The inflation of Edwardian England, and its recurrent economic crises, paved the way for much of the far-reaching industrial legislation. Unemployment insurance and the minimum wage campaign cannot be understood outside the context of damaging industrial unrest, particularly after 1910. In Syndicalism, the government faced a challenge to the entire structure of industrial organization, and its response was conceived partly in terms of short-run palliatives. Political philosophers may provide the signposts, but practical politicians more readily react to the crisis of the moment. Many of the Liberal reforms are, thus, pragmatic rather than reflective. In this sense, what we can now see as 'welfarism' had 'birth-pangs' induced by economic and social tension and a real fear of the consequences of doing nothing.

Given that the response was essentially pragmatic, we should beware of grandiloquent claims that the Liberal Party created the Welfare State between 1906 and 1914. This hypothesis is shaky on two main grounds. First, the legislation was piecemeal; second, permissive enactments were still the main order of the day. Lloyd George introduced much of his legislation as avowedly experimental. Unemployment insurance related only to the most vulnerable trades; sickness benefits applied only to the insured, not their families; pensions were only available to the non-pauperized over-seventies; medical provision was grudging and limited; secondary education was available only to a small, though growing, minority of poor children. One could go on, but the point seems clear that these reforms hardly instituted a system of welfare which aimed to provide 'from the cradle to the grave'. The Liberals did not even dismantle the poor law, with its hated associations of degradation and humiliation. Rather the new services were expected to operate alongside the old. Liberal legislation certainly provided a basis for future initiatives; but the way was hardly so clearly charted, in insurance, education, or other fields, that post-war developments were pre-ordained. Ironically, perhaps the most radical reforms of all—Lloyd George's 1913 land reform proposals, which included a land commission to redistribute property and provide central government funds for the purpose—were aborted by the advent of war, though their passage was by no means certain, given the parlous Liberal majority. These proposals were not taken up again after 1918.

The fuss created by compulsory schemes of insurance has obscured the fact that the Liberal Party had by no means abandoned permissive legislation. It enacted or permitted to remain on the statute book much more permissive than mandatory legislation. It also worked increasingly through the new County and County Borough Councils. Minimum standards of public health had been imposed on local authorities since the 1870s, but exactly how much each spent in improving facilities beyond the bare minimum was its own decision, and that of its rate-payers at the ballot box. Though education authorities were forced in 1907 to take a quarter of their secondary-school pupils from the poorer sections of the community on pain of loss of part of their government grant, the allocation of most of that grant was at local, rather than central, disposal. Likewise money for free school meals was a local concern before 1914. Housing schemes were bedevilled by a lack of central direction, and Burns's Housing and Town Planning Act of 1909 did little to right the balance. Local authorities were in most cases unable or unwilling to put in hand enough slum clearance and housing schemes because of lack of central direction and lack of central funds.

In general, the Government relied too much on local authorities and those local authorities produced patchwork schemes. In one sense, such reliance signified that the Liberal Party was by no means in the control of progressives, like Lloyd George and Churchill, who wished to increase central direction of public life. The Prime Minister, H. H. Asquith, was deeply suspicious of where such policies might lead, while many from the individualist wing of the Party, men like R. B. S. Haldane, Sir Edward Grey and even the eccentric Harold Cox, loathed greater State controls. Pure individualism being no longer viable, however, they were prepared to compromise by seeing greater powers in the hands of the local authorities. Some of these authorities, notably the London County Council, produced highly imaginative welfare schemes which anticipated those of the 1940s. Others, like their nineteenth-century predecessors, remained extremely reluctant to spend rate-payers' money on anything more than the bare minimum. Of course, State responsibilities, administered either centrally or locally, grew markedly during this period. Many of the policies which saw the light of day, such as pensions and insurance, were integral to the establishment of the Welfare State. By themselves, however, they did not herald its advent. For that more compulsory and universal provision was needed, and this the Liberal coalition neither could nor would provide. The road from individualism to collectivism had been completed. Although the map had been bought and the route partially charted, the additional journey to welfarism still lay ahead.

Notes

1. Quoted in L. Robbins, *The Theory of Economic Policy* (1965 ed.), p. 43.
2. E. J. Hobsbawm, *Industry and Empire* (1968), p. 197.
3. G. S. R. Kitson Clark, *An Expanding Society: Britain, 1830–1900* (1967), p. 162.
4. Harold Perkin, *The Origins of Modern English Society, 1780–1880* (1969), pp. 437–40, and 'Individualism Versus Collectivism in Nineteenth-Century Britain: A False Antithesis', *Journal of British Studies* vol. xvii (1977).
5. Horace Mann, 'On the Cost and Organisation of the Civil Service', *Journal of the Royal Statistical Society*, vol. xxxii (1869), p. 38.
6. *The Times*, 1 March 1847 and see below 8e.
7. D. N. McCloskey, 'Did Victorian Britain Fail?', *Economic History Review* (2nd series), vol. xxiii (1970), pp. 446–60.
8. See below, 9g and 9h.
9. *Hansard* (3rd series), vol. cclxxxiv (1884), col. 1689.
10. See below, 9f.
11. Calculations from B. R. Mitchell and P. Deane, *Abstract of British Historical Statistics* (1962), pp. 8–10 and 396–9.

Note on abbreviations

Unless otherwise stated all *Hansard* and *Parliamentary Papers* references are to the House of Commons rather than the Lords.

Part One

State intervention: the tempering of individualism c. 1830–c. 1870

1 The new political economy: expositors and popularizers

Any inquiry into *laissez faire* ideologies must begin with the great Scottish political economist Adam Smith (1723–90). His masterwork, *Inquiry into the Nature and Causes of the Wealth of Nations* (1776), postulated that national prosperity was to be achieved and secured by permitting the free play of market forces to determine an objective price. The primacy of the market ensures that profitable investment takes place in areas where demand is sufficiently strong. Thus the individual pursuit of men's self-interest, rationalized and harmonized by the market, ensures the continued prosperity of the community at large. Smith's exhortations to government to abandon the numerous restrictions and tolls on commerce and industry were vigorously if selectively adopted by generations of political leaders from Pitt the Younger to Gladstone. Smith by no means envisaged stripping government of all responsibilities, however. It was essential for government to provide basic services which individuals were unwilling or unable to offer to the market. This might extend even to State education (1a). Smith's writings on the economy enormously influenced Jeremy Bentham (1748–1832) and the school of utilitarian philosophers, who sought to ensure the greatest happiness of the greatest number. Most, like J. R. McCulloch (1789–1864), accepted that the government's duty was to promote free trade in order to guarantee profitable investment, thus ensuring full employment and decent wages. Though he scorned the utility of working men combining to adjust wages, he conceded that in times of crisis they must be offered more help than would be available from the market. *Laissez-faire* and self-help were the norm, but were not applicable in all circumstances (1b). Nassau Senior (1790–1864), a Benthamite thinker and an influential political figure on poor law and factory questions, was likewise guarded on the subject of government responsibility. Although self-reliance was a safe general guide, there were occasions on which government intervention was absolutely necessary (1c). John Stuart Mill (1806–73), educated in rigorously utilitarian fashion by his father James Mill, accepted *laissez-faire* precepts almost as a matter of course, though with similar caveats to those expressed by Senior. Towards the end of his life, however, he came to the radically different view that man's liberty to pursue his own self-interest is closely circumscribed by his environment (1d). Thus, he looked away from the Benthamites and anticipated, among others, the Fabian socialists.

It is necessary, therefore, to qualify the extent to which leading political economists accepted pure *laissez-faire*. The popularizers were much less guarded, and undoubtedly in many sections of society, more influential. Harriet Martineau's (1802–76) sublimely self-confident writings made up in directness what they lacked in intellectual finesse, and her message was deliberately, redundantly, clear (1e). James Wilson's (1805–60) *Economist*, which did so much to bolster the anti-corn law crusade from 1843, frequently carried articles condemning government intervention as pernicious, and asserting an incautious *laissez-faire* doctrine which would have alarmed both Smith and Bentham (1f). Samuel Smiles (1812–1904) produced, in *Self-Help*, one of the major best-sellers of the Victorian age. It is a series of rags-to-riches stories, with the accent heavily on sturdy independence, work and thrift (1g).

Suggestions for further reading

Central to the debate on *laissez-faire* are L. Robbins, *The Theory of English Classical Political Economy* (1952) and E. Halévy, *The Growth of Philosophic Radicalism* (1928). See also the very perceptive chapter 10 of S. G. Checkland, *The Rise of Industrial Society in England, 1815–1855* (1964) and A. W. Coats (ed.), *The Classical Economists and Economic Policy* (1971). On Harriet Martineau, see R. K. Webb, *Harriet Martineau* (1960) and on Smiles, A. Briggs, *Victorian People* (1954), chapter 5.

1a   The duties of government

Adam Smith, *Wealth of Nations* (1776), Everyman ed. 1910, vol. ii, pp. 180–1, 211, 297–8.

According to the system of natural liberty, the sovereign has only three duties to attend to; three duties of great importance, indeed, but plain and intelligible to common understandings: first, the duty of protecting the society from the violence and invasion of other independent societies; secondly, the duty of protecting, as far as possible, every member of the society from the injustice or oppression of every other member of it, or the duty of establishing an exact administration of justice; and, thirdly, the

duty of erecting and maintaining certain public works and certain public
institutions which it can never be for the interest of any individual, or
small number of individuals, to erect and maintain; because the profit
could never repay the expense to any individual or small number of
individuals, though it may frequently do much more than repay it to a
great society .... After the public institutions and public works necessary
for the defence of the society, and for the administration of justice ... the
other works and institutions of this kind are chiefly those for facilitating
the commerce of the society ... such as good roads, bridges, navigable
canals, harbours etc., ... and those for promoting the instruction of the
people. The institutions for instruction are of two kinds: those for the
education of the youth, and those for the instruction of people of all ages
.... The expense of maintaining good roads and communications is, no
doubt, beneficial to the whole society, and may, therefore, without any
injustice, be defrayed by the general contribution of the whole society ....
The expense of the institutions for education and religious instruction is
likewise, no doubt, beneficial to the whole society, and may, therefore,
without injustice, be defrayed by the general contribution of the whole
society. This expense, however, might perhaps with equal propriety, and
even with some advantage, be defrayed altogether by those who receive the
immediate benefit of such education and instruction, or by the voluntary
contribution of those who think they have occasion for either the one or
the other.

1b The limits of laissez-faire

J. R. McCulloch, *Principles of Political Economy* (1825).

It may ... be laid down as a general rule that the more individuals are
thrown on their own resources, and the less they are taught to rely on
extrinsic and adventitious assistance, the more industrious and economical
will they become, and the greater, consequently, will be the amount of
public wealth. But, even in mechanics, the engineer must allow for the
friction and resistance of matter; and it is still more necessary that the
economist should make a corresponding allowance, seeing that he has to
deal not only with natural powers, but with human beings enjoying

political privileges and imbued with the strongest feelings, passions and prejudices. Although, therefore, the general principle as to self-reliance be stated above, the economist or the politician who should propose carrying it out to its full extent in all cases and at all hazards, would be fitter for bedlam than for the closet or the cabinet. When any great number of work people are thrown out of employment, they must be provided for by extraneous assistance in one way or another; so that the various questions with respect to a voluntary and compulsory provision for the destitute poor are as necessary parts of this science as the theories of rent and profit.

1c   A classical economist expounds the Utilitarian principle

Nassau Senior, *Industrial Efficiency and Social Economy*, 1848, ed. S. L. Levy, 1928, vol. ii, pp. 301–3.

The only rational foundation of government, the only foundation of a right to govern and of a correlative duty to obey, is expediency – the general benefit of the community. It is the duty of a government to do whatever is conducive to the welfare of the governed. The only limit to this duty is its power. And as the supreme government of an independent state is necessarily absolute, the only limit to its power is physical or moral inability. And whatever it is its duty to do it must necessarily have a right to do ....

It is obviously expedient that a government should protect the persons and the property of its subjects. But if it can also be shown to be expedient that a government should perform any other functions, it must also be its duty and its right to perform them. The expediency may be more difficult of proof, and until that proof has been given, the duty and the right do not arise. But as soon as the proof has been given they are perfect. It is true that in such matters a government may make mistakes. It may believe its interference to be useful when it is really mischievous. There is no government which does not make such mistakes; and the more it interferes the more liable it must be to them. On the other hand, its refusal or neglect to interfere may also be founded on error. It may be passively wrong as well as actively wrong. The advance of political knowledge must diminish both these errors; but it appears to me that the most fatal of all errors would be the general admission of the proposition that a government has no right to interfere for any purpose except that of affording protection, for such an admission would prevent our profiting by experience, and even from acquiring it ....

The greatest objection to the extension of government interference [is] its tendency to keep the people in leading strings, and to deprive them of the power to manage their own common affairs, by depriving them of the practice without which the arts of administration cannot be acquired.

1d A philosopher, schooled in classical economics, comes to accept socialism

John Stuart Mill, *Principles of Political Economy*, (1848), Penguin, ed. Winch, 1970, pp. 306–7, 310, 314.

Whatever theory we adopt respecting the foundation of the social union, and under whatever political institutions we live, there is a circle around every individual human being, which no government, be it of one, or a few, or of the many, ought to be permitted to overstep ... the point to be determined is, where the limit should be placed .... I apprehend that it ought to include all that part which concerns only the life, whether inward or outward, of the individual, and does not affect the interests of others .... Even in those portions of conduct which do affect the interest of others, the onus of making out a case always lies on the defenders of legal prohibitions .... Scarcely any degree of utility, short of absolute necessity, will justify a prohibitory regulation, unless it can also be made to recommend itself to the general conscience ....

In all the more advanced communities, the great majority of things are worse done by the intervention of government, than the individuals most interested in the matter would do them, or cause them to be done, if left to themselves. The grounds of this truth are expressed with tolerable exactness in the popular dictum, that people understand their own business and their own interests better, and care for them more, than the government does or can be expected to do. This maxim holds true throughout the greater part of the business of life, and wherever it is true we ought to condemn every kind of government intervention that conflicts with it ... *Laissez-faire*, in short, should be the general practice: every departure from it, unless required by some great good, is a certain evil.

John Stuart Mill, *Autobiography* (1873), ed. H. J. Laski, 1924, pp. 194–6.

In this third period ... of my mental progress ... my opinions gained ... in breadth and depth, I understood many things, and those which I had understood before, I now understood more thoroughly ... in the days of my most extreme Benthamism ... I had seen little further than the old school of political economists into the possibilities of fundamental improvement of social arrangements. Private property, as now understood, and inheritance, appeared to me, as to them, the *dernier mot* of legislation: and I looked no further than to mitigating the inequalities consequent on those institutions, by getting rid of primogeniture and entails....

[But now] our ideal of improvement ... would class us decidedly under the general designation of socialists ... we ... looked forward to a time when society will no longer be divided into the idle and the industrious; when the rule that they who do not work shall not eat, will be applied not to paupers only, but impartially to all; when the division of the produce of labour, instead of depending, as in so great a degree it now does, on the accident of birth, will be made by concert on an acknowledged principle of justice .... The social problem of the future was considered to be, how to unite the greatest individual liberty of action, with a common ownership in the raw material of the globe, and an equal participation of all in the benefits of combined labour .... The deep-rooted selfishness which forms the general character of the existing state of society, is *so* deeply rooted, only because the whole course of existing institutions tends to foster it.

1e Non-interventionist homilies for ordinary folk

Harriet Martineau, *Illustrations of Political Economy*, 9 vols (1832–4), Brooke and Brooke Farm, vol. i, p. 105, vol. vi, p. 144, vol. ix, pp. 21–2, 54.

' ... surely it is hard upon the small farmer to go down in the world in spite of all his labour; and it does not seem fair that he should be driven out of the market by his neighbours because he begins the world with less capital than they.'

'Begging your pardon, my dear, that is a more foolish remark than I should have expected from you. When we reason upon subjects of this kind it is not our business to take the part of one class against another, but to discover what is for the general good; which is, in the long run, the same as the good of individuals. We are not taking the part of the large farmers against the small ... nor of the small against the large ...; but the question is, how the most regular and plentiful supply of food can be brought to market. If it be clear that this is done by cultivation on an extensive scale, we ought not to wish for the continuance of small landed properties, but rather that their owners may apply their labour and capital where they will meet with a better return. We are sorry for the little farmers ... but the more clearly we see that they suffer through a mistake, the more anxious we must be that the mistake should be rectified.'

'I am sure', said Mr. Malton, 'it gives me great concern to see a man like Norton growing poorer and poorer each year; but I know that it is partly his own fault, because he must see that his mode of tillage can never answer. If I had his lot now in my own hands, I would serve him, not by doing anything to his two fields but by employing him on good wages ... he would soon be in possession of the comforts of life, and might lay by a provision for his old age; while at the same time, he would be serving me and society at large by giving up his land to be made more productive.'

'I am aware,' said I, 'that an industrious labourer is a benefactor to society.'

'And what more honourable title need a man desire?', exclaimed my father. 'Is it not better to deserve this title, and to possess the comforts of life, than to starve on the empty name of a landed proprietor?'

'Summary of Principles'
Free competition cannot fail to benefit all parties:
    Consumers, by securing the greatest practicable improvement and cheapness of the article
      Producers, by the consequent perpetual extension of demand; – and
      Society at large, by determining capital to its natural channels

PRODUCTION being the great end in the employment of labour and capital, that application of both which secures the largest production is the best.
    Large capitals, well managed, produce in a larger proportion than small ....
    Large capitals, therefore, are preferable to an equal aggregate amount of small capitals ....
    The interests of capitalists best determines the extent of capital; and any interference of the law is, therefore, unnecessary ....
    Combination of labourers against capitalists ... cannot secure a permanent rise of wages unless the supply of labour falls short of the demand; – in which case, strikes are usually unnecessary.
    Nothing can permanently affect the rate of wages which does not affect the proportion of the population to capital.
    Legislative interference does not affect this proportion, and is therefore useless.

1f Individuals are best able to look after their own interests

'Who is to blame for the Condition of the People?',
The Economist, 21 November 1846.

The principle that each man is responsible to nature for his own actions is undeniable ....

The state, because it assumes to provide for the welfare of the people ... makes itself unwisely responsible for it. The collateral and permanent effects of legislation ... are so very complicated, and very often so much more important than the direct and temporary effects, that to make good laws seems a work fit rather for God than man. One of those collateral effects seldom thought of ... is the general helplessness of the masses, which is sure to be induced by the state undertaking to provide for their welfare. They come to rely on it and take no care for themselves. They trust in it, and become its dependents .... We consider the mental degradation of the masses – the extinction amongst them of the spirit of enterprise and of self-reliance with the annihilation of the feeling of independence ... which is everywhere the consequence of the perpetual interference of the State, to be one of the most disastrous, though collateral, effects of the legislation which is intended to benefit the people ....

The desire for happiness, or what is called self-interest, is universal .... Relying on self-interest, enlightened by knowledge and religion, to achieve the welfare of the whole, by achieving the welfare of the individual, we endeavoured to show that, while there is a great chance of individuals providing for their own welfare as individuals, there is almost an infinity of chances against their promoting the welfare of the community, when they attempt to do that by commercial and economical legislation.

1g 'Heaven helps those who help themselves'

Samuel Smiles, *Self Help* (1859), London, 1908 ed. pp. 1–3

'Heaven helps those who help themselves' is a well-tried maxim, embodying in a small compass the results of vast human experience. The spirit of self-help is the root of all genuine growth in the individual; and, exhibited in the lives of the many, it constitutes the true source of national vigour and strength. Help from without is often enfeebling in its effects, but help from within invariably invigorates. Whatever is done *for* men or classes, to a certain extent takes away the stimulus and necessity of doing for themselves; and where men are subjected to over-guidance and over-government, the inevitable tendency is to render them comparatively helpless.

Even the best institutions can give a man no active help. Perhaps the most they can do is to leave him free to develop himself and improve his individual condition. But in all times men have been prone to believe that their happiness and well-being were to be secured by means of institutions rather than by their own conduct. Hence the value of legislation as an agent in human advancement has usually been much over-estimated .... Moreover, it is every day becoming more clearly understood, that the function of government is negative and restrictive, rather than positive and active; being resolvable principally into protection — protection of life, liberty and property. Laws, wisely administered, will secure men in the enjoyment of the fruits of their labour, whether of mind or body, at a comparatively small personal sacrifice; but no laws, however stringent, can make the idle industrious, the thriftless provident, or the drunken sober. Such reforms can only be effected by means of individual action, economy, and self-denial; by better habits, rather than by greater rights.

National progress is the sum of individual industry, energy, and uprightness, as national decay is of individual idleness, selfishness, and vice .... The highest patriotism and philanthropy consists, not so much in altering laws and modifying institutions, as in helping and stimulating men to elevate and improve themselves by their own free and independent individual action.

2 The critics of laissez-faire

The utilitarian school of political economists was more strenuously opposed than is sometimes realized. Economic *laissez-faire* was attacked as vicious, materialistic, redundant and ultimately self-destructive by Tory philanthropists, apologists for the aristocracy, literary social critics, some evangelical churchmen, and proto-socialists. It is interesting to speculate why, given the range of this opposition, the 'Manchester School' captured the minds of most men of influence to such an extent that some historians have dubbed the period 1830–70 one of pure *laissez-faire*.

Best known are the barbs of the 'social novelists'. Mrs Elizabeth Gaskell (1810–65), coming to the industrial north as an outsider like the Hale family in her *North and South*, paints a sympathetic picture of the travails of working men bemused by the dictates of the 'laws of trade'. *Mary Barton* contains an eloquent statement of the limitations of *laissez-faire* (2e). Dickens's (1812–70) strictures, deriving from a much closer knowledge of the capital than of the main centres of industrial production, nevertheless had considerable influence. In *Hard Times*, dedicated to Thomas Carlyle, he poked fun at manufacturers' dread of any restrictions on their liberty to make profits. *Our Mutual Friend* contains an ironic attack on the complacent hypocrisy of Mr Podsnap's self-help philosophy (2f).

Many critics concentrated on the materialism of *laissez-faire*. The Christian Socialists, who emerged at the end of the 1840s as perhaps the most impressive group to stiffen the sinews of the Established Church, argued that the Manchester School exalted the pursuit of wealth to the detriment of the notion of the perfectability of man (2g). Charles Kingsley (1819–75), a leading Christian Socialist himself, looked to the reassertion of paternalism as the antidote to *laissez-faire*. In this, he came close to some of the ideas of Thomas Carlyle (1795–1881). One of the most impressive writers of his age on social matters, Carlyle's *Signs of the Times*, *Chartism* and *Past and Present* were important contributions to the attack on unfettered industrialism — a word Carlyle himself invented. Like Kingsley, Carlyle warned against the distorting perspective of 'this Mammon-gospel' in making supply and demand 'the one Law of Nature' (2c).

In some ways, the most intellectually coherent critics were the 'old' Tories, like David Robinson and Rev. Edward Edwards, who contributed scathing attacks on the new political economy in *Blackwood's Edinburgh Review*. Though now largely ignored by historians, *Blackwood's* in the 1820s had a comfortably larger circulation than either the *Edinburgh* or *Quarterly* Reviews. Edwards pointed to the class antagonism inherent in *laissez-faire*, and suggested that incautious acceptance of such speculative schemes would destroy the fabric of society itself (2b). Disraeli's (1804–81) social novels belong to his 'Young England' period of Tory philanthropy in the 1840s. In *Sybil*, he suggested that the only salvation for capitalism lay in its catering for the well-being of the workforce just as much as for the pursuit of profit (2d).

Thomas Hodgskin is celebrated as one of the earliest socialist writers. He used the labour theory of value against political economists in arguing that the only valid property was that generated by the sweat of the labourer's brow. This conceded, Hodgskin would defend the rights of property as strenuously as anyone (2a).

Suggestions for further reading

On the social novelists, see L. Cazamian, *The Social Novel in England, 1830–50* (1973). Raymond Williams has some perceptive points on Thomas Carlyle in *Culture and Society 1780–1850* (Penguin ed., 1961). For Christian Socialism, see Owen Chadwick, *The Victorian Church* (2 vols, 1966–70), vol. 1, chapter 5, section 3. The Blackwood's economists are retrieved from unjustified oblivion in Harold Perkin, *The Origins of Modern English Society* (1969), esp. chapter 8, sections 1 and 2.

2a   An early socialist attacks political economy and capitalism

Thomas Hodgskin, *Labour Defended against the Claims of Capital* (1825), 1922 ed., pp. 71–3, 82–3.

Betwixt him who produces food and him who produces clothing ... and him who uses them, in steps the capitalist, who neither makes them nor uses them, and appropriates to himself the produce of both. With as niggard a hand as possible he transfers to each a part of the produce of the other, keeping to himself the larger share. Gradually and successively has he insinuated himself betwixt them, expanding in bulk as he has been nourished by their increasingly productive labours, and separating them so widely from each other that neither can see whence that supply is drawn which each receives through the capitalist. While he despoils both, so completely does he exclude one from the view of the other that both believe they are indebted to him for subsistence. He is the *middleman* of all labourers .... Capitalists may well be pleased with a science which both justifies their claims and holds them up to our admiration, as the great means of civilising and improving the world ....

Though the defective nature of the claims of capital may now be satisfactorily proved, the question as to the wages of labour is by no means decided. Political economists, indeed, who have insisted very strongly on the necessity of giving security to property, and have ably demonstrated how much that security promotes general happiness, will not hesitate to agree with me when I say that whatever labour produces ought to belong to it .... I take it for granted ... that they will henceforth maintain that the whole produce of labour ought to belong to the labourer.

2b   An Old-Tory rebuttal of free trade nostrums

Blackwood's Edinburgh Review, vol. xxvii (1830), pp. 561–2 (article by Edward Edwards).

There is indeed nothing in the conduct of the advocates of Free Trade so deserving of reprehension, as the hypocritical pretences with which they attempt to disguise or conceal the real object of their measures. If we credit their professions, this amiable and enlightened tribe of philosophers has nothing in view except the public good, and the improvement of the condition of the industrious classes. There is, however, room to think, that they over-estimate the ignorance and blindness of the community in supposing that the mass of our population can be much longer hoodwinked by this flimsy pretence. If the effect of this system had been at any time a matter of doubt, recent and dear-bought experience has taught the working-classes, that the free competition of foreign labour *must* diminish the compensation which they can expect to receive for their toil. The artisans and mechanics of this country have probably by this time become pretty well convinced, that the importation and consumption of the produce of foreign labour has no tendency to ameliorate their condition; and that they at least form no portion of that public whom the Free Trade system is said to benefit. We must, however, be allowed to assure the labouring and industrious classes, that they constitute no portion of that public, of whom the Whigs and the Economists talk so loudly and so frequently. In the vocabulary of this sect, the personification called 'the public' includes only the idle capitalists, the consuming classes, the 'fruges consumere nati'; but has no reference whatever to the working portion of the community. The Whig Economists regard this class merely as beasts of burden, as animal machinery produced by nature for the purpose of 'hewing wood and drawing water' in the service of non-productive and consuming classes. We apprehend, however, that the moment is arriving, when the Free Traders will no longer find shelter from public scorn and indignation, under the hollow and false pretence of intending to benefit the working classes. The time is approaching when they must cease to insult the understandings of those whom they have irreparably injured.

2c The nemesis of laissez-faire

Thomas Carlyle, *Past and Present* (1843), Everyman ed. 1912, pp. 177–80.

In brief, all this Mammon-Gospel, of Supply-and-demand, Competition, Laissez-faire, and Devil take the hindmost, begins to be one of the shabbiest Gospels ever preached; or altogether the shabbiest ... who shall regret to see the entirely transient, and at best somewhat despicable life strangled out of *it*? ...

Laissez-faire, Supply-and-demand, – one begins to be weary of all that. Leave all to egoism, to ravenous greed of money, of pleasure, of applause:– it is the Gospel of Despair! ...

All this dire misery, therefore; all this of our poor Workhouse Workmen, of our Chartisms, Trades-strikes, Corn-Laws, Toryisms, and the general downbreak of Laissez-faire in these days, – may we not regard it as a voice from the dumb bosom of Nature, saying to us: 'Behold! supply-and-demand is not the one Law of Nature; Cash-payment is not the sole nexus of man with man, – how far from it! Deep, far deeper than Supply-and-demand, are Laws, Obligations sacred as Man's Life itself: these also, if you will continue to do work, you shall now learn and obey. He that will learn them, behold Nature is on his side, he shall yet work and prosper with noble rewards. He that will not learn them, Nature is against him, he shall not be able to work in Nature's empire, – not in hers. Perpetual mutiny, contention, hatred, isolation, execration shall wait on his footsteps, till all men discern that the thing which he attains, however golden it look or be, is not success, but the want of success.'

2d   Disraeli on the evils of unrestrained competition and the need for paternalism in industry

Sybil (1845), Penguin ed. 1954, pp. 177–8, 179–81.

The man seated himself at his loom; he commenced his daily task ....

Then why am I here? Why am I, and six hundred thousand subjects of the Queen, honest, loyal, and industrious, why are we, after manfully struggling for years, and each year sinking lower in the scale, why are we driven from our innocent happy homes, our country cottages that we loved, first to bide in close towns without comforts, and gradually to crouch into cellars, or find a squalid lair like this, without even the common necessaries of existence; first the ordinary conveniences of life, then raiment, and, at length, food, vanishing from us.

It is that the capitalist has found a slave that has supplanted the labour and ingenuity of man. Once he was an artisan: at the best, he now only watches machines; and even that occupation slips from his grasp, to the woman and the child. The capitalist flourishes, he amasses immense wealth; we sink, lower and lower; lower than the beasts of burthen; for they are fed better than we are, cared for more. And it is just, for according to the present system they are more precious. And yet they tell us that the interests of Capital and of Labour are identical.

The factory was about a mile distant from their cottage, which belonged indeed to Mr Trafford, and had been built by him .... With gentle blood in his veins, and old English feelings, he imbibed, at an early period of his career, a correct conception of the relations which should subsist between the employer and the employed. He felt that between them there should be other ties than the payment and the receipt of wages ....

He became very opulent, and he lost no time in carrying into life and being the plans which he had brooded over in the years when his good thoughts were limited to dreams .... At Mr. Trafford's, by an ingenious process, not unlike that which is practised in the House of Commons, the ventilation was also carried on from below, so that the whole building was kept at a steady temperature, and little susceptible to atmospheric influence. The physical advantages of thus carrying on the whole work in one chamber are great: in the improved health of the people, the security against dangerous accidents to women and youth, and the reduced fatigue resulting from not having to ascend and descend, and carry materials to the higher rooms. But the moral advantages resulting from superior inspection and general observation are not less important: the child works under the eye of the parent, the parent under that of the superior workman; the inspector or employer at a glance can behold all.

When the workpeople of Mr. Trafford left his factory they were not forgotten. Deeply had he pondered on the influence of the employer on the health and content of his workpeople. He knew well that the domestic virtues are dependent on the existence of a home, and one of his first efforts had been to build a village where every family might be well lodged. Though he was the principal proprietor, and proud of that character, he nevertheless encouraged his workmen to purchase the fee: there were some who had saved sufficient money to effect this; proud of their house and their little garden, and of the horticultural society, where its produce permitted them to be annual competitors. In every street there was a well: behind every factory were the public baths; the schools were under the direction of the perpetual curate of the church, which Mr. Trafford, though a Roman Catholic, has raised and endowed. In the midst of this village, surrounded by beautiful gardens, which gave an impulse to the horticulture of the community, was the house of Trafford himself, who comprehended his position too well to withdraw himself with vulgar exclusiveness from his real dependants, but recognized the baronial principle, reviving in a new form, and adapted to the softer manners and more ingenious circumstances of the times.

And what was the influence of such an employer and such a system of employment on the morals and manners of the employed? Great; infinitely beneficial. The connexion of a labourer with his place of work, whether agricultural or manufacturing, is itself a vast advantage. Proximity to the employer brings cleanliness and order, because it brings observation and encouragement. In the settlement of Trafford crime was positively unknown, and offences were very slight. There was not a single person in the village of a reprobate character. The men were well clad; the women had a blooming cheek; drunkenness was unknown; while the moral condition of the softer sex was proportionately elevated.

2e   Unrestrained capitalism drives a weaver to murder and despair

Elizabeth Gaskell, *Mary Barton* (1848), Penguin ed. 1970, pp. 456–7.

[This scene takes place after John Barton's death, as his workmates and employer muse on the tragedy.]

'For he was a loving man before he grew mad with seeing such as he was slighted, as if Christ himself had not been poor. At one time, I've heard him say, he felt kindly towards every man, rich or poor, because he thought they were all men alike. But latterly he grew aggravated with the sorrows and suffering that he saw, and which he thought the masters might help if they would.'

'That's the notion you've all of you got,' said Mr. Carson. 'Now, how in the world can we help it? We cannot regulate the demand for labour. No man or set of men can do it. It depends on events which God alone can control. When there is no market for our goods, we suffer just as much as you can do.'

'Not as much, I'm sure, sir; though I'm not given to Political Economy, I know that much. I'm wanting in learning, I'm aware; but I can use my eyes. I never see the Masters getting thin and haggard for want of food; I hardly ever see them making much change in their way of living, though I don't doubt they've go to do it in bad times. But it's in things for show they cut short; while for such as me, it's in things for life we've to stint. For sure, sir, you'll own it's come to a hard pass when a man would give ought in the world for work to keep his children from starving and can't get a bit, if he's ever so willing to labour ....'

Job Legh pondered for a few moments.

'It's true it was a sore time for the hand-loom weavers when power-looms came in: them new-fangled things make a man's life like a lottery; and yet I'll never misdoubt that power-looms and railways, and all such-like inventions, are the gifts of God. I have lived long enough, too, to see that it is part of His plan to send suffering to bring out a higher good; .... But I'm clear about this, when God gives a blessing to be enjoyed, He gives it with a duty to be done; and the duty of the happy is to help the suffering to bear their woe.'

'Still, facts have proved and are daily proving how much better it is for every man to be independent of help, and self-reliant,' said Mr. Carson, thoughtfully.

'You can never work facts as you would fixed quantities, and say, given two facts, and the product is so and so. God has given men feelings and passions which cannot be worked into the problem, because they are for ever changing, and uncertain. God has also made some weak; not in any one way but in all. One is weak in body, another in mind, another in steadiness of purpose, a fourth can't tell right from wrong, and so on; or if he can tell the right, he wants strength to hold by it. Now to my thinking, them that is strong in any of God's gifts is meant to help the weak, — be hanged to the facts! I ask your pardon, sir: I can't rightly explain the meaning that is in me. I'm like a tap as won't run, but keeps letting it out drop by drop, so that you've no notion of the force of what's within.'

2f   Charles Dickens on industrialism and the pressure of facts

Hard Times (1854), Penguin ed. 1969, Book II, chapter 1, pp. 145–6.

A sunny midsummer day. There was such a thing sometimes, even in Coketown.

Seen from a distance in such weather, Coketown lay shrouded in a haze of its own, which appeared impervious to the sun's rays. You only knew the town was there, because you knew there could have been no such sulky blotch upon the prospect without a town .... The wonder was, it was there at all. It had been ruined so often, that it was amazing how it had borne so many shocks. Surely there never was such fragile china-ware as that of which the millers of Coketown were made. Handle them never so lightly, and they fell to pieces with such ease that you might suspect them of having been flawed before. They were ruined, when they were required to send labouring children to school; they were ruined, when inspectors were appointed to look into their works; they were ruined, when such inspectors considered it doubtful whether they were quite justified in chopping people up with their machinery; they were utterly undone, when it was hinted that perhaps they need not always make quite so much smoke .... Whenever a Coketowner felt he was ill-used – that is to say, whenever he was not left entirely alone, and it was proposed to hold him accountable for the consequences of any of his acts – he was sure to come out with the awful menace, that he would 'sooner pitch his property into the Atlantic'. This had terrified the Home Secretary within an inch of his life, on several occasions.

However, the Coketowners were so patriotic after all, that they never had pitched their property into the Atlantic yet, but, on the contrary, had been kind enough to take mighty good care of it. So there it was, in the haze yonder; and it increased and multiplied.

Our Mutual Friend (1864), Penguin ed. 1971, Book I, chapter 11, pp. 186–8.

'There is not,' said Mr. Podsnap, flushing angrily, 'there is not a country in the world, sir, where so noble a provision is made for the poor as in this country.'

The meek man was quite willing to concede that, but perhaps it rendered the matter even worse, as showing that there must be something appallingly wrong somewhere.

'Where?' said Mr. Podsnap.

The meek man hinted, Wouldn't it be well to try, very seriously, to find out where?

'Ah!' said Mr. Podsnap. 'Easy to say somewhere; not so easy to say where! But I see what you are driving at. I knew it from the first. Centralization. No. Never with my consent. Not English.'

An approving murmur arose from the heads of tribes; as saying, 'There you have him! Hold him!'

He was not aware (the meek man submitted of himself) that he was driving at any ization. He had no favourite ization that he knew of. But he certainly was more staggered by these terrible occurrences than he was by names, of howsoever so many syllables. Might he ask, was dying of destitution and neglect necessarily English? ... Mr. Podsnap felt that the time had come for flushing and flourishing this meek man down for good. So he said:

'I must decline to pursue this painful discussion. It is not pleasant to my feelings. It is repugnant to my feelings. I have said that I do not admit these things. I have also said that if they do occur (not that I admit it), the fault lies with the sufferers themselves. It is not for *me*' – Mr. Podsnap pointed 'me' forcibly, as adding by implication, though it may be all very well for *you*— 'it is not for me to impugn the workings of Providence. I know better than that, I trust, and I have mentioned what the intentions of Providence are. Besides,' said Mr. Podsnap, flushing high up among his hair-brushes, with a strong consciousness of personal affront, 'the subject is a very disagreeable one. I will go so far as to say it is an odious one. It is not one to be introduced among our wives and young persons, and I' – He finished with that flourish of his arm which added more expressively than any words. 'And I remove it from the face of the earth.'

2g   A Christian ginger-group attacks economic orthodoxies

'The Aims of Political Economy', *Christian Socialist*, 18 January 1851

According to some writers, we should imagine that utility was measured according to the *wealth produced. Value, labour, capital, wages, profit, rent, etc.* are the substantives of their science; and the production of wealth appears to be the end, the sum and substance, the object of their desires.

We deny, from beginning to end, this view of political economy ....

We assert ... that the welfare of *man* is the end of political economy ....

The whole system of modern manufacture, with its factory slavery; its gaunt and sallow faces; its half-clad hunger; its female degradation; its abortions and ricketty children; its dens of pestilence and abomination; its ignorance, brutality and drunkenness; its vice in all its hideous forms of infidelity, helpless poverty, and mad despair – these, and if it were possible, worse than these are the sure fruits of making man the workman of mammon, instead of making wealth the servant of humanity for the relief of man's estate.

The day is not far distant when the *Labour* of England will hold his (her?) Court of Justice; let those who may, await the sentence of the tribunal.

That system of political economy which makes *wealth* and not *man*, the ultimatum, is based on a monstrous fallacy – on a fallacy so slavish and so detestable, that the wonder is how accomplished and personally amiable men can be found as its abettors.

The fallacy is, in taking the *rents of the landlords, and the profits of the capitalists*, as the measures of good and evil, instead of taking the *condition of the cultivators, and the condition of the labourers* (the many) as the sure index of the character of a system ....

Man is the stable element. *His* condition is the standard; *his* improvement is a good; *his* deterioration is an evil .... Man is not useful as he produces wealth, but wealth useful as it sustains man, ameliorates his condition ... gives opportunities for his further cultivation, and aids in the great scheme of human regeneration.

3 Factory legislation

In the 1830s and 1840s the factory question put into clear focus the general debate on the desirability and limitations of State intervention. From it emerged three pieces of legislation, imposing on employers increasingly stringent conditions for the employment of women and children. The 1833 Factory Act, which differed from its predecessors in 1802 and 1819 in containing provision for government inspection to ensure that its provisions were effected, excluded all children under nine years of age from textile factories, and set a maximum of forty-eight hours a week on children between nine and thirteen. Young persons of thirteen to eighteen might work a maximum of sixty-nine hours. Further agitation secured an Act in 1844 which limited employment of children under thirteen to six-and-a-half hours. For the first time, the labour of women in factories was regulated. No woman, or young person under eighteen, must work longer than twelve hours a day. In 1847 a ten-hour day in factories was secured for women and children, though the existence of relay-working provided a loophole for some manufacturers to exploit for a few more years (3f).

The factory movement was largely spearheaded by Tory philanthropists and paternalists, such as Shaftesbury, Oastler and Fielden, genuinely concerned, of course, with conditions of labour, but equally worried about the challenge to traditional authority represented by a factory-owning and commercial *nouveau riche*. Against them, many factory owners argued that legislative restriction was unnecessary, and was resented even by parents of factory children. The utilitarian economists moved cautiously to ensure that the case for State intervention was incontrovertibly made, and that the proposed remedy would be efficacious. J. R. McCulloch was convinced (3b) that the 1832 Sadler Committee on factory conditions had been selective in its use of evidence and presented a hopelessly biased case for State intervention. The Factory Commission of 1833, appointed in the wake of the furore caused by Sadler's report, by contrast, was anxious to prove that conditions in factories were no worse, and often rather better, than elsewhere (3a). Legislative intervention was justified, however, on the grounds that children required protection as they were not free agents, able to bargain on equal terms in a free market. The legitimate grounds for government intervention with trade and industry were the subject of extensive debate when the 1844 Factory Bill was considered (3e). Members were in general extremely reluctant to tamper with the, largely chimerical, notion that adult males were free to bargain for the best terms when offering themselves in the free labour market. Viscount Howick (later 3rd Earl Grey), however, argued a much more interventionist role for government. The *Westminster Review* accepted that factory legislation involved a new conception of the duties of government (3d).

The role of inspectors was crucial. Many manufacturers began to argue that because inspectors made improper use of the powers delegated to them, their influence should be diminished. The argument, dear to the hearts of anti-interventionists, that centralized controls and commissions represented a new despotism serviced by spies, could then be advanced. Disputes over the proper interpretation of the law by the most active and able factory inspector, Leonard Horner, led to an interesting altercation in 1854–5 when a factory masters association was formed (3g & h). The *Westminster Review* had argued in 1836 that the powers of the first factory inspectors, and the enormity of the task that a mere four were called on to execute, vitiated the effectiveness of the 1833 Act (3c).

Suggestions for further reading

Numerous general textbooks devote space to factory reform, but the fullest account is J. T. Ward, *The Factory Movement, 1830–1855* (1962).

3a Legislative intervention on child labour in factories is justified

First Report of the Commission of Enquiry into Factories, *Parliamentary Papers*, 1833, vol. xx, pp. 35–6, 55–6, 75.

From the whole of the evidence laid before us of which we have thus endeavoured to exhibit the material points we find –

1st That the children employed in all the principal branches of manufacture throughout the Kingdom work the same number of hours as the adults.

2nd That the effects of labour during such hours are, in a great number of cases,

> Permanent deterioration of the physical constitution The production of disease often wholly irremediable: and The partial or entire exclusion (by reason of excessive fatigue) from the means of obtaining adequate education and acquiring useful habits, or of profiting by those means when afforded.

3rd That at the age when children suffer these injuries from the labour they undergo, they are not free agents but are let out to hire, the wages they earn being received and appropriated by their parents and guardians ....

In recommending legislative restriction of the labour of children, as not being free agents, and not being able to protect themselves, we have been careful not to lose sight of the practical limits within which alone any general rule admits of application. We have not found these limits in the greater or lesser intensity, or in the greater or lesser unwholesomeness of infant labour in factories. It appears in evidence, that of all employments to which children are subjected, those carried on in factories are amongst the least laborious, and of all departments of in-door labour, amongst the least unwholesome. It is in evidence, that boys employed in collieries are subjected at a very early age to very severe labour, that cases of deformity are more common and accidents more frequent amongst them than amongst children employed in factories. Hand-loom weavers, frame-work knitters, lace runners, and work-people engaged in other lines of domestic manufacture, are in most cases worked at earlier ages, and for longer hours and for less wages, than the body of children employed in factories ....

We are induced ... briefly to state the grounds which appear to justify that interference with factories, as distinguished from collieries, or from establishments of a domestic nature.

Children employed in factories, as a distinct class, form a very considerable proportion of the infant population. We have found that the numbers are rapidly increasing, not only in proportion to the increase of the population employed in manufacturing industry, but, in consequence of the tendency of improvements in machinery to throw more and more of the work upon children, to the displacement of adult labour. The children so employed are assembled together in large numbers .... Their daily entrance into and dismissal from the factories takes place with the regularity of military discipline ....

The restrictions we venture to propose ... are, that children under nine years of age shall not be employed in mills or factories .... That until the commencement of the fourteenth year the hours of labour during any one day shall not in any case exceed eight. That until the commencement of the fourteenth year children shall not in any case be allowed to work at night; that is to say, between the hours of ten at night and five in the morning ....

Since the whole of our recommendations have for their object the care and benefit of children, we have been desirous of devising means for securing the occupation of a portion of the time abridged from their hours of labour to their own advantage. We think the best mode of accomplishing this object will be the occupation, suppose of three (or four) hours of every day in education ... this ... will serve two ulterior objectives of considerable importance: first, it will be the best means of preventing the employment of the same child in two different factories on the same day ... and secondly, it will better qualify the persons so educated to adapt themselves to other employments, if in after life the vicissitudes of trade or other causes should render it desirable that they should find other means of support ....

THOMAS TOOKE
25 June 1833   EDWIN CHADWICK
THOMAS SOUTHWOOD SMITH

3b   A political economist attacks the Sadler Factory Report

Edinburgh Review, vol. lxi (1835), pp. 463–4 (review by J. R. McCulloch).

Children, that is young persons between the ages of nine and fourteen years, as well as adults, are largely employed in factories; and while the health and morals of the latter are said to suffer severely, the former have been described as being stunted in their growth, and rendered decrepit and miserable for life, by the prolonged confinement, drudgery and ill treatment to which they are exposed. These representations of the ruinous effects of what has been called white *slavery*, after being circulated in speeches, tracts, petitions, and dissertations, were at length embodied in

Mr. Sadler's famous Factory Report, which, we believe, contains more false statements, and exaggerated and fallacious representations, than any other document of the kind ever laid before the Legislature. The discussions to which their Report, and the proposal that grew out of it, for limiting factory labour to ten hours a-day, gave rise, induced Government to enquire on the spot into the actual condition of the labourers, and especially the children employed in factories. This Commission collected a great deal of valuable and authentic information; and much light has since been thrown on the question of factory labour. We do not say ... that the statements and representations as to its pernicious influence have been proved to be *wholly* destitute of foundation; but we believe ... that they have been grossly exaggerated. That abuses have existed in some factories is certain; but these have been rare instances; and, speaking generally, factory workpeople, including non-adults, are as healthy and contented as any class of the community obliged to earn their bread in the sweat of their brow.

We do not, however, know that we should object to the total exclusion of children, from nine to thirteen years of age, from factories, provided we had any reasonable security that they would be moderately well attended to and instructed at home. But no such security is to be looked for .... Were they turned out of the factories, few would either go to the country or to school. Four-fifths of them would be thrown loose upon the streets, to acquire a taste for idleness, and to be early initiated in the vicious practices prevalent amongst the dregs of the populace, in Manchester, Glasgow, Leeds and other great towns. Whatever may be the state of society in these towns, we hesitate not to say, that *it would have been ten times worse but for the factories*. They have been the best and most important academies. Besides taking children out of harm's way, they have imbued them with regular, orderly, and industrious habits.

3c   The need for centralized control of factory regulations

Westminster Review, vol. xxvi (1836), pp. 207–10.

To enforce the provisions of this Act [1833] against ... powerful interests, the only machinery created by the statute consists of four inspectors for the whole of the kingdom, to whom, by the authority of the Home Office, superintendents have been added, who act under the inspectors. The sole authority for enforcing the Act is lodged in the inspectors who are responsible to the Secretary of State for the Home Department. This agency is inadequate to enforce the uniform and strict observance of the law, among others, for the following reasons:

1. The experience of each inspector is limited to a part of the field over the whole of which the law is to be enforced, and each is but little acquainted with the circumstances which are not prominent in his own district.

2. Each inspector is impressed the most forcibly by the representations which are made to him in his own district ... and it is impossible that he can have so clear an apprehension of what may be peculiar to other districts ....

3. The consequence is, that each inspector adopts a different view, necessarily a partial, and so far an incorrect one, as to what is expedient or inexpedient, practicable or impracticable. Accordingly, the reports of the different inspectors are full of the most conflicting statements in reference to the expediency or inexpediency, practicability or impracticability of almost all the main provisions of the Act which it is their duty by every means at their command to enforce ....

4. There is another consideration which will have weight .... The inspector enters the mill with no hostile intention. He merely goes to see that certain enactments are obeyed which the Legislature has ordained. It is in the interest of the mill-owner to treat him with courtesy; it is equally in the interest of the inspector to return the civility he receives, because he knows that his labour will be lessened by the co-operation of the mill-

owner. A friendly intercourse is thus likely to arise between them which will increase with the frequency and intimacy of their inter-communication. A bias in favour of the mill-owner will thus be apt to take possession of the inspector's mind .... To such influences all men placed in such a position must be exposed: but from such interests, which are sinister interests, a central authority is free ....

From the whole it follows that it is expedient to appoint a central authority to which the inspectors should report, and which should frame regulations for their guidance. The advantages of such a central control are:

1. That whatever regulations might be issued would be founded on an accurate knowledge of *all* the circumstances which called for their enforcement ....

2. Uniformity would be given to the working of the whole measure ... there should be one law for all, and that .... law should be rigidly enforced on all. Not, indeed, that there should be one law in the sense of those who would restrict the adult labour of all the factories in the kingdom to that exact time which they had found it convenient to work their own mills; but one law framed on the great interests common to all ....

3. Responsibility would be concentrated. The factory inspector is responsible only for what takes place in his own district. No one inspector, nor all the inspectors together, are responsible for the proper working of the statute in all the districts; nor are they bound to report to a competent authority why it does not work, if it does not, and to suggest the remedies which their observation and experience may have led them to discover ....
For the working of the Poor Law Act, the Legislature has appointed a Central Board of Poor Law Commissioners and a body of Assistant Commissioners .... For the working of the Factory Act, the Legislature has appointed only what is analogous to the Assistant Commissioners, and has omitted to appoint a Central Board, a superintending and controlling body.

3d   Factory legislation as a 'new era in our social life'

Westminster Review, vol. xxxviii (1842), pp. 86–7.

... legislation to control industry expressly on behalf of humanity and public morals, marks a new era in our social life. The absence of such legislation, prior to the first act of factory regulation, affords no argument to prove, on the one hand, its needlessness, or, on the other, that there has been any remarkable improvement in the moral perceptions of our legislature. It has been called into existence, in fact, by the change in our industry, consequent upon the increased use of machinery. Whether or not we may assume, from the fact of the moral relations of the young with their employers, under the old systems of industry, being brought little under public notice, that there was little demanding the interference of the legislature, it was certainly the obvious change effected in the manufacturing system by the factories which brought these relations under legislative regulation.

It may safely be asserted that, in a community sufficiently advanced in civilization to undertake to preserve every one of its members from absolute destitution by laws for the relief of the poor, every child has a moral right to maintenance and education, exempt from any such amount of labour as shall prevent its attaining a physical development, and a religious, moral, and intellectual cultivation, sufficient to enable it to provide for its own future wants and happiness with benefit to the community at large. No encroachment upon this right can be accompanied by countervailing advantages either to the individual or to the community at large, whatever may be the convenience to the parents or guardians of the child or to its employer; and all labour or restraint interfering with this right is 'undue,' as is legally asserted by the existing Factories Regulation Act.

3e   Debates on the factory question

Hansard (3rd series), vol. lxxiv, cols 613–50 *passim*, (1844).

J. A. Roebuck: I take it as a general rule, the result of experience, that the labouring man has the greatest interest in forming a wise contract for himself .... Experience has shown that we ought not in any manner to interfere with private rights where private interests were strong and armed with a peculiar knowledge, and where the parties were best calculated to think for themselves on any question. That is the general principle. If any interference took place a reason should be shown. The *onus* lies on those who come to the conclusion that interference is necessary to show what the circumstances are which justify that interference .... I will now place before the House my position distinctly, – that they ought not to interfere with the power of persons to contract ... the noble Lord [Ashley] says, that there are a peculiar class of men in the country – the factory labourers, who have peculiar interests, and are altogether in a condition which calls for legislative interference. The noble Lord says, that their peculiar condition arises from overwork and underpay, and thereupon he gathers together a huge heap – an indigested mass, and flings it at the House, evidence which he thinks shows great misery and immorality, and degradation in the factories .... Now there is this remarkable fact as to the noble Lord's argument – that there is between his premises and his conclusions no connexion whatever. It is not enough to show that there is an evil. Having made out the evil ... it must be shown by the noble Lord that the measure proposed by him is a remedy .... What the House requires is, not only to prove the evil but also to show the efficacy of the remedy.

Sir James Graham: Since the last discussion on this subject, Mr. Horner, an inspector of the cotton districts, had, by his direction, visited several factories, and he would state the result of [Mr. Horner's] inquiries. In nine factories, of the work people employed, Mr. Horner found that more than 50 per cent were females, and of them nearly 70 per cent were above eighteen, while $27^1/_2$ per cent were married women. The hon. and learned

Gentleman himself had laid down the principle that though they ought not to interfere with parties able to decide and judge for themselves, yet when that was not the case, as in the instance of children, it was right for the Legislature. A question then arose upon the Returns as to whether there was not something peculiar in the situation of female adults which brought them, if not quite within the limit at least to the very verge of that principle. Did they decide and judge for themselves? So far as married women were concerned, the Law held distinctly the reverse. The Law held that they were under such control that they could not decide and judge for themselves, and to the female sex generally many of the rights of freedom are denied. The most important consideration of all was, that the restriction which had been already imposed upon the labour of children and young persons had driven those who sought to evade the Law in working machinery for more than twelve hours, by the force of legislation to avail themselves of the lower paid labour of females, in order to work beyond the limited time. Married women might clearly be influenced by their husbands, for the sake of gaining higher wages, thus to overwork themselves, and generally as to females, considering that they were the weaker portion of the community, having a claim by nature on our compassion and on our care, he thought the House would feel they were more peculiarly entitled to the protection of the Legislature.

Henry Labouchere: ... he would ... confine himself to the Question ... whether there was any justification for the House assenting to a principle hitherto unheard of and unadmitted in the legislation of this or any other country − namely, that they should, by direct legislation, limit the hours of labour of the adult population ... it was most inexpedient and highly dangerous to embark in this course of legislation ... all this proceeded on what he held to be a false principle − namely, that there was something in the factory labour of this country that was worse than the average nature of employment to which the labouring population were subject; and so far from that being the case, he believed that there were many favourable circumstances attending it ... he found in the Reports, and other evidence to which they could have access, that the employment of females in factories was spoken of as a favourite employment, and it was very difficult to get a young woman in the factory districts to become a domestic servant. That was a practical answer to all the cases selected to produce a feeling in that House against factory labour for females .... He held it most important to keep the correct principles of legislation in view in this matter. He was not one of those who would say that they never might modify principles abstractedly correct so as to do more good than harm;

but this he would say that they never could widely depart from them without danger ... if the House sanctioned the principle, he was afraid ... they could not oppose any interference with labour hereafter.

Viscount Howick: It has been said by a writer, whose authority has and ought to have the greatest weight with the House, that

> The property which every man has in his own labour, as it is the original foundation of all other property, so it is the most sacred and inviolable. The patrimony of a poor man lies in the strength and dexterity of his hands; and to hinder him from employing this strength and dexterity in what manner he thinks proper, without injury to his neighbour, is a plain violation of this most sacred property. It is a manifest encroachment upon the just liberty both of the workman and of those who might be disposed to employ him.

The House will easily recognise this passage as a quotation from the *Wealth of Nations*; this I believe to be the authority on which you rely when you assert that principle is violated by the kind of legislation which is now proposed; but, for my own part, while I subscribe to the principle in the sense in which it was meant to be laid down by the distinguished author I have quoted, I utterly deny that it applies to the question now before us ... I agree ... with Adam Smith ... that restrictions upon the freedom of industry, if intended to increase the wealth of a particular class, are unjust—if that of the whole community, are impolitic and defeat their own aim; but I contend that you altogether misapply the maxim of leaving industry to itself when you use it as an argument against regulations of which the object is, not to increase the productive power of the country, or to take the fruits of a man's labour from himself and give it to another, but, on the contrary, to guard the labourer himself and the community from evils against which the mere pursuit of wealth affords us no security. The mere increase of a nation's wealth is not the only—it ought not even to be the first and highest object of a Government. The welfare, both moral and physical of the great body of the people, I conceive to be the true concern of the Government .... There are some who believe that if a government maintains the honour and interests of a nation in its relations with foreign countries, and protects the lives and property of its subjects from violence or wrong, it accomplishes all, or almost all, that can be reasonably expected from it .... In the present state of the country and of society, it seems to me that we have too many convincing and alarming proofs that this view of the duties of the supreme authority of the State is a wrong one, and that far more is required from the Government and the Legislature.

More especially when we look to the present state of the manufacturing districts we must feel that such is the case .... When we look at the dense masses of population that are there collected, or rather heaped together, without any adequate provision either for their moral or physical well-being; when we learn, as by recent enquiries we have learnt (I must say for one, to my astonishment and dismay) – when we learn what abuses prevail, and how much misery exists amongst the thousands of human beings crowded together in the busy seats of our commercial and manufacturing industry; when we consider this state of things, surely we must feel that we have trusted too much in a case where it does not apply, to the maxim that men should be left to take care of their own interests; and that it would have been well if even at the price of some sacrifice of productive power and of national wealth the State had earlier interfered, and had taken measures which should have opposed some check to so vast an increase of population without some corresponding increase in the machinery for maintaining order and decency, and of diffusing the blessings of education and of religion.

3f   The 1847 Factory Act

'An Act to limit the Hours of Labour of young Persons and Females in Factories' (10 & 11 Vic., c.29).

clause 2   'Be it enacted, That from the First Day of *May* One thousand eight hundred and forty-eight no Person under the Age of Eighteen Years shall be employed in any such Mill or Factory ... for more than Ten Hours in any One Day, nor more than Fifty-eight hours in any One Week.... '

clause 3   'And be it enacted, That the Restrictions respectively by this Act imposed as regards the working of Persons under the Age of Eighteen Years shall extend to Females above the Age of Eighteen Years.'

3g   The duties of factory inspectors

Report of Inspectors of Factories, October 1854: Leonard Horner, pp. 5–7.

Very little attention has been paid to the recommendations ... whereby danger from horizontal shafts revolving at a height of more than seven feet from the floor might be prevented, which were communicated to all occupiers of factories by the circular letter of the 15th March last .... In some instances they have in one form or another been adopted, particularly the strap-hooks or hangers, by which the lapping of straps round the shaft, a frequent cause of fatal accidents, is completely prevented. Nowhere have I seen this more effectually accomplished than in the large cotton mill of Messrs. Dugdale, Brothers, near Burnley. I have seen many shafts *less* than seven feet from the floor, which within the last few months have been securely fenced by being surrounded with a case, sometimes of iron and frequently of wood. Mr. Sub-inspector Jones, in his report of a recent visit to one of the factories of Messrs. Ormond and Hardcastle, the most extensive of the cotton spinners and manufacturers in Bolton, says 'the whole of the horizontal shafting is now securely fenced with strong *wooden* casing.' If shafts *less* than seven feet from the floor can thus be securely fenced by iron or wood casings, those *more* than seven feet can surely also be guarded. These facts show very clearly that the statements made to your Lordship by the deputation of mill occupiers last March, that it is nearly impossible to case horizontal shafts at all, and that if it were done with wood the danger of setting the mill on fire would be extreme, are not entitled to any weight. It is strange that these gentlemen should have forgotten that a very large proportion of the vertical shafts in mills have for years been cased with wood, and it would be difficult to prove that there is more risk of the case of a horizontal shaft catching fire than that of a vertical one.

Two fatal accidents from horizontal shafts, left without any description of guard to prevent the strap from falling upon the shaft, or coiling round it, have recently occurred; and, although they happened after the 31st of October, I think it material that the occurrences themselves, the proceedings taken in consequence, and the results, should be made known without delay.

On the 10th of November I received a report from Mr. Rowntree, certifying surgeon, at Oldham, that on the 3d of that month Henry Glenny, aged 22, employed in the factory of Messrs. Folson and Collins, of Oldham, while engaged in his ordinary work had been killed. I forthwith directed Mr. Sub-inspector Graham to go to the factory, and investigate the cause of the man's death. It arose from his foot getting tangled in a strap of the machine at which he was working; and, the strap having lapped round the horizontal shaft that drives the machine, the man was dragged up, his skull was fractured, and he died immediately. Mr. Graham further reported that there were no guide-hooks or other contrivance to prevent the strap falling on the shaft, and lapping; if there had been, the accident could not have happened.

An information was laid by Mr. Graham against Messrs. Folson and Collins, under sections 21., 73., and 60. of 7 Vic. c.15., for having neglected to fence securely the said horizontal shaft, as required by law. The complaint was heard at Oldham petty sessions on the 30th ult., by the Rev. T. S. Mills (chairman), and Messrs. Platt, Worthington, Wright, and Barlow. Mr. Graham reported to me that when the hearing was concluded the magistrates retired, and that when they came into court the Chairman announced that the case was dismissed, without giving any reason for the decision. That the shaft had not been fenced was proved, and thus an enactment which is as clear and imperative as any other in the Act was set aside.

3h   Fears of factory legislation and inspection

'Report of the Executive Committee of the National Association of Factory Occupiers' (Manchester, 1855), pp. 3, 18–19.

Objects: 'To watch over Factory Legislation with a view to prevent any increase of the present unfair and injudicious enactments; to obtain an amendment of the present Factory Laws and their Administration; and to protect the members of the Association from improper prosecutions and legal proceedings instituted or promoted by the Factory Inspectors, or by other parties .... '

If the duty of the inspectors is confined to a blind and unreasoning enforcement of the law – if the judicial element is altogether excluded from their office, and in their reports and proceedings, they are only expected to appear as *partizans* of the law or the *pretended* interests of humanity, excluding from their regard all considerations of fair play to factory occupiers—in what respect do they differ from mere spies and informers and wherefore the necessity of having gentlemen of their class to perform duties which are quite within the capacity of an ordinary policeman? ... If anyone will be at the pains to look through their periodical reports to the government, he cannot fail to observe the growing tendency the Inspectors exhibit to magnify the importance of their office, by depreciating the characters of the mill owners, and by exaggerated accounts of accidents and offences; how carefully they abstain from attaching deserved blame to the factory workers, who are themselves very frequently the cause of the accidents attributed to the inhumanity of their employers; how little their exertions are directed to the promotion of confidence and harmony between employer and employed; how greedily they seek to increase the occasions of office in order to swell their tables of prosecutions and convictions; and how little pleasure they seem to take in the innocence of their fellow creatures.

4 Poverty and the new poor law

Poverty was the central social issue at the beginning of the period. At the same time as the industrial revolution was providing new jobs, largely in the north of England, a rapidly rising population resulted in growing structural underemployment in the rural sector of the economy. This brought lower wages, longer periods of unemployment or underemployment and much misery to agricultural labourers, particularly in the south. The natural resort of distressed Englishmen was to the old poor law. As poverty increased, poor law expenditure rose dramatically, from about £2,000,000 in 1784 to £7,871,000 at its pre-reform peak in 1817. Under such pressure, the viability of the old system of poor relief was called in question. Influenced by the view of Rev. Thomas Malthus (1766–1834) that increasing population pressure would destroy the delicate balance between people and available food supplies, resulting in famine and death, the political economists began their attack. They concentrated on the apparent wastefulness of expedients such as cash allowances to supplement inadequate wages – the Speenhamland system – which had been introduced into many southern counties during the food crises of 1793–1815. The main burden of their charge was that the old poor law encouraged both procreation and idleness, thus exacerbating the problem it was designed to alleviate. In particular, as David Ricardo (1772–1823) argued, it interfered with the sacred laws of supply and demand, and opened up the horrendous prospect of massively increased public expenditure to no practical purpose (4a).

It was clear that some remedy must be found, but the precise nature of the radical solution eventually enshrined in the Poor Law Amendment Act, 1834, was largely dictated by Edwin Chadwick (1800–90) and Nassau Senior (1790–1864). They were the best informed and most influential voices on the parliamentary commission of inquiry into the operation of the poor laws, which sat from 1832 to 1834. Both men were influenced by the Benthamite school of Utilitarian efficiency, and they presented large quantities of evidence – which most historians now admit to be partial and selective – to show that the old system engendered yet more poverty. It should be dismantled entirely in order to institute a new scheme, under

central supervision, the cardinal principles of which were that outdoor
relief – wage supplementation and the like – should be abolished, and that
poor relief inside the workhouse should be sufficiently unpleasant to deter
applications from all but the truly destitute (4b). Thus was born the famous
philosophy of 'less eligibility' of poor relief. So well, indeed, did the
framers of the 1834 Act do their work that the stigma of 'going on the
parish' remained with the working classes for the next hundred years, and
was in large part responsible for the reluctance of many to accept State-
supported welfare reforms early in the twentieth century. Senior argued
that the new system was both rational and in the best interests of the poor
themselves.

The 1834 Act, though it had an easy passage in parliament, soon stirred
up controversy. Designed to cope with structural underemployment in the
rural areas, it was singularly ill-equipped to deal with massive but short-
term slumps in the industrial north resulting in unemployment on a huge
scale. It is now clear that, here in particular, the tidy-minded solutions of
Chadwick were widely evaded, and outdoor relief continued to be offered
by the new Boards of Guardians. Where the full rigour of 1834 was
effected, however, there is no doubt that 'less eligibility' bit deep and left
ugly wounds for future generations to heal(4f&g). There were also
differing views about the extent to which the new law reduced poor law
expenditure and improved the moral fibre of the labourers (4c).

Chadwick and the poor law commissioners found themselves under
much attack for foisting on the community a centralized bureaucracy
which ran counter to 'English' desires for self-government and lack of
controls (4d). *The Times*, no friend of Utilitarian nostrums, saw the return
of the Star Chamber as the natural culmination of this pernicious example
of government growth. The commissioners, both in the 1830s and 1860s,
attempted to allay suspicions, while pointing to measurable improvements
and lower poor rates (4d & i). The Lancashire cotton famine of the early
1860s provided an excellent example of a situation with which the
reformed poor law was not equipped to deal. Largely on the initiative of the
leader of the Opposition, and extensive Lancashire landowner, the Earl of
Derby (1799–1869), parliament passed a pioneer, if largely unsuccessful,
Public Works Act (4h), designed to circumvent the poor law temporarily
by financing a wide range of relief schemes to find work for the
unemployed.

Suggestions for further reading

The literature on this subject, and the controversies it excites, is vast. Readers are advised to
consult two excellent introductory pamphlets: J.D. Marshall, *The Old Poor Law, 1795–1834*

(1968) and M.E. Rose, *The Relief of Poverty, 1834–1914* (1972); both have good annotated
bibliographies. See also the excellent symposium, D. Fraser (ed.), *The New Poor Law in the
Nineteenth Century* (1976). On the cotton famine, see W.O. Henderson, *The Lancashire
Cotton Famine, 1861–1865* (1934).

4a   The withering rays of political economy illuminate the old poor law

D. Ricardo, *Principles of Political Economy and Taxation* (1817), Penguin ed.
1971, pp. 115–16, 126.

The power of the labourer to support himself, and the family which may
be necessary to keep up the number of labourers, does not depend on the
quantity of money which he may receive for wages, but on the quantity of
food, necessaries and conveniences become essential to him from habit,
which that money will purchase. The natural price of labour, therefore,
depends on the price of food, necessaries, and conveniences required for the
support of the labourer and his family ....

The market price of labour is the price which is really paid for it, from
the natural operation of the proportion of the supply and the demand;
labour is dear when it is scarce, and cheap when it is plentiful. However
much the market price of labour may deviate from its natural price, it has,
like commodities, a tendency to conform to it.

It is when the market price of labour exceeds its natural price, that the
condition of the labourer is flourishing and happy, that he has it in his
power to command a greater proportion of the necessaries and enjoyments
of life, and therefore to rear a healthy and numerous family. When,
however, by the encouragement which high wages give to the increase of
population, the number of labourers is increased, wages again fall to their
natural price, and indeed from a re-action sometimes fall below it.

When the market price of labour is below its natural price, the condition
of the labourers is most wretched: then poverty deprives them of those
comforts which custom renders absolute necessaries. It is only after their
privations have reduced their number, or the demand for labour has
increased, that the market price of labour will rise to its natural price, and

that the labourer will have the moderate comforts which the natural rate of wages will afford ....

Like all other contracts, wages should be left to the fair and free competition of the market, and should never be controlled by the interference of the legislature.

The clear and direct tendency of the poor law, is in direct opposition to these obvious principles: it is not, as the legislature benevolently intended, to amend the condition of the poor, but to deteriorate the condition of both poor and rich; instead of making the poor rich, they are calculated to make the rich poor; and whilst the present laws are in force, it is quite in the natural order of things that the fund for the maintenance of the poor should progressively increase, till it has absorbed all the net revenue of the country, or at least so much of it as the state shall leave to us, after satisfying its own never failing demands for the public expenditure.

4b   The 1834 Poor Law Report

Parliamentary Papers, 1834 vol. xvii, in S.G. and E.O.A. Checkland (eds), *The Poor Law Report of 1834* (1974), pp. 335, 375, 418–19, 438–9

The first and most essential of all conditions; a principle which we find universally admitted, even by those whose practice is at variance with it, is that his [the pauper's] situation on the whole shall not be made really or apparently so eligible as the situation of the independent labourer of the lowest class. Throughout the evidence it is shown that in proportion as the condition of any pauper class is elevated above the condition of independent labourers, the condition of the independent class is depressed; their industry is impaired, their employment becomes unsteady, and its remuneration in wages is diminished. Such persons, therefore, are under the strongest inducements to quit the less eligible class of labourers and enter the more eligible class of paupers .... Every penny bestowed that tends to render the condition of the pauper more eligible than that of the independent labourer, is a bounty on indolence and vice. We have found that as the poor's rates are at present administered, they operated as bounties of this description, to the amount of several millions annually ....

The chief specific measures which we recommend ... are –

First, that except as to medical attendance, and subject to the exception respecting apprenticeship ... all relief whatever to able-bodied persons or to their families otherwise than in well-regulated workhouses ... shall be declared unlawful and shall cease, in manner and at periods hereafter specified; and that all relief afforded in respect of children under the age of sixteen shall be considered as afforded to their parents ....

We recommend ... the appointment of a Central Board to control the administration of the Poor Laws, with such assistant Commissioners as may be found requisite; and that the Commissioners be empowered and directed to frame and enforce regulations for the government of workhouses, and as to the nature and amount of the relief to be given and the labour to be exacted in them, and that such regulations shall, as far as may be practicable, be uniform throughout the country ....

We recommend that the Central Board be empowered to cause any number of parishes which they may think convenient to be incorporated for the purpose of workhouse management, and for providing new workhouses where necessary ....

4c Two views of the effects of the new poor law

Edwin Chadwick, *An Article on the Principles and Progress of the Poor Law Amendment Act* (1837), p. 45 (Report from the auditor of the Uckfield (Sussex) Poor Law Union).

When the overseers met in vestry, in November, for the purpose of making a rate for the winter half-year, it was found that, instead of a 5s. or 6s. book, as had hitherto been the case, a rate of 1s. 6d. would be amply sufficient; it was much doubted whether it would have been necessary to have made a rate at all, had it not been to meet the sum assessed for the county rate ....

Here, then, was upwards of £1,000 left in the hands of the ratepayers, to meet the demands of such labourers as were willing to earn it; on the other hand, there were two houses for able-bodied men who were out of employment, with regular hours, regular diet, no beer, no tobacco, strict supervision, with the *sedentary*, and, therefore, to the agricultural labourer, *irksome*, employment of picking oakum.

The effect was almost magical: the ratepayers, who had been most violently opposed to the Union, had now substantial proofs in their own pockets of its advantages, and the labourers, as well those who deserved that name, as those who had hitherto been only known by it, began to think, to use their own expression, it was high time 'to look out'. Employment was now sought after – the farmers were reminded of their reduction – their feelings were appealed to – they honourably answered the demand, without taking advantage of circumstances to reduce the wages, and the gratitude of the workman was evinced by his civility, his attention, and his industry.

Mr J.H. Cutler's speech to Birmingham Town Council, 1 December 1840, reprinted in G.R.W. Baxter, *Book of Bastiles* (1841), p. 536.

It was said, that the management of the New Poor-Law was more economical than under the old; and, with a view to prove this, Mr. Weale, the Assistant-Commissioner stated, that the average cost of the population of Aston, is only 2s.8½d., while in Birmingham [under the old system] it is 5s.5½d. a-head. Now, this was extraordinary, but he should like to know how the parish of Aston could keep their poor at a cost of 2s.2d. a-head, that being the net cost of the maintenance, exclusive of the other expenses attendant upon the establishment. He found, however, upon unquestionable authority, that the poor under the New Law, in 1836, amounted to 4,254,000, or a burden on each of the population of nearly 7s.7d. Where, then, was this boasted economy under the new arrangement? It evaporated immediately the test was applied! Let them go to Manchester, where the cost, taking into calculation the population of the poor, was 6s.6d., thus showing a difference of 1s.6d. in favour of the old system.

4d   The Poor Law Commission justifies itself

Report of the Poor Law Commissioners on the continuance of the
Commission, Parliamentary Papers, 1840, vol. xvii, pp. 180–2.

We would here beg leave to recall to your Lordship's memory the state of
England, immediately before the passing of the Poor Law Amendment Act
.... The amount of the Poor-rates had become grievously oppressive in
most parts of the country, and in some places had become nearly
intolerable, so as to threaten the abandonment of the land by the
proprietors .... Various contrivances for compounding relief with wages
had enabled the predominant interest in each locality to force their weaker
neighbours to contribute to a common fund from which they did not
derive an equal benefit, and had converted the state of the labourer into a
condition little superior to that of predial servitude. The consequences of
this perversion of the natural relations of employer and workmen were
developed in the agrarian disturbances and fires of 1830 and 1831 .... Now
although the Poor Law Commission has existed for little more than five
years, the causes of evil which we have just described have been
extinguished. Systematic relief of able-bodied men in aid of wages, only
exists in a few Unions which do not yet possess an efficient workhouse. All
the other pernicious varieties of the old method of relief, which are
described by the Commission of Inquiry as being then in full vigour – the
allowance system, the roundsman system, the labour-rate system – have
ceased ....

The objection most commonly made to the existence of the Poor Law
Commission consists in the assertion that its powers are *unconstitutional and
arbitrary* ....

With respect to the *centralized authority* which is the objection to the Poor
Law Commission, as an innovation inconsistent with the general spirit of
the constitution, we may observe that this objection appears to assume that
nearly the entire administration of the United Kingdom is conducted by
local authorities, bound together by no common tie except the general law,

and acknowledging no common superior except the Crown and Parliament. This assumption, however, is not consistent with fact.

4e   The 'excessive powers' of the commission attacked

William Smith Marriott, Letter to the *Sussex Express*, 13 February 1841, reprinted in G.R.W. Baxter, *Book of Bastiles* (1841), p. 288.

I think you will concur with me in sentiments of astonishment and alarm in observing the announced intention of the Whig Radical Government to continue the unconstitutional and excessive powers of the triumvirate of Somerset-house, with all their satellites, for ten years longer! ... I would call upon you, Sir, and the Conservative press, which I rejoice to say is generally opposed to this measure, I would call upon parishes, and Boards of Guardians, and the gentry and yeomanry of England, whom this law practically declares to be incapable of managing their own affairs, and I would call upon the clergy whom I believe to be opposed to enactments, the cruelty of which, pressing upon their poorer brethren, none know better than they. I would call upon all these by remonstrance and petitions to use their legitimate influence to prevent the enactment of a measure which is founded neither on *humane* nor on *Christian principles*. The Scripture says, 'If a man *will not* work, neither shall he eat'. The Poor-Law Commissioners say, 'If a man cannot work, neither shall he eat', unless, indeed, he will accept the bread of affliction, and the water of bitterness, in a Union workhouse. I speak not of the idle and the profligate, who bring their sufferings on themselves, but of honest, industrious labourers, whose poverty is their only crime ....

I have spoken of the powers of the Commissioners as excessive, and shall I not be borne out in this assertion by any one who has ever attended a Board of Guardians, and listened to any one of their imperial edicts, commencing with 'Now we, the Poor-Law Commissioners, hereby order and command', and ending with 'E. Chadwick!', leaving nothing to Guardians and rate-payers, the former of whom by their name are supposed to *protect the poor*, and the latter − who raise the funds for their maintenance – leaving nothing to them, I say, but to carry the orders of their masters, however they may disapprove of them, into execution and to pay whatever money is required without presuming to ask for what purpose it is intended? ...

That the powers of the Commissioners are *unconstitutional* is clear from the fact that they are *above the law*, for they are commissioned, not so much to see that an Act of Parliament is carried into effect, as from time to time, to make fresh orders which are to have the authority of law, and to give arbitrary interpretations of their own, to every one of its provisions.

4f 'Poverty is in England punished with greater severity than crime!'

Richard Oastler, *The Fleet Papers* (4 vols, 1841–4), vol. i, pp. 191–2.

... it is sworn by the Governor of the Millbank Penitentiary, that the felons there 'who are sick, are allowed wine, or any other nourishment which the medical officer may deem necessary.'

Compare the dietary of that prison with a dietary table before me, which is signed 'Edwin Chadwick'. My blood freezes as I write that name! – ...

Dietary at the Penitentiary

'The average daily allowance to each prisoner is a pint of gruel for breakfast, a pint of broth for supper, one pound and a half of bread, and five ounces of meat without bone, to be weighed after cooking, and potatoes or other vegetables.'

Thus swears the Governor; – yet thus does the heartless 'Edwin Chadwick' order for England's industrious, honest poor!

For able bodied		Men	Women
Breakfast and supper	Bread	6 ozs	5 ozs
	Cheese or butter	1 oz	1 oz
Dinner, 2 days	Suet pudding and		
	vegetables	1 lb	10 ozs

Dinner, 1 day	Meat and vegetables	1 lb	10 ozs
Dinner, 4 days	Bread	7 ozs	7 ozs
	Cheese	1 oz	1 oz

(signed) EDWIN CHADWICK

So that, under the accursed New Poor Law, poverty is in England punished with greater severity than crime! ... I can do more. My heart bleeds – my head is bewildered. The sins of England make me tremble for my native land! Under the operation of the new Poor Law, England is reduced to a state of horrid barbarism.

4g   'Less eligibility' in action

Report of a Committee of Guardians into the working of Milnthorpe (Westmorland) workhouse, 27 April 1842. Cumbria County Record Office (Kendal), WSPU/K Minute Book 1842–6, pp. 15–16.

With respect to the practice, lately commenced here, of giving a money grant, weekly, in lieu of Tobacco and Snuff, we strongly recommend that this allowance of money should be *at once discontinued*, as the practice is found to lead to irregular and sometimes debasing habits in the recipients .... We further recommend, with regard to Tobacco and Snuff, that the former practice of giving to old Men and Women above Sixty, a small quantity should again be resumed; but the Master is requested to give it as sparingly as possible, and only in cases where the habitual use is inveterate.

With regard to *premium upon earnings* we recommend as a general rule that the present practice of giving One half of the total amount of these premiums weekly *in Money* should be *discontinued*; and in lieu thereof that in every case where the premium *exceeds* three pence, only three pence of that gross sum shall be given to the paupers weekly, and the residue be retained by the Master for the use of the pauper when he may desire to leave the House, or if he die there, to cover the expences of his funeral .... We further find with regard to premiums that many of them are too high; That the rate of earnings of the Paupers employed in Heckling, Spinning, Balling & Boxing and Stonebreaking be reduced.

4h   The poor law and the Lancashire cotton famine

Public Works (Manufacturing Districts) Act, 1863 (26 & 27 Vic., c. 70).

Whereas ... by reason of the closing of Mills and Factories in certain Parts of the Country great numbers of the labouring and manufacturing classes had been thrown out of Employment, Provision was made to enable Boards of Guardians of certain Unions to obtain temporary aid to meet the extraordinary Demands for Relief therein ....

For the purposes of Loans under this Act, the Commissioners of Her Majesty's Treasury may, from Time to Time ... cause to be issued out of the Consolidated Fund ... any Sum ... not exceeding two hundred thousand Pounds ... to be at the Disposal of the Public Works Loan Commissioners ....

[The money to finance public works schemes, such as paving streets, improving water supplies, improving common land as places of recreation etc.]

Hansard (3rd series), vol. clxxii (1863), cols 344–6, House of Lords, 7 July 1863.

Earl of Derby: I am not disposed in any way to object to this Bill, which I think is founded on a right principle, and is calculated to afford considerable relief in the manufacturing districts ... a Bill like this, which will remove many of the difficulties which we have had in finding employments ... for the distressed operatives ... must be acceptable to those who have taken a part in the administration of relief to our suffering fellow-countrymen. As a general rule, the intervention of the Government, in matters of this kind, may not be considered desirable; but this Bill is an exception which, under the circumstances, demands our approval.

4i Poor law administration supported in the 1860s

Report of the Select Committee on Poor Relief, *Parliamentary Papers*, vol. ix (1864), pp. 197–8.

CONTINUANCE OF A CENTRAL AUTHORITY

Your Committee then proceeded to examine several witnesses upon the subject of the expediency of the continuance of the central authority. The witnesses consisted principally of chairmen and vice-chairmen of Boards of Guardians, and of clerks to Poor Law Unions. Your Committee found that the concurrence of opinion in favour of the existence and continuance of a central Board was almost unanimous. Mr. Adamson, clerk to the guardians of the Salford Union, says, 'I am satisfied that without a central authority abuses would creep in in the administration of the law, as they did before the passing of the Poor Law Amendment Act.' ...

Mr. Bowring, clerk to the Guardians of the City of London Union, states, 'I do not think that there is any person in the kingdom, knowing anything about the administration of the Poor Law, who would dispense with the Poor Law Board. If the central authority were dispensed with, you would come back to the state of anarchy and confusion which existed previous to 1832 and 1833; and I am afraid that it would be even worse, for you would have Boards of Guardians with large funds, instead of churchwardens and overseers with small funds. I think it would conform with the opinion of the country generally if a proposition were made to make the Board a permanent establishment.' ...

POWER OF POOR LAW BOARD TO ISSUE GENERAL ORDERS

The power to make orders for the management of the poor and administration of the laws for their relief was conferred upon the central authority by the 4 & 5 Will. 4, c.76, sect. 15; and in exercise of that power they have issued several orders regulating the administration of outdoor relief, the chief of which are the order of 21 December 1844, usually

known as the Prohibitory Order; and the out-door relief regulation order
of the 14th of December 1852. The former of these orders is in force in the
agricultural, and the latter in the manufacturing, unions, and each order
contains such numerous exceptions as to provide for all cases to which the
general rule would be inapplicable .... Your Committee do not consider
that any advantage could result from confiding any further powers to the
guardians in respect to grants of outdoor relief; and being, moreover, of
opinion that the authority vested in the Central Board to regulate the
administration of the laws for the relief of the poor has been exercised with
general advantage, have agreed to the following resolution; viz.:-

That the power of issuing General Orders now possessed by the Poor
Law Board is salutary and useful, and should be continued.

5 Public health

In many northern cities, the industrial revolution produced powerful reasons for State intervention, in the form of an overcrowded population living in squalid, poorly constructed and insanitary homes. The new towns and cities had grown too rapidly for comfortable assimilation within the existing framework. They lacked even basic sanitary amenities, such as a proper water supply, and there was no adequate local government provision. Medical men were not slow to point out the connection between dirt and disease. J.P. Kay (later famous as the educational administrator Sir James Kay-Shuttleworth) presented a harrowing picture of early nineteenth-century Manchester (5a). It is noticeable, however, that Kay drew attention to the moral failings of the working classes, and suggested that much could be achieved by the directed development of more sober and provident habits. Edwin Chadwick's 1842 *Sanitary.Report* (5b) took the argument several stages further. With a wealth of statistical evidence, he demonstrated the differential effects on life expectancy of being born into a particular class and living in a particular environment. Chadwick viewed the problem partly in terms of the diminished efficiency of the nation as a consequence of high mortality rates and frequent debilitating illnesses, but his *Report* called unequivocally for the adoption of uniform standards to protect public health and to improve the moral condition of the industrial population. He also sketched out a programme of action on drainage, filth-removal and water supply.

Chadwick's *Report* led to the establishment of a parliamentary Health of Towns Commission. This produced further evidence in 1844 and 1845 pointing in the same direction. By no means all interested parties, however, were prepared to accept the Chadwick formula. The principle of local autonomy was held sacred by many; and while certain far-seeing authorities were prepared to put his solutions into immediate practice, others held back. Liverpool, for example, appointed a Medical Officer of Health with wide advisory and regulatory powers as early as 1846, while Birmingham saw no need to do so until compelled by parliament in 1872. Most commonly, public health initiatives were taken by means of local Acts of Parliament, such as that adopted by Rochdale in 1853 (5e). Thus, a series of piecemeal solutions was reached—some satisfactory, others not.

Most professionals, like the sanitary engineer W.A. Guy (5c), accepted the need for central supervision. Local initiative in matters of this magnitude was seen as 'a popular delusion'. Nevertheless, the Public Health Act of 1848 showed great deference to local wishes. A central Board of Health was established, with Chadwick its salaried commissioner. Its role was essentially advisory, however, and local authorities were not compelled to adopt sanitary measures unless their death rate was 23 per 1000 or higher. In 1848, 23 per 1000 was exactly the average mortality rate in England and Wales, though, of course, considerably inflated by much worse figures in certain northern cities. Cautious as it was, the Act represented an important development in social policy, in that central government was prepared selectively to adopt compulsory powers with the aim of ensuring minimum standards. The Tory *Quarterly Review* (5d) attempted to dispel alarm about the degree of centralization implied. Chadwick's inquisitorial methods were to prove deeply offensive to local sensitivities, however, and he was dismissed from his post in 1854. The general Board of Health was wound up in 1858, and assimilated within a newly created medical department of the Privy Council, and the Local Government Act Office. Its demise, ironically though not insignificantly, coincided with a period of considerable development in local sanitary schemes.

If there was a leading spirit behind the public health movement after Chadwick's removal, it was surely London's first MOH and, from 1858, medical officer to the Privy Council department, John Simon (1816–1904). He pressed continually for improvements to local sanitary measures, and argued that local interests were not well served by penny-pinching councillors more concerned to keep down the rates than to ensure adequate sanitary provision for all, including the non-rate-paying poor (5g). He was also involved in the campaign to secure legislation against the adulteration of food (5f). An ineffective Adulteration of Foods Act was passed in 1860, the precursor of more far-reaching legislation in 1872 and 1875, by which local authorities were enjoined to employ public analysts to test food. The Alkali Act, 1863, was similarly the first of a series of enactments to deal with acid gas pollution, affecting fields and livestock adjacent to chemical soda works. The legislation was passed under pressure from leading landowners, such as the Earl of Derby (1799–1869) (5h).

Though overshadowed by amending legislation in 1875, the 1866 Sanitary Act (5i) may be seen as Simon's crowning achievement. Badly drafted as it was, this enshrined the vital principle of uniform and universal provision of sanitary protection, with compulsory powers of enforcement on local authorities. Individual dwellings were brought within the purview of nuisance control as the scope of legislation was widened. It is surely significant that the two most important sanitary statutes of the period were passed, in 1848 and 1866, at a time of serious national concern over epidemics of cholera — water-borne and affecting working and middle classes alike—whereas typhus and other scourges of an overcrowded and insanitary population visited the poor in disproportionate numbers. At all events, it was in the field of public health that the State moved first from permissive to selective and carefully controlled compulsory legislation.

Suggestions for further reading

S.E. Finer, *The Life and Times of Edwin Chadwick* (1952) and R. Lambert, *Sir John Simon, 1816–1904, and English Social Administration* (1963), cover the ground admirably through the medium of wide-ranging biographies of the most influential figures.

5a   The causes of preventable disease

J.P. Kay, *The Moral and Physical Condition of the Working Classes Employed in the Cotton Manufacture of Manchester* (1832), Cass ed. 1970, pp. 28–9 77–82.

The state of the streets powerfully affects the health of their inhabitants. Sporadic cases of typhus chiefly appear in those which are narrow, ill ventilated, unpaved, or which contain heaps of refuse, or stagnant pools. The confined air and noxious exhalations, which abound in such places, depress the health of the people, and on this account contagious diseases are also most rapidly propagated there. The operation of these causes is exceedingly promoted by their reflex influence on the manners. The houses, in such situations, are uncleanly, ill provided with furniture; an air of discomfort if not of squalid and loathsome wretchedness pervades them, they are often dilapidated, badly drained, damp: and the habits of their tenants are gross—they are ill-fed, ill-clothed, and uneconomical—at once spendthrifts and destitute—denying themselves the comforts of life, in order that they may wallow in the unrestrained licence of animal appetite. An intimate connexion subsists, among the poor, between the cleanliness of the street and that of the house and person. Uneconomical habits, and dissipation are almost inseparably allied; and they are so frequently connected with uncleanliness, that we cannot consider their concomitance as altogether accidental .... When the health is depressed by the concurrence of these causes, contagious diseases spread with a fatal malignancy among the population subjected to their influence. The records of the Fever Hospital of Manchester, prove that typhus prevails almost exclusively in such situations.

Believing that the natural tendency of unrestricted commerce ... is to develop the energies of society, to increase the comforts and luxuries of life and to *elevate the physical condition* of every member of the social body, we have exposed, with a faithful, though a friendly hand, the condition of the lower orders connected with manufactures of this town, because we conceive that the evils affecting them result *from foreign and accidental causes* ....

The evils affecting the working classes, *so far from being the necessary results of the commercial system, furnish evidence of a disease which impairs its energies, if it does not threaten its vitality* ....

Want of cleanliness, of forethought, and economy, are found in almost invariable alliance with dissipation, reckless habits, and disease. The population gradually becomes physically less efficient as the producers of wealth – morally so from idleness – politically *worthless* as having few desires to satisfy, and *noxious* as dissipators of capital accumulated. Were such manners to prevail, the horrors of pauperism would accumulate. A debilitated race would be rapidly multiplied. Morality would afford no check to the increase of the population: crime and disease would be its only obstacles .... A dense mass, impotent alike of great moral or physical efforts, would accumulate .... They would drag on an unhappy existence, vibrating between the pangs of hunger and the delirium of dissipation – alternately exhausted by severe and oppressive toil, or enervated by supine sloth.

5b The Chadwick prescription for public health

Edwin Chadwick, *Report on the Sanitary Conditions of the Labouring Population of Great Britain* (1842), 1965 ed. by M.W. Flinn, pp. 78, 228–9, 422–5.

It appears that fever, after its ravages amongst the infant population, falls with the greatest intensity on the adult population in the vigour of life. The periods at which the ravages of the other diseases, consumption, small-pox, and measles take place, are sufficiently well known. The proportions in which the diseases have prevailed in the several counties will be found deserving of peculiar attention.

A conception may be formed of the aggregate effects of the several causes of mortality from the fact, that of the deaths caused during one year in England and Wales by epidemic, endemic, and contagious diseases, including fever, typhus, and scarlatina, amounting to 56,461, the great proportion of which are proved to be preventible, it may be said that the effect is as if the whole county of Westmorland, now containing 56,469 souls, or the whole county of Huntingdonshire, or any other equivalent district, were entirely depopulated annually, and were only occupied again by the growth of a new and feeble population living under the fears of a similar visitation. The annual slaughter in England and Wales from preventible causes of typhus which attacks persons in the vigour of life, appears to be double the amount of what was suffered by the Allied Armies in the battle of Waterloo ....

CLASSES	Total No. of Deaths under 20 Years of Age	Proportion of Deaths which occurred at the under-mentioned periods of Age			Proportion of Deaths under 20 Years to Total Deaths
		Between 0–5	Between 5–10	Between 10–20	
Gentry and Professional Persons, Children of					
Manchester	21	1 in 3	1 in 24	1 in 54	1 in 3
Leeds	20	1 in 5	1 in 26	1 in 40	1 in 4
Liverpool	61	1 in 3	1 in 11	1 in 23	1 in 2½
Bath	32	1 in 11	1 in 12	1 in 31	1 in 4½
Bethnal Green	33	1 in 5	1 in 20	1 in 13	1 in 3
Strand Union	21	1 in 6	1 in 29	1 in 29	1 in 4
Kendal Union	15	1 in 7	1 in 26	1 in 9	1 in 3
County of Wilts (Unions of)	25	1 in 9	1 in 40	1 in 13	1 in 5
County of Rutland (Unions of)	4	1 in 4	—	—	1 in 7
Total	232	1 in 5	1 in 19	1 in 19	1 in 3½
Farmers, Tradesmen, and Persons similarly circumstanced, Children of					
Manchester	444	1 in 2	1 in 18	1 in 27	1 in 2
Leeds	425	1 in 2	1 in 18	1 in 18	1 in 2
Liverpool	1,033	1 in 2	1 in 19	1 in 33	1 in 1¾
Bath	78	1 in 4	1 in 24	1 in 30	1 in 3
Bethnal Green	142	1 in 2	1 in 20	1 in 28	1 in 2
Strand Union	99	1 in 3	1 in 20	1 in 25	1 in 2
Kendal Union	47	1 in 4	1 in 35	1 in 14	1 in 3
County of Wilts (Unions of)	54	1 in 7	1 in 27	1 in 15	1 in 4
County of Rutland (Unions of)	174	1 in 3	1 in 30	1 in 17	1 in 3
Total	2,496	1 in 2¼	1 in 20	1 in 23	1 in 2
Agricultural and other Labourers, Artisans, and Servants, Children of					
Manchester	3,106	1 in 2	1 in 22	1 in 19	1 in 1½
Leeds	2,245	1 in 2	1 in 14	1 in 14	1 in 1½
Liverpool	4,004	1 in 1½	1 in 15	1 in 33	1 in 1¼
Bath	508	1 in 2	1 in 19	1 in 18	1 in 1¾
Bethnal Green	908	1 in 2	1 in 15	1 in 30	1 in 1½
Strand Union	367	1 in 2	1 in 14	1 in 23	1 in 2
Kendal Union	186	1 in 3	1 in 19	1 in 11	1 in 2
County of Wilts (Unions of)	954	1 in 3	1 in 21	1 in 14	1 in 2
County of Rutland (Unions of)	293	1 in 3	1 in 18	1 in 18	1 in 2¼
Total	12,571	1 in 2	1 in 17	1 in 20	1 in 1½

CLASSES	Total No. of Deaths which occurred between 20 and 60	Proportion of Deaths which occurred at the under-mentioned periods of Age				Proportion of Deaths from 20 to 60 to Total Deaths
		Between 20–30	Between 30–40	Between 40–50	Between 50–60	
Gentry and Professional Persons and their Families						
Manchester	13	1 in 18	1 in 14	1 in 18	1 in 18	1 in 4
Leeds	28	1 in 11	1 in 10	1 in 16	1 in 10	1 in 3
Liverpool	34	1 in 46	1 in 15	1 in 23	1 in 9	1 in 4
Bath	29	1 in 29	1 in 24	1 in 24	1 in 12	1 in 5
Bethnal Green	21	1 in 25	1 in 17	1 in 25	1 in 14	1 in 5
Strand Union	37	1 in 9	1 in 9	1 in 10	1 in 11	1 in 2¼
Kendal Union	18	1 in 13	1 in 13	1 in 7	1 in 17	1 in 3
County of Wilts (Unions of)	32	1 in 15	1 in 15	1 in 17	1 in 13	1 in 4
County of Rutland (Unions of)	7	1 in 14	1 in 14	1 in 14	1 in 28	1 in 4
Total	219	1 in 17	1 in 14	1 in 16	1 in 12	1 in 4
Tradesmen, Farmers, &c						
Manchester	220	1 in 14	1 in 11	1 in 13	1 in 18	1 in 3¼
Leeds	238	1 in 12	1 in 14	1 in 14	1 in 19	1 in 3½
Liverpool	481	1 in 22	1 in 13	1 in 14	1 in 13	1 in 3½
Bath	109	1 in 11	1 in 7	1 in 9	1 in 9	1 in 2¼
Bethnal Green	92	1 in 15	1 in 11	1 in 12	1 in 11	1 in 3
Strand Union	71	1 in 16	1 in 22	1 in 10	1 in 9	1 in 3
Kendal Union	43	1 in 8	1 in 14	1 in 17	1 in 17	1 in 3
County of Wilts (Unions of)	65	1 in 22	1 in 14	1 in 10	1 in 12	1 in 3½
County of Rutland (Unions of)	108	1 in 15	1 in 16	1 in 19	1 in 19	1 in 4
Total	1,427	1 in 15	1 in 12	1 in 13	1 in 14	1 in 3½
Agricultural Labourers, Operatives, Servants, &c.						
Manchester	1,149	1 in 16	1 in 14	1 in 18	1 in 17	1 in 4
Leeds	773	1 in 14	1 in 16	1 in 20	1 in 22	1 in 4½
Liverpool	1,205	1 in 17	1 in 18	1 in 17	1 in 24	1 in 4½
Bath	258	1 in 12	1 in 14	1 in 13	1 in 17	1 in 3
Bethnal Green	228	1 in 18	1 in 23	1 in 21	1 in 31	1 in 5½
Strand Union	212	1 in 13	1 in 12	1 in 13	1 in 13	1 in 3
Kendal Union	113	1 in 13	1 in 14	1 in 18	1 in 14	1 in 3¾
County of Wilts (Unions of)	492	1 in 13	1 in 18	1 in 18	1 in 19	1 in 4
County of Rutland (Unions of)	157	1 in 12	1 in 18	1 in 18	1 in 27	1 in 4
Total	4,587	1 in 15	1 in 17	1 in 18	1 in 20	1 in 4

First, as to the extent and operation of the evils which are the subject of the inquiry:-

That the various forms of epidemic, endemic, and other disease caused, or aggravated, or propagated chiefly amongst the labouring classes by atmospheric impurities produced by decomposing animal and vegetable substances, by damp and filth, and close and overcrowded dwellings prevail amongst the population in every part of the kingdom, whether dwelling in separate houses, in rural villages, in small towns, in the larger towns—as they have been found to prevail in the lowest districts of the metropolis.

That such disease, wherever its attacks are frequent, is always found in connexion with the physical circumstances above specified, and that where those circumstances are removed by drainage, proper cleansing, better ventilation, and other means of diminishing atmospheric impurity, the frequency and intensity of such disease is abated; and where the removal of the noxious agencies appears to be complete, such disease almost entirely disappears ....

Secondly. As to the means by which the present sanitary condition of the labouring classes may be improved:—

The primary and most important measures, and at the same time the most practicable, and within the recognized province of public administration, are drainage, the removal of all refuse of habitations, streets, and roads, and the improvement of the supplies of water ....

That for the protection of the labouring classes and of the ratepayers against inefficiency and waste in all new structural arrangements for the protection of the public health, and to ensure public confidence that the expenditure will be beneficial, securities should be taken that all new local public works are devised and conducted by responsible officers qualified by the possession of the science and skill of civil engineers ....

The advantages of uniformity in legislation and in the executive machinery, and of doing the same things in the same way (choosing the best), and calling the same officers, proceedings, and things by the same names, will only be appreciated by those who have observed the extensive public loss occasioned by the legislation for towns which makes them independent of beneficent, as of what perhaps might have been deemed formerly aggressive legislation.

5c   The advantages of central direction in public health

'The Sanitary Question', *Fraser's Magazine*, vol. xxxvi (1847), p. 371 (article by W.A. Guy).

The utter failure of the system of local self-government for sanitary purposes is notorious to all who have taken any pains to inquire into the subject. Even if the parochial system were perfect for all other purposes of administration, it must necessarily fail when applied to some of the chief measures of sanitary improvement. Drainage, especially, which is of vast importance to health, cannot be carried out by parishes. It presupposes an extensive area selected for that special object, surveyed and laid out with a scientific skill and judgement which few parishes have in their command, and which popular election is extremely unlikely to ensure.

We look upon local self-government, then — at least for sanitary purposes, whether the governing body be a parish vestry or a town council—as a popular delusion, condemned by common sense and everyday experience. We are not advocates for the opposite system of centralisation, as that term is generally understood, but if we had to make our choice between the two systems, we should prefer the most unpopular. We would rather trust to the central government than to the local authorities. The one is about as pure as the other, but government nomination would secure a better class of officers than parish election.

5d   A warm reception for the 1848 Public Health Act

'Sanitary Consolidation – Centralization-Local Self-government',
Quarterly Review, vol xxxviii (1850), pp. 436–7, 441–2.

And first—to strike at once into the heart of the debate – let us meet the charge of 'Centralization', or the alleged tendency of the new Sanitary system to supersede Local Self-government by the arbitrary rule of a Metropolitan Board. To reduce this question to its proper terms, we must begin by laying down a well-marked preliminary distinction – that, namely, which exists between Local self-government, as it affects the *mass* of residents in any district, and as it concerns the *functionaries*, often corrupt and ignorant, by whom they are rated and ruled. Obviously, wherever district rates are squandered by jobbing or incompetent Local boards, the corrective intervention of a Central power, so far from diminishing, may tend largely to increase, the *real* self-governing power of the place, as measured by the control of the population over the expenditure of their own funds ....

Centralization is, in fact ... legitimate, provided that its action be based on ascertained public requirement, national or provincial. It is only when these limitations are disregarded, when the exception becomes the rule, and when, in opposition to the public wish, the imperial power exercises by its nominees a direct and permanent sway over local affairs, that Centralization becomes excessive and obnoxious ....

These distinctions have been clearly kept in view by the framers of that admirable sanitary code, the Public Health Act of 1848; an act which embodies the main principles laid down by Sir Robert Peel's Commission of Inquiry into the means of improving the Health of Towns; – and which will remain, we believe, an imperishable monument of that great statesman's far-reaching sagacity. This masterly enactment, while it places the *general* sanitary interests of the country under the care of a Metropolitan Board (the pretext of the anti-centralization cry), also recognises the principle of Local Self-government, by the simultaneous institution of District boards, elected by the ratepayers, to whom they are consequently responsible, and liable to central interference only in one of two cases: first, on an appeal or petition, emanating from district itself, and signed by not less than one-tenth of the ratepayers; secondly, on a duly certified district mortality exceeding the high annual rate of 23 in 1000. Even, indeed, when the regulating power of the Central authority is thus called forth, either by the express prayer of a suffering district, or by a mortality prejudicial to society at large, its operation is surrounded by official delays and restrictions, designed to afford time for local deliberation, and popular concurrence ....

5e   Local initiative in public health

The Rochdale Improvement Act, 1853 (16 & 17 Vic., c. 210) (copy in Manchester Central Reference Library).

... it is expedient that further Provision be made for the Election of Commissioners, the widening, paving and altering of Streets, the cleansing of the River Roche, the Drainage and general Improvement of the Town, the Extension of the Limits for the Supply of Gas for private Consumption, the Formation of a Cemetery for the Burial of the Dead, and the other Purposes for which Provision is made by this Act....

X. That the Commissioners for executing this Act ... shall be called 'The Rochdale Improvement Commissioners' ... with Power to purchase, take, hold, and dispose of Lands and other Property for the Purposes but subject to the Restrictions of this Act, and to put this Act in all respects into execution....

XIII. That ... the Qualification for a Commissioner shall be his being of full Age, and the Owner or Occupier of any Tenement within the Town which was rated in the then last Rate ... on a net yearly Value of Twenty Pounds or upwards....

XCVII. That the Commissioners, from Time to Time, as they think proper, may cleanse and otherwise improve the River Roche within the Town, and for such Purpose may remove or alter the Town Mill Weir on that River, and erect such other proper and sufficient Works as may be requisite....

XCIX. That the Commissioners may order any Land vested in them to be laid into any Street for the widening and rendering more commodious the same, or to be otherwise disposed of for making or improving any Street as they think proper....

CI. That, except with the Consent of the Commissioners, any new Street within the Town shall not be made of less Width than, if a Carriage Road, Thirty Feet, or, if not a Carriage Road, Ten Feet....

CXIX. That the Commissioners from Time to Time may make, alter, and remove, in such Places within the Town as they think fit, any public Privies or Waterclosets, and may maintain and cleanse the same, and make such Regulations for the Use thereof....

CXXII. That if any Person discharge the Smoke of any Furnace or Fireplace or any Steam from any Building (otherwise than from the Top of the same) into any Street within the Town, every Person so offending shall for every such Offence forfeit any Sum not exceeding Forty Shillings ....

5f   Sir John Simon on the evils of food adulteration

Simon, *Reports Relating to the Sanitary Condition of London* (1854) Preface, pp. xii–xiii, xxvii–xxxi.

Probably on no point of political economy is there more general concurrence of opinion, than against any legislative interference with the price of labour. But I would venture to submit, for the consideration of abler judges than myself, that before wages can be safely left to find their own level in the struggles of an unrestricted competition, the law should be rendered absolute and available in safeguards for the ignorant poor – first, against those deteriorations of staple food which enable the retailer to disguise starvation to his customers by apparent cheapenings of bulk; secondly, against those conditions of lodgment which are inconsistent with decency and health .... such evils as I denounce are not the more to be tolerated for their rising in unwilling Pauperism, rather than in willing Filth....

If – as is rumoured, the approaching reconstitution of the General Board of Health is ... to give it a Parliamentary President, that member of the Government ought to be open to challenge in respect of every matter relating to health .... He must be able to justify or to exterminate adulterations of food; to shew that alum ought to be in our loaves, or to banish it for ever; to shew that Copper is wholesome for dessert, or to give us our olives and greengages without it; to shew that red-lead is an estimable condiment, or to divert it from our pepper-pots and curries .... Into the hands of this new minister ... would devolve the guardianship of public health against combined commercial interests, or imcompetent administration.

5g Simon on the inadequacies of local sanitary administration

Sir John Simon, *Public Health Reports* (1887), vol. i, pp. 482, 486 (being Papers presented to the President of the General Board of Health, June 1858).

My own seven years' experience in the service of a local sanitary authority has given me a strong belief in the general disposition of such authorities to exert themselves efficiently against the causes of premature death, when but once they have become fully and publicly informed of the existence and fatality of such causes. *Fully informed*, I say;—because the non-removal of evils which occasion so much human misery commonly depends much less on the supineness of the local authority, as its primary cause, than on the absence of local consciousness as to the real facts of the case. *Publicly informed*, I say;—because local sanitary authorities, exercising their powers virtually without control, and being, like individual men, not incapable of indolence and error, peculiarly require that their fulfilment of very important duties should be subject to public criticism. Failing this check, it is unquestionable that the existing constitution of such authorities must sometimes endanger the objects for which they are constituted. Elected on the principle of being the representatives of rate-payers, the members are sometimes a little apt to forget that, for sanitary purposes, they are also the appointed guardians of masses of human beings whose lives are at stake in the business. They do not always remember that the interests of life are at least as sacred as the separate interests of pocket. And this danger especially deserves to be guarded against; for it has not infrequently happened that local owners of low house-property have procured themselves to be elected members of sanitary boards with a view to the protection of their own unworthy interests by systematic resistance to sanitary improvement....

... sanitary neglect is a mistaken parsimony. Fever and cholera are costly items to count against the cheapness of filthy residence and ditch-drawn drinking-water: widowhood and orphanage make it expensive to sanction unventilated workplaces and needlessly fatal occupations.

5h   The Alkali Act, 1863

Hansard, (3rd series), vol. clxx, cols 169–70 (1863), House of Lords, 16 April 1863.

Lord Stanley of Alderley: The main object of the [Select Committee] enquiry was, as to the means of preventing the injury occasioned in various ways, and especially to vegetation, by alkali works in the manufacture of soda, by the muriatic gas evolved in the process. This gas had a great affinity for water, and this circumstance afforded a mode, which was adopted in some of the best regulated works, for remedying the evil. It was very much to the credit of the manufacturers connected with the trade that they expressed a readiness to be subject to legislation on the subject. The Committee, therefore, recommended that the manufacturers engaged in this branch of business should be compelled to adopt such machinery as would provide for the condensation of this gas, and that this machinery should be under the supervision of inspectors ... appointed by Government.... The power and position of England depended to a very great extent upon her manufacturing freedom, and he firmly believed her pre-eminence had been created and established mainly through freedom from legislative interference with the great departments of industry ....
Their Lordships ... would regret if any legislation with a view to enable owners of land to recover damages from the manufacturers with greater facility than at present, should be attended with injury to so important an interest. In this case, however, a remedy had been tried; it had been shown

to be effective, it had been adopted without inconvenience, and the manufacterers knew that it might, to a certain extent, bring them even a profit, as the condensed gas created muriatic acid, which was a marketable commodity and of great use in many branches of manufacture ....

The Alkali Act, 1863 (26 & 27 Vic., c. 124).

4. If any Alkali works is carried on in contravention of this Section [prescribing conditions for suitable condensation] the Owner of that Work shall ... be subject in respect of the First Conviction to a Penalty not exceeding Fifty Pounds, and in respect of every Offence after a previous Conviction to a penalty not exceeding One hundred Pounds.

5i   The Sanitary Act, 1866

29 & 30 Vic., c. 90.

... 10. If a Dwelling House ... is without a Drain ... sufficient for effectual drainage, the Sewer Authority may by Notice require the Owner of such House within a reasonable Time ... to make a sufficient Drain emptying into any Sewer the Sewer Authority is entitled to use....

19. The Word 'Nuisances' ... shall include,

1. Any House ... so overcrowed as to be dangerous or prejudicial to the Health of the Inmates.

2. Any Factory, Workshop or Workplace ... not kept in a cleanly state, or not ventilated in such a Manner as to render harmless as far as practicable any Gases, Vapours, Dust, or other Impurities.

3. Any Fireplace or Furnace which does not as far as practicable consume the Smoke arising from the Combustible used....

22. If the Nuisance Authority shall be of opinion, upon the Certificate of any legally qualified Medical Practitioner, that the cleansing or disinfecting of any House ... would tend to prevent or check infectious or contagious Disease, it shall ... give Notice ... requiring the Owner or Occupier ... to cleanse and disinfect the same....

35. On Application of One of her Majesty's Principal Secretaries of

State by the Nuisance Authority ... the Secretary of State may ... declare the following Enactment to be in force in the District of such Nuisance Authority....

1. For fixing the Number of Persons who may occupy a House or Part of a House which is let in Lodgings or occupied by Members of more than One Family.

2. For the Registration of Houses thus let....

3. For the Inspection of such Houses and the keeping the Same in a cleanly and wholesome State

4. For enforcing therein the Provision of Privy Accomodation ... and the cleansing and Ventilation of the common Passages and Staircases.

5. For the cleansing and lime-whiting at stated Times of such Premises.

The Nuisance Authority may provide for the Enforcement of the above Regulations by Penalties not exceeding Forty Shillings for any One Offence.

6 Education

The reasons for State intervention in education were similar to those in the field of public health. Just as the conjunction of dirt and disease called for advice, guidance and, eventually, compulsion, so the threat of large numbers of working people crowded together in an alien environment, far from the traditional benefits and obligations of a village community, suggested a need for education to inure the community to its new role and attendant obligations. The State saw education primarily as a problem of order. The first parliamentary grant for education was made in 1833 (6a). Though payable to assist the voluntary efforts of Church schools, who dominated elementary education provision, it marked the beginnings of State support; and this would lead eventually to a State system of education.

In 1839 the first education inspectors were appointed, though only after vetting by diocesan administrations, to ensure that the State got value for the money expended to support what still remained a voluntary system of education. Not surprisingly, the inspectorate contained a disproportionate number of Anglican clergymen. Their reports were often intelligent and illuminating (6b), though it may legitimately be queried how far men, whose previous experience had been largely rural, were qualified to pronounce on essentially urban problems. The Secretary of the Committee of the Privy Council on Education was J.P. Kay (later Kay-Shuttleworth) (1804–77), and he established, between 1839 and 1849, a small, efficient bureaucracy of supervision. In 1846 an important pupil-teacher training scheme (6c) was introduced, the precursor of State training for teachers and a decisive blow to the monitorial system of the voluntary schools, by which older, untrained pupils taught the younger, thus easing the task of the teacher though by no means ensuring high standards of attainment.

By the mid-1840s, the extent to which the State should assume responsibility for education was a much-debated question, the more so as the education budget grew. The initial £20,000 grant in 1833 had increased to £100,000 by 1847 and would exceed £800,000 in 1861. Rev. W.H. Milman recognized that popular education must eventually be State-controlled, though he was concerned to ensure that efficient Church schools should not be prejudiced by the development (6d). Edward Baines Jnr (1800–90), a leading Congregationalist and editor of the influential *Leeds Mercury*, spoke for many dissenters in seeing State education as no more desirable than Anglican indoctrination, and productive of greater long-term dangers through excessive government control. By 1867 he had accepted that a purely voluntary system was no longer tenable (6e).

When R.R.W. Lingen (1819–1905) replaced Kay-Shuttleworth as Secretary of the Committee on Education in 1849, he began a process of reorientation. Inspectors, who under the Kay-Shuttleworth regime had been encouraged to express their views freely, were subjected to tighter controls. Lingen and Robert Lowe (1811–92), Vice-President of the Education Department, used the evidence of the Newcastle Commission on Popular Education (1858–61) to establish a 'payment by results' capitation system in the famous Revised Code of 1861. Grants to schools were made on the basis of 12s. per pupil per annum, 4s. of which was paid on proof of regular attendance and 8s. on satisfactory performance in annual tests, geared rigidly to the '3 Rs'. The new Code stirred up furious controversy. Lowe was able to point to massive savings on the education budget as the State imposed basic standards and refused to support either those who fell below them or those who, in Lowe's revealing words, were being educated 'above their station and business in life' (6g). Kay-Shuttleworth came out of retirement to attack the Code (6h). He believed that it stifled genuine educational development, imposed an inappropriate uniformity and produced savings to the exchequer which were both illusory and, in the long term, dangerous. Moreover, it encouraged the mere rote-learning and fact-grubbing satirized by Dickens in *Hard Times* (6f).

The Revised Code has met with almost universal condemnation. It did, however, clip the wings of many Church schools in that it imposed essentially secular standards of attainment and in some ways smoothed the path of the Board Schools in the 1870s. When the noncomformist-influenced National Education League, formed in 1869, pointed out the alarming deficiencies of the voluntary system, which reached fewer than 20 per cent of pupils in most urban areas, it advocated free, compulsory education in schools no longer under the control of the Anglicans (6i). The Elementary Education Act, 1870, emanated from a Liberal Party subject to many countervailing pressures, and was inevitably a compromise. It was designed only to fill the gaps left by the voluntary system, and it by no means pushed the Church out of education. Instead, voluntary schools were still to be supported, but supplemented by elementary 'Board Schools' established in areas where there was a need for them, and financed

partly by local rate-payers and partly by the State (6j). In 1870 the State
was not prepared to acknowledge an obligation to provide either
compulsory or free elementary education; though these developments,
when they came in the next twenty-one years, were then seen as the
logical outcome of this Act.

Suggestions for further reading

The best short introduction is Gillian Sutherland, *Elementary Education in the Nineteenth
Century* (Hist. Assoc. pamphlet, G76, 1971). See also John Hurt, *Education in Evolution*
(1971). On the early inspectorate, Richard Johnson, 'Educational Policy and Social Control
in Early Victorian England', *Past and Present*, Vol. 49 (1970), pp. 96–119 is particularly
valuable.

6a   Debates on the first government grant for education

Hansard (3rd series), vol. xx, cols 140, 143, 733–5, 30 July and 17 August
1833.

J. A. Roebuck: I propose a Resolution, by which this House will
acknowledge as a principle of Government, that the education of the people
is a matter of national concern; that, as such, it ought to be the object of
the most immediate, continued, and sedulous attention on the part of the
Legislature....

One of the first and one of the most important results from a proper
education of the people, would be a thorough understanding on their part
of the circumstances on which their happiness depended, and of the powers
by which those circumstances were controlled. They would learn what a
government could, and ... could not do to relieve their distresses—they
would learn what depended on themselves, what on others—what evils
resulted from evil authority, what from popular ignorance and popular
vice. Of all the knowledge that can be conferred on a people, this is the
most essential....

On the vote of £20,000 for the purposes of education.... The House
divided—Ayes 50; Noes 26; Majority 24

William Cobbett: could not consent to take from the people a single farthing in the way of taxes ... in order to teach the working classes reading and writing. He was sure he should not be accused of a wish to degrade them, or to deprive them of any advantages, but he thought the word education was much mistaken. Education was the knowledge necessary for the situation in life in which a man was placed. Take two men for instance— suppose one of them to be able to plough, and the other able to plough, and make hurdles and be a good shepherd. If the first man knew how to read as well as to plough, and the other man did not know how to read, even then, he should say, that the latter was the better man ... what became of the benefits of education? ... Nothing but to increase the number of schoolmasters and-schoolmistresses—that new race of idlers....

6b An Inspector investigates educational deprivation

Minutes of the Committee of Council on Education, 1846, *Parliamentary Papers*, 1847, vol. xlv, p. 134 (Report of Rev. Henry Moseley).

I have generally found the worst schools in those districts where the best are required, I mean those districts where the people are poorest and the most ignorant. This is one of the evils of the entire dependence of education on local resources for its support. It manifests itself particularly in localities on which mining operations are encroaching, in which those persons who draw from them their wealth rarely reside, and from which the gentry have fled. In districts like these, the clergyman occupies a new and anomolous position. The social edifice in which, in other and more favoured localities, he occupies the most honoured place, stands here in ruins. There is nothing to fill up the space between him and the industrial masses, unless it be the class of small shopkeepers, colliery clerks and victuallers. It is a desolate position....

Of a school situated in a district like this, I have recorded in my diary the following note, 'It seems as though the schools ... were graduated according to the moral and intellectual debasement of the people: an ignorant and a demoralized population and a bad school go together', and very inferior teaching seems to be thought good enough for very coarse ignorant people. The place is squalid, unthrifty-looking and wretched, and so is the school. The master has lost one arm and does not wear a coat, very seldom changes his shirt, and, I should think, never combs his hair. He says that he is allowed to take *private pupils*, teaching them, not as he does the rest (whom he obviously neglects), but on what he calls the "commercial plan"…. '

6c   The development of education policy and the inspectorate

Minutes of the Committee of Council on Education, August–December 1846. *Parliamentary Papers*, 1847, vol. xlv, pp. 1–2.

Resolved That it would be highly expedient that all the schools which are under the inspection of the Privy Council should be visited at least once in each year; that the existing number of Inspectors appears to be insufficient, as, notwithstanding their constant assiduity in the discharge of the duties intrusted to them, it is found impossible to make arrangements for the inspection of schools oftener than once in two years….

Their Lordships had further under their consideration [evidence] representing the very early age at which the children acting as assistants to schoolmasters are withdrawn from school to manual labour, and the advantages which would arise if such scholars as might be distinguished by proficiency and good conduct were apprenticed to skilful masters, to be instructed and trained, so as to be prepared to complete their education as schoolmasters in a Normal School….

Pupil Teachers—Qualifications of Candidates

The following qualifications will be required from candidates for apprenticeship:—

They must be at least thirteen years of age, and must not be subject to any bodily infirmity likely to impair their usefulness as pupil teachers.

In schools connected with the Church of England, the clergymen and managers, and, in other schools, the managers, must certify that the moral character of the candidates and of their families justify an expectation that the instruction and training of the school will be seconded by their own efforts and by the example of their parents. If this cannot be certified of the family, the apprentice will be required to board in some approved household.

Candidates will also be required,—

1. To read with fluency, ease, and expression.

2. To write in a neat hand, with correct spelling and punctuation, a simple prose narrative slowly read to them.

3. To write from dictation sums in the first four rules of arithmetic, simple and compound; to work them correctly, and to know the tables of weights and measures.

4. To point out the parts of speech in a simple sentence.

5. To have an elementary knowledge of geography.

6. *In schools connected with the Church of England* they will be required to repeat the catechism, and to show that they understand its meaning, and are acquainted with the outlines of scripture history. The parochial clergyman will also assist in this part of the examination.

In other schools the state of religious knowledge will be certified by the managers.

7. To teach a junior class to the satisfaction of the Inspectors.

8. Girls should also be able to sew neatly and to knit.

6d   Popular education properly 'an affair of the State'

'The Education of the People', *Quarterly Review*, vol. lxxviii (1846), pp. 396, 418–9 (article by Rev. W.H. Milman).

Sooner or later, popular education must be an affair of the State;—of the State, not merely as making grants to different societies, and demanding the right of inspection over schools which receive such grants; but as establishing some system administered by an efficient and responsible board (a department, if it shall seem most convenient, of the Privy

Council), for providing masters to work on some well-matured plans, with books under a proper supervision, and paid, at least in great part, by the State, or by compulsory and equal local assessments. The schoolmaster must become a public functionary, duly qualified for his office, and under due control....

The real peril and difficulty is lest the State education, whether by public grant or parochial or district taxation, should diminish the amount of voluntary subscriptions in the cause of education, or do injury otherwise to existing institutions.... The last thing to be desired would be to supplant, even by more efficient foundations, schools which have grown out of the wants of the spot, are endeared to the associations and knit up with the sympathies of the poor, and, in some instances, maintained even prodigally by the munificence of their neighbours. The State school will at first, of necessity, be as a stranger in the land. Let it not come between the kindly intercourse, the mutual good understanding of rich and poor, the Christian love on the one hand, the Christian gratitude on the other. Let those rural schools which stand in their little gardens at the park-gates of our nobility and our gentry, which are daily visited by the ladies of the 'great house,' as well as the wife or daughter of the parson, and are fully, even lavishly supported, it may be as a sort of amiable luxury of charity—let all these remain inviolate—if inspected, inspected only with the most tender consideration. Even if such schools be in some instances deficient in quickening the intelligence of the peasant children, they do a vast deal of good: they expand and soften their hearts—they bind together rich and poor by stronger ties even than the more full appreciation of their common interests.

6e   Edward Baines changes his mind on the efficacy of State education

Edward Baines, *An Alarm to the Nation on the Unjust, Unconstitutional and Dangerous Measure of State Education* (1847), pp. 2–3.

NAKED Despotism is a clumsy form of government which we have no reason to fear in England. The more refined despotism of modern Europe derives its support from the numberless state-functionaries, and especially from the dependence of the ministers of religion and schoolmasters, of every sect and rank, upon the Government, which thus spreads its silent influence like a net over the *interests and opinions*, over the *rising and mature* MIND of the people. It is this species of Government influence which we have to apprehend in England, and which is not the less dangerous because compatible with all the forms of a free Constitution. Nor is it the less to be feared, because it makes its first approaches in the seductive guise of an extension of education....

I do not charge the Ministers with any purpose hostile to freedom. But I do charge them with designs which, in my judgement, are inconsistent with freedom, and of deadly influence on the mental vigour, the independent spirit, and the voluntary religion of the people. *I fear it is their wish to bring the ministers of religion of every sect into the condition of State-pensioners. I fear it is their wish to have every School in the land under Government inspection, and virtually subject to Government control....*

Edward Baines to Sir James Kay-Shuttleworth, 19 October 1867 (unpublished letter, Leeds City Archives, Baines Papers, 52/11).

I confess to a strong distrust of government action and a passionate love for voluntary action and self-reliance. But though the passion still rules, I now acknowledge that it was allowed no absolute sway; and as a practical man I was compelled to abandon the purely voluntary system, as untenable in competition with that which combines voluntary action and State aid. Nor would I withhold the commendation due to the Minutes in Council for merits intrinsically their own and especially for retaining the voluntary and religious elements and for Inspection....

6f   Dickens attacks facts without understanding

Hard Times (1854), Penguin ed. 1969, pp. 47–48.

'Now, what I want is, Facts. Teach these boys and girls nothing but Facts. Facts alone are wanted in life. Plant nothing else, and root out everything else. You can only form the minds of reasoning animals upon Facts: nothing else will ever be of any service to them. This is the principle on which I bring up my own children, and this is the principle on which I bring up these children. Stick to Facts, sir!'

The scene was a plain, bare, monotonous vault of a schoolroom, and the speaker's square forefinger emphasized his observations by underscoring every sentence with a line on the schoolmaster's sleeve....

'In this life, we want nothing but Facts, sir; nothing but Facts!'

The speaker, and the schoolmaster, and the third grown person present, all backed a little, and swept with their eyes the inclined plan of little vessels then and there arranged in order, ready to have imperial gallons of facts poured into them until they were full to the brim.

Thomas Gradgrind, sir. A man of realities. A man of fact and calculations. A man who proceeds upon the principle that two and two are four, and nothing over, and who is not to be talked into allowing for anything over. Thomas Gradgrind, sir—peremptorily Thomas—Thomas Gradgrind. With a rule and a pair of scales, and the multiplication table always in his pocket, sir, ready to weigh and measure any parcel of human nature, and tell you exactly what it comes to. It is a mere question of figures, a case of simple arithmetic....

In such terms Mr. Gradgrind always mentally introduced himself, whether to his private circle of acquaintance, or to the public in general. In such terms, no doubt, substituting the words 'boys and girls', for 'sir', Thomas Gradgrind now presented Thomas Gradgrind to the little pitchers before him, who were to be filled so full of facts.

Indeed ... he seemed a kind of cannon loaded to the muzzle with facts, and prepared to blow them clean out of the regions of childhood at one discharge. He seemed a galvanizing apparatus, too, charged with a grim mechanical substitute for the tender young imaginations that were to be stormed away.

6g   Robert Lowe defends the Revised Code

Hansard (3rd series), vol. clxv, cols 206–7, 229–30, 237–8, 13 February 1862

I now proceed to ... the question of expense ... it is our duty, and one we ought zealously to discharge, in administering whatever system of Education may be decided upon, to take care there is no extravagance, that the public get an equivalent for the expenditure, and that there is no gross and flagrant inequality in the grants made to schools.... The fact is that a great many of these schools are receiving under the present system a great deal more than they are entitled to, and no system can be entitled to support that does not make provision for diminishing that inequality....

The true principle is not to lower your standard to meet cases which are at present below it, but to do what you can to induce them to amend themselves, and if they will not ... to leave them to the unaided support of voluntary efforts, but not to degrade the whole system for their sake.... We know that there will be a loss where teaching is inefficient. That is our principle, that where the teaching is inefficient the schools should lose. I cannot promise the House that this system will be an economical one, and I cannot promise that it will be an efficient one, but I can promise that it shall be either one or the other. If it is not cheap, it shall be efficient; if it is not efficient it shall be cheap. The present is neither one nor the other....

Now it is said, that by this plan we are degrading education.... The truth is, what we fix is a *minimum* of education, not a *maximum*. We propose to give no grant for the attendance of children at school, unless they can read, write and cipher; but we do not say that they shall learn no more. We do not object to any amount of learning; the only question is, how much of that knowledge ought we to pay for. Consider that the age at which the poor man's child leaves school is generally about eleven; if we ask that during his time of schooling he shall be taught to read, write and cipher, is not that enough? In so doing we think that, so far from degrading education, we, by requiring more labour and industry in the schools, are really raising it. It must never be forgotten that those for whom this system is designed are the children of persons who are not able to pay for the teaching. We do not profess to give these children an education that will raise them above their station and business in life; that is not our object, but to give them an education that may fit them for that business....

6h An influential attack on the Revised Code

J. Kay-Shuttleworth, *Four Periods of Public Education* (1862), pp. 577–8, 582–3, 635.

The vindication of the Revised Code is based on the denial that the existing system secures adequate results. By implication it attributes this alleged failure to a misdirection of effort. The teachers are too highly instructed,—they are above their work,—their daily instruction as apprentices and their residence in college must be shortened,—their education must be lowered to the level of their work,—that level is the teaching of reading, writing, and arithmetic, to scholars early absorbed by labour in agriculture or manufactures. This work ought to be done before eleven. No working man's child need be paid for after that age. The teachers have been mischievously pampered and protected. 'Hitherto,' says the Vice-president [Lowe], 'we have been living under a system of bounties and protections; now we prefer to have a little free trade.' The teachers must, like corn and cotton, be subject to the law of supply and demand. They and the managers must make the best bargains they can....

The last twenty-five years has witnessed a great municipal and religious revolution;—the last fifteen years a still greater change in education.

When schools were planted twenty years ago in towns, villages, and rural parishes, almost the only teachers were either untrained men, who from some defect of body or health had been driven from the rougher struggles of life or muscular toil, or were self-taught Sunday School teachers, trained for three or six months in some central Model School.

They had to struggle, aided only by monitors under thirteen years of age, with the untamed brutishness of the wild or pauperised immigrant population,—with the semi-barbarism of children from coarse sensual homes,—with the utter want of consciousness in the population that humble learning could do their children any good,—with the then extravagant and harsh claims of an unorganised system of manufacturing and mining labour,—with the absence of previous training in the home or infant school,—with the late age at which children with no school-habits, savage, ignorant, incapable, wayward, or wild, came under their care,—with irregularity of attendance,—short school attendance in each year, and brief school time altogether,—constant migration of families,—and overwhelming ill-paid duties.

To grapple with these evils, the Government resolved to create a new machinery of public education. This new trained machinery of apprenticed pupil teachers, assistant and certificated teachers, has come into existence chiefly since 1847....

This corps of teachers has been like the raw recruits of an army suddenly raised—brought into the field in successive battalions, on the verge of an immature manhood, and placed, as soon as drilled, in the front of difficulties and dangers. They have had to take up everywhere the work of the untrained masters. They have been the pioneers of civilisation. Fourteen years have barely elapsed since their first companies took up their position, and their ranks are still full of the last batches of raw recruits. The schools hitherto founded have met the wants of barely one-half of the population. Every year has been adding to the experience of the Inspectors of schools, and of managers and teachers. But schools are not universal, and are not yet thoroughly efficient....

To give the people a worse education from motives of short-sighted economy, would be, in these respects, utterly inconsistent with all preceding national policy. The idea that an ignorant, brutish people is either more subordinate or more easily controlled than a people loyal by conviction and contented from experience and reason, is exploded. The notion that the mass of the people are the sources of national wealth merely as beasts of burthen—that the nation has no interest in their intelligence, inventive capacity, morality, and fitness for the duties of freemen and citizens,— is a doctrine which would find no advocates. No Chancellor of the Exchequer would dare to avow that their sensuality was a prolific source of revenue which he could not afford to check. Why, then, is education to be discouraged by regulations which cut off all aid to children under seven and after eleven years of age? Why are the annual grants to be reduced two-fifths at one blow? Why are the stipends, training, and qualifications of schoolmasters to be lowered? Why is instruction in the school to be mainly concentrated on the three lower elements?

6i Bedrock support for the National Education League

Report of a Conference of Nonconformist Ministers, held at Leeds (Leeds, 1870), pp. 2–5 (Copy in Leeds Central Library).

Address from the Major of Leeds, W. Glover Joy:
The League proposes to provide for every child, free, compulsory, undenominational, but not a godless Education: as the School boards have power to grant the use of the school rooms for the giving of religious instruction out of school hours, and also to permit the reading of the Scriptures in the schools, provided that no child shall be present at such reading if his parents or guardians disapprove, thus separating, not excluding, religious teaching....

If, after thirty years' trial, the Denominational System had met the requirements of the country, we should not have been in the state we now are; but it has not. The nation is dissatisfied with it, and, in my mind there is little doubt it will eventually cease to exist....

Now shall the present state of things continue and be perpetuated, or shall we heartily fall in with the League, and never rest till every child in the kingdom has primary education, without the possibility of proselyting influences being brought to bear upon him by anyone, (applause) and thus endeavour to break down sectarian and unchristian differences instead of perpetuating and extending them? (Hear, hear)....

Give us a dissolution of Parliament on this Educational Question, and the voters of this Kingdom will speak out as they never spoke before, and they will say, give us free, undenominational, compulsory Education for our children. We ask no more, we will take no less. (Great applause)

6j   The Elementary Education Act, 1870

33 & 34 Vic., c.75

Supply of Schools

5. There shall be provided for every school district a sufficient amount of accommodation in public elementary schools ... available for all the children resident in such district for whose elementary education efficient and suitable provision is not otherwise made, and where there is an insufficient amount of such accommodation, in this Act referred to as 'public school accommodation,' the deficiency shall be supplied in manner provided by this Act.

6. Where the Education Department, in the manner provided by this Act, are satisfied and have given public notice that there is an insufficient amount of public school accommodation for any school district, and the deficiency is not supplied as hereinafter required, a school board shall be formed for such district and shall supply such deficiency, and in case of default by the school board the Education Department shall cause the duty of such board to be performed in manner provided by this Act.

7. Every elementary school which is conducted in accordance with the following regulations shall be a public elementary school within the meaning of this Act; and every public elementary school shall be conducted in accordance with the following regulations (a copy of which regulations shall be conspicuously put up in every such school); namely,

(1.)   It shall not be required, as a condition of any child being admitted into or continuing in the school, that he shall attend or abstain from attending any Sunday school, or any place of religious worship, or that he shall attend any religious observance or any instruction in religious subjects in the school or elsewhere, from which observance or instruction he may be withdrawn by his parent, or that he shall, if withdrawn by his parent, attend the school on any day exclusively set apart for religious observance by the religious body to which his parent belongs.

(2.)   The time or times during which any religious observance is practised or instruction in religious subjects is given at any meeting of the school shall be either at the beginning or at the end or at the beginning and the end of such meeting, and shall be inserted in a time table to be approved by the Education Department, and to be kept permanently and conspicuously affixed in every school-room; and any scholar may be withdrawn by his parent from such observance or instruction without forfeiting any of the other benefits of the school.

(3.) The school shall be open at all times to the inspection of any of Her Majesty's inspectors, so, however, that it shall be no part of the duties of such inspector to inquire into any instruction in religious subjects given at such school, or to examine any scholar therein in religious knowledge or in any religious subject or book.

7 Aspects of self-help

Self-help was the Victorial ideal. There were advantages in members of the working class insuring themselves against sickness, old age and temporary unemployment, both in fewer calls upon the poor law and, crucially, in fostering a spirit of thrift, independence and self-reliance perfectly in tune with the competitive ethic of the age. There were many avenues for self-help, most of them approved by government. There were burial and collecting societies, building societies, savings banks and a flourishing co-operative movement. The best known were friendly societies which offered a range of benefits against regular contributions (7a). Registration of friendly societies had begun in 1793, but the Victorian period saw significant developments aimed at protecting members' funds against incompetent actuarial calculations, fraud or other loss. The Friendly Societies Act, 1855, extended the protection offered to members of registered societies and the work of John Tidd Pratt (1797–1870), the first registrar of friendly societies, was important in establishing securely founded organizations. In many places, particularly the north-west, friendly societies were active social centres as well as mutual protection agencies. By 1872 they had over $1\frac{1}{4}$m members, and though they recruited far more skilled than unskilled workers, they had at least five times as many members as did trade unions at the same time.

Working people also put any surplus income into savings banks (7b). These seem to have been particularly popular with domestic servants, and many deposits were made on behalf of children. For the very poor, particularly in Scotland and the north of England, the 'penny savings banks' were established to deal with smaller deposits. Some of the small banks proved insecure, however. To meet this problem and also to increase the range of opportunities open to small investors, the Liberal Government utilized existing machinery to create the Post Office Savings Banks from 1861 (7c). This development proved very popular. The number of POSB accounts grew from an average of 663,000 in 1863–8 to 5,776,000 in 1891–5 of which by the mid-1890s, just over half were held by women and children.

The early fortunes of the co-operative movement had been closely tied to the socialist vision of Robert Owen. Co-operative trading was designed as an escape from, and effective antidote to, capitalism. Eventually, co-operation would subdue competition to create a society of equal shares in which distinctions between rich and poor, middle and working classes were swept away. Ironically, as this utopian vision faded, the co-operative trading scheme survived, not only as a viable adjunct to capitalism but, to many middle-class observers, as an important stabilizing element in society. W.N. Molesworth noted with satisfaction that the Rochdale co-operators, who developed the idea of a dividend on purchases, were not egalitarians (7d). They sought their own well-being, but without any desire to restructure society.

All forms of self-help depended on the availability of an adequate and regular income from which appropriate provision could be made. Henry Mayhew (1812–87), the journalist and writer, was one of the very few middle-class observers of Victorian working conditions to appreciate that the structure of the labour market depended to a large extent on casual, irregular labour. Casual labourers, immensely important in London where Mayhew's work was concentrated, were usually quite unable to make the far-sighted provision which self-help required (7e). It is not surprising that self-help philosophy was more readily accepted among skilled workers and regular earners than among the casual and poorly paid members of the working class.

Suggestions for further reading

P. H. J. H. Gosden, *Self-Help* (1973) is a good introduction. On Mayhew, see E. P. Thompson and Eileen Yeo (eds), *The Unknown Mayhew* (1971).

7a   The principles of friendly societies

J. Tidd Pratt, *Suggestions for the Establishment of Friendly Societies* (1855), pp. 3–4.

Friendly Societies exercise a highly beneficial influence on the welfare of the Industrious Classes, and through the industrious classes they influence in some degree the whole mass of society; and it is hoped that if defects are pointed out, and improvements suggested, they may, in some degree, be placed on a more permanent basis.

Friendly Societies are formed on the principle of mutual insurance. Each member contributes a certain sum by weekly or monthly subscriptions while he is in health, for which he expects to receive from the society a certain provision or allowance when he is incapacitated for work by accident, sickness, or old age. Nothing, it is obvious, can be more unexceptionable than the principle of these associations. Owing to the general exemption from sickness until a comparatively late period of life, if a number of individuals under 30 or 35 years of age form themselves into a society, and subscribe each a small sum from their surplus savings, they are able to secure a comfortable provision for themselves in the event of their becoming unfit for labour. Any single individual who should trust to his own unassisted efforts for support would, it is plain, be placed in a very different situation from those who are members of a Friendly Society; for, however industrious and parsimonious, he might not be able to accomplish his object, inasmuch as the occurrence of any accident, or an obstinate fit of sickness, might, by throwing him out of employment, and forcing him to consume the savings he had accumulated against old age, reduce him to a state of indigence, and oblige him to become dependent on the bounty of others. Whenever a liability to any unfavourable contingency exists, the best and cheapest way of obviating its effects is by uniting with others ....

7b Savings banks

William Lewis, *A History of the Banks for Savings* (1866), pp. 8–12, 98–9.

Of the hundreds of charitable and benevolent agencies set on foot to improve the condition of the English artisan we can speak only in the aggregate .... Under the influence of properly organised and properly conducted societies ... there is a sensible improvement in public morals among the masses of the people. Within the memory of the present generation lewdness, profanity and vulgarity polluted the atmosphere of most large workshops .... Then their hours of idleness were hours of mischief; in them the old proverb of 'an idle brain' being 'the devil's workshop' was fully exemplified; bull-baiting, cock-fighting, low drinking, and gambling were their amusements .... To say that all this is changed would be idle, but that much of it is changed is beyond doubt ....

The good results of such habits to the industrious classes themselves and to all portions of society are neither few nor doubtful. The pursuit of economy and thrift will beget, as a matter of course, self-dependence; and so soon as men become socially independent they also become self-relying and self-supplying. 'Few men come to the parish who have ever saved money', said one large employer of labour before a Committee of the House of Commons on Poor Laws .... But the good work does not stop here. 'In proportion as our men save money', said another large employer, 'their morals are improved; then they come to see that they have a stake in the country and behave better'....

One of the most positive proofs of the increase in the provident habits of the people between 1828 and 1844 is to be found in the increase in the number of small depositors. In 1828 the number of depositors in Savings Banks who had not subscribed more than £20 was 203,604. In 1844 they had increased to 564,642....

But ... we see more in Savings Banks than that they enabled many in times of hardship by a wise foresight to escape much that others suffered. We see in the progress of these banks undoubted evidence of the increasing prosperity of the Country, in relation at any rate to the poorer classes; and they are among the direct agents in creating that prosperity. Savings Banks created and then fostered habits of economy and frugality, and every man won over to the pursuit and practice of these habits increased the sum of prosperity manifest during the period we are considering.

7c   The establishment of Post Office Savings Banks

Hansard (3rd series), vol. clxi, cols 262–3, 8 February 1861.

W.E. Gladstone: The establishment of savings banks has undoubtedly been of immense service to the humbler classes throughout the country.... The main question, that of the liability of the trustees to the depositors, was one which had ... baffled the skill of those who had attempted to deal with it. Under those circumstances, they proposed to avail themselves of another description of machinery already in existence, simple in form, and recommended by its incomparable convenience, for the purpose of carrying out more effectively the objects for which savings banks had been set on foot. Of those institutions there were only about 600 scattered throughout the country, and of that number but a small proportion were open for a sufficient number of hours in the week. Looking, however, to the Post Office Department, he found that it comprised between 2,000 and 3,000 money order offices ... and that every one ... was open six days in the week for not less than eight or ten hours each day. Now, there was a machinery ready to hand and admirably adapted for extending the usefulness of the savings bank system....

The rate of interest which was now paid on deposits in savings banks stood at the somewhat high rate of £3 5s. per cent, and he proposed that under the operation of the scheme to which he was asking the assent of the Committee it should be fixed at £2 10s., with power to increase that amount within certain limits....

7d Co-operation

W.N. Molesworth, 'On the Extent and Results of Co-Operative Trading Associations at Rochdale', *Journal of the Royal Statistical Society*, vol. xxiv (1861), pp. 507–14.

The objects of this Society are the social and intellectual advancement of its members; it provides them with groceries, butcher's meat, drapery goods, clothing, shoes, clogs etc.... The capital is raised in £1 shares; each member being allowed to take not less than 5, and not more than 100, payable at once or by instalments of 3s 3d. per quarter. The profits are divided quarterly as follows:—1st. Interest at 5 per cent per annum, on all paid-up shares; 2nd. 2½ per cent off net profits for educational purposes, the remainder divided amongst the members in proportion to money expended. For the intellectual improvement of the members, there is a library consisting of more than 3,000 volumes.... The newsroom is well supplied with newspapers and periodicals, fitted up in a neat and careful manner and furnished with maps, globes, microscopes, telescope etc. The newsroom and library are free to all members....

It may, perhaps, provoke a smile to find ... 'social and intellectual advancement' placed in such close juxtaposition with 'groceries, butcher's meat, drapery goods, clothing, shoes and clogs'. But there is a real and very close connexion between these two classes of things. Men must be provided with the necessaries of life, or they will be unable to devote attention to their social and intellectual advancement; and the more abundantly their material wants are supplied, and the more they are released from care and anxiety about these wants, the more time will they have at their disposal to devote to their mental and spiritual improvement; and the greater, as a general rule, will be their intellectual, social, moral, ay, and I would even add, their religious progress....

	Membership	Funds	Profits
1844	28	£28	—
1851	630	£2,785	£990
1860	3,450	£37,710	£15,906

I cannot, of course, speak for all of them, but as far as I have had an opportunity of observing them, I have been struck by the absence of that levelling spirit, and of that desire for self-aggrandizement which has characterized some of the working-class attempts to elevate themselves. The chief ambition ... appears to me to be to raise themselves by raising the class to which they belong, without desiring to leave it, and without the slightest wish to depress or injure any other class. Their object and ambition appears to be that the working class should be well fed, well clothed, well housed, well washed, well educated—in a word that they should be respectable and respected. If any taint of the socialist and communist theories in which the society originated still cleaves to them, it is being rapidly worked off, and will, I am persuaded, shortly disappear.

7e   The fallacies of self-help for the casual poor

Henry Mayhew, *London Labour and the London Poor* (4 vols, 1861), vol. ii, p. 367.

All casual labour, as I have said, is necessarily *uncertain* labour; and wherever uncertainty exists, there can be no foresight or pro-vidence.... Pro-vidence, therefore, is simply the result of certainty, and whatever tends to increase our faith in the uniform sequences of outward events, as well as our reliance on the means we have of avoiding the evils connected with them, necessarily tends to make us more prudent. Where the means of sustenance and comfort are fixed, the human being becomes conscious of what he has to depend upon; and if he feel *assured* that such means may fail him in old age or in sickness, and be fully impressed with the *certainty* of suffering from either, he will immediately proceed to make some provision against the time of adversity or infirmity. If, however, his means be *uncertain*—abundant at one time, and deficient at another—a spirit of speculation or gambling with the future will be induced, and the individual get to believe in 'luck' and 'fate' as the arbiters of his happiness rather than to look upon himself as 'the architect of his fortunes' – trusting to 'chance' rather than his own powers and foresight to relieve him at the hour of necessity....

The ordinary effects of uncertain labour, then, are to drive the labourers to improvidence, recklessness, and pauperism.

Even in the classes which we do not rank among labourers, as, for instance, authors, artists, musicians, actors, uncertainty or irregularity of employment and remuneration produces a spirit of wastefulness and carelessness. The steady and daily accruing gains of trade and of some of the professions form a certain and staple income; while in other professions, where a large sum may be realized at one time, and then no money be earned until after an interval, incomings are rapidly spent, and the interval is one of suffering. This is part of the very nature, the very essence, of the casualty of employment and the delay of remuneration. The past privation gives a zest to the present enjoyment; while the present enjoyment renders the past privation faint as a remembrance and unimpressive as a warning....

It is easy enough for men in smooth circumstances to say, 'the privation is a man's own fault, since, to avoid it, he has but to apportion the sum he may receive in a lump over the interval of non-recompense which he knows will follow.' Such a course as this, experience and human nature have shown not to be easy – perhaps, with a few exceptions, not to be possible. It is the starving and not the well-fed man that is in danger of surfeiting himself.

8 The growth and professionalization of government

The considerable extension of government intervention from the 1830s onwards demanded an efficient civil service to administer it. Not surprisingly, there was considerable criticism of a patronage system strained by the recruitment of ever more candidates.

In 1853 the Chancellor of the Exchequer, W.E. Gladstone (1809–98), asked Sir Stafford Northcote (later Lord Iddesleigh, 1818–87) and Sir Charles Trevelyan (1807–86) to study the recruitment pattern and suggest changes. Their Report (8a) was influential, though it should be said that patronage appointments to the government service in the 1830s and 1840s, including men like Chadwick, Kay-Shuttleworth and Horner, had taken considerable pains to ensure that their staffs were efficient. Many of the Northcote-Trevelyan recommendations, therefore, were only reformulations of existing practice in the best-run departments. Moreover, open competition was not properly accepted in the civil service until after 1870. Trevelyan himself was at pains to point out that, since the best education was only available to those already privileged, his reforms would merely secure the more efficient recruitment of men from within the existing élite (8c). *The Times* nevertheless welcomed what it saw as the final nail in the coffin of patronage (8b).

In any age it is wrong to see civil servants as mere executants of politicians' will. Permanent officials were usually in an excellent position to influence policy, and they by no means accepted political castration when they entered government service. R. R. W. Lingen's unpublished confidential memorandum (8d) is typical of informed pressure brought to bear on politicians in a highly charged field. Lingen, as Secretary of the Privy Council Committee on Education, developed while in post very strong views on the role of the Church in education; and he was not afraid to push them under the noses of his political masters. Expertly informed pressure from permanent officials was an important factor in the formulation of policy.

This, in fact, was one aspect of many which worried critics of government growth like Joshua Toulmin Smith (1816–69). This lawyer and antiquary wrote several tracts designed to show that recent developments fatally undermined local self-government and imposed a pernicious tyranny on the British people (8e). Tom Taylor, the dramatist and sometime editor of *Punch* (1817–80), who was also in charge of the Local Government Act Office in the 1850s and 1860s, answered the charge (8f). No Benthamite, indeed no uncritical accepter of any received doctrine, he still came to the view that, given the scale of the problems faced, central government was too deferential to the principle of local self-government.

By the end of the 1860s, it was possible to discern a changing attitude towards the role of government and the scope of the tasks it could legitimately undertake. Both the *Pall Mall Gazette* (8g) and Stafford Northcote (8i) were groping towards an as yet barely articulated philsophy essential to the acceptance of collectivism in the next generation: that the State was no longer merely the holder of the ring, intervening only to avert great evils. Its intervention in social questions was a positive good, and there was an increasing range of issues which could only be tackled by decisive government activity. Horace Mann, organizer of the Census and Registrar of the General Register Office, was right in 1869 when he argued that the experience of State intervention hitherto would persuade observers in the 1870s and beyond that there should be more of it, not less (8h).

Suggestions for further reading

The growth of government in nineteenth-century Britain is a complicated and controversial subject. A sound introduction is Arthur Taylor, *Laissez-Faire and State Intervention in Nineteenth-Century Britain* (1972). Two sides of one of the central arguments are put by Oliver MacDonagh, *A Pattern of Government Growth* (1961) and Jenifer Hart, 'Nineteenth-Century Social Reform: A Tory Interpretation of History', *Past and Present*, vol. 31 (1965), pp. 39–60. See also O. MacDonagh, *Early Victorian Government, 1830–70* (1977), pp. 197–213.

8a   The Northcote-Trevelyan Report, November 1853

Parliamentary Papers, 1854, vol. xxvi pp. 1–3.

Summary of our Recommendations

Upon a review of the recommendations contained in this paper it will be seen that the objects which we have principally in view are these:

1. To provide, by a proper system of examination, for the supply of the public service with a thoroughly efficient class of men.

2. To encourage industry and foster merit, by teaching all public servants to look forward to promotion according to their deserts, and to expect the highest prizes if they can qualify themselves for them.

3. To mitigate the evils which result from the fragmentary character of the Service, and to introduce into it some elements of unity, by placing the first appointments upon a uniform footing, opening the way to the promotion of public officers to staff appointments in other departments than their own....

It cannot be necessary to enter into any lengthened argument for the purpose of showing the high importance of the Permanent Civil Service of the country in the present-day. The great and increasing accumulation of public business, and the consequent pressure upon the Government, need only be alluded to....

It would be natural to expect that so important a profession would attract into its ranks the ablest and most ambitious of the youth of the country; that the keenest emulation would prevail among those who have entered it; and that such as were endowed with superior qualifications would rapidly rise to distinction and public eminence. Such, however, is by no means the case. Admission into the Civil Service is indeed eagerly sought after, but it is for the unambitious, and the indolent or incapable, that it is chiefly desired. Those whose abilities do not warrant an expectation that they will succeed in the open professions, where they must encounter the competition of their contemporaries ... where they may obtain an honourable livelihood with little labour, and with no risk; where their success depends upon their simply avoiding any flagrant misconduct, and attending with moderate regularity to routine duties; and in which they are secured against the ordinary consequences of old age, or failing health, by an arrangement which provides them with the means of supporting themselves after they have become incapacitated.

8b   Civil service reform welcomed

The Times, 9 February 1854.

The proposed reforms in the civil service are so obviously just and beneficial that decency will demand acquiescence and even approval....

It is proposed to throw open upwards of 16,000 salaried places to the general competition of the country.... It is proposed, as, indeed, is the necessary consequence of such a change, to sweep away for ever the entire system of patronage, which has hitherto been considered essential to party government—to put an end to the barter of places for support, and to all that network of solicitation and intrigue which involves even high minded men, and proves how much morality is a thing of custom.

The present state of things is this—a quarter of a century ago since, a popular movement ... overwhelmed an old world of privileges and pensions. Giant sinecurists have passed away as a race.... But in our political inundation one high tableland escaped, and the civil service is a relic of the world which preceded the Reform Bill. Incapacity, indifference and idleness are reported to be the characteristics of a body appointed chiefly through private interest or political venality....

The plan advocated by the Government is one the importance of which all classes ought to feel.... Nothing less is proposed than the creation of a new liberal profession, as freely open to all as the Church, the bar, or the hospital. From the time this measure receives the royal assent, it will be the fault of the people if the public service do not become their birthright, according to the talent, education, and industry of each, without any hindrance from those sinister influences which have hitherto, as a general rule, made access dependent on a powerful connexion or a seared conscience.

8c   Sir Charles Trevelyan's estimate of the impact of competitive examinations on the civil service

British Library, Department of Manuscripts, Add. MSS. 44,580 f.103.
Reprinted in E. Hughes, 'Sir Charles Trevelyan and Civil Service
Reform', *Eng. Hist. Rev.*, vol. lxiv (1949), p. 72.

The effect of a system of open competition will be to secure for the public offices generally and especially for the principal offices the best portion of the best educated of our youth.

Who are so successful in carrying off the prizes at competing scholarships, fellowships etc. as the most expensively educated young men? Almost invariably, the sons of gentlemen, or those who by force of cultivation, good training and good society have acquired the feelings and habits of gentlemen. The tendency of the measure will, I am confident, be decidedly *aristocratic*, but it will be so in a good sense by securing for the public service those who are, in a true sense οι αριδτοι [the best]. At present, a mixed multitude is sent up, a large proportion of whom, owing to the operation of political and personal patronage, are of an inferior rank of society.... *and they are, in general, the least eligible of their respective ranks.* The idle and useless, the fool of the family, the consumptive, the hypochondriac, those who have a tendency to insanity, are the sort of young men commonly 'provided for' as the term is, in a public office.... All this will be remedied by the proposed arrangement.

8d A leading civil servant influences policy and pushes his own views

Internal memorandum of R. R. W. Lingen on Representation of the Committee of the Council on Education in the House of Commons, 6 June 1855, Public Record Office, Ed. 24/53.

1. Members complain that the H. of Commons is not efficiently informed of the proceedings of a Department by which such large, and annually increasing, funds are administered.

2. The Home Secretary, notoriously, is too much occupied to be able to answer, except at Second Hand, for more than the general outlines and principles of the Education Department.

3. The Conclusion therefore, is drawn that there ought to be a direct and special representation of the Department in the H. of Commons ....

6. An obvious change might therefore appear to be to make the Secretary's office a Parliamentary one ....

7. Speaking generally .... think this would be the best step which could be taken .... It would effectively put the Education Department in rapport with the H. of Commons, indeed generally with the Legislature ....

I do not hold the same opinion so long as it is not consciously determined to incur the pretty certain breaking-up of the present system, which is, in the very essence of it, something quite unparliamentary. The public with which the Department deals is not a political, but a religious, one, and a religious one in fragments. Take each fragment by itself, Church, Wesleyan, Roman Catholic etc. and talk to any of their leading men—and you see, in a moment, how they dread and shrink from, any system which subjects the Congregation to any civic and undenominational power, no matter whether that power be Vestry, Town Council, Board of Guardians, or House of Commons. 'Find us the money, and leave us to ourselves' is the prayer of each and all of them ....

My conviction is the same now as it has been for years past; that there is only one solution of the question viz, to separate secular and religious instructions, and in effect to take the former out of the hands of the Congregations, making it a purely civil matter.

Between the present state of things and that consummation, I see not only prolonged contests and difficulties, but also this additional fact, that nearly all the people who at this moment are willing and able to work in the matter are willing and able to work in one way only, viz, as members of religious bodies, and not as simple citizens.

The Parliamentary Secretaryship appears to me to be a step towards precipitating the contest between the present and a more public system, which, some way or other, I think not only inevitable, but desirable. I would create the Secretaryship as soon as I had made up my mind that it was no longer worth while to delay the agitation of a final settlement.

8e   An attack on the growth of and centralized government commissions

J. Toulmin Smith, *Government by Commissions Illegal and Pernicious* (1849), pp. 174–5.

... it is not the *evidence* but the *reports* of Commissions, as disseminated through the newspapers and in other ways well known to the initiated, which are read.... So sycophantic or indolent, or both, are the minds of those who alone attach any importance to these Commissions that they swallow the reports as 'authority,' seldom thinking of looking into the evidence, picked and *ex-parte* as that necessarily is. This is precisely what is reckoned upon in order to be able to carry out the ultimate ends for which those reports are foisted on the public, with the object of creating a false and factitious subservience to 'authority,' instead of a real and healthy formation of *opinion*.

There will always, then, be a large class to which these Commissions may safely look for support and to be quoted as admirable contrivances. The class is increasing: that fact is unquestionable. The tendency of the whole system is to depress individual thought and effort; to impose upon it under specious pretences of authority; to cramp the development of individual ideas and check the individual search after truth; to induce men (too ready to be so induced) to accept any *vade mecum* which may offer itself, instead of themselves earnestly battling with the questions until the truth has been won by self-exertion; to make men, in short, depend on the thoughts of other men rather than on those which earnest careful inquiry has led themselves to form. The class must increase the wider the system spreads; and the two mutually re-act to increase and spread each other.

8f   Central control justified by a prominent government official

Tom Taylor, 'On Central and Local Action in relation to Town Improvement', *Transactions of the National Association for the Promotion of Social Science*, vol. i (1857), pp. 476–7.

I cannot agree with Mr. Smith that the prevailing under-estimate and neglect of local duties are the result of 'attempts made of late years to overlay the institutions of England, alike in working and in spirit, by the system of bureaucracy and functionarism'. So far as such a system can be said to exist, I cannot but consider it rather as a result than as a cause of the neglect of local duties.

Mr. Smith appears to think that in every department of the Government lurk certain mysterious enemies of everything ancient, and English, and local, always on the look-out to curtail a parochial power here, a corporate function there, equally greedy of authority and public pence—true 'hungry officials', devoid alike of capacity and honesty, equally deficient in a sense of public duty and respect for private morality.

I am inclined to think—it may be because I am myself a servant in one of these departments which Mr. Smith considers more peculiarly peopled by these official ogres—that Mr. Smith, on this point, is labouring under a delusion which tends to impair the value of his books and to limit the good effect of his meritorious labours. There may, of course, be a mischievous and mistaken 'centralism', just as there is a spurious 'localism'—the one striving to establish Procrustean systems of its own, to weaken local liberty, and to substitute for the healthy variety of independent action a vicious and shortsighted uniformity regulated from the centre, just as the other seeks to establish the rule of unmitigated selfishness and penny wisdom under the specious mask of local liberty ....

I should be inclined to assert that in the general working of central departments, charged with duties which bring them into contact with local authorities, the tendency is rather to over-timidity than to excessive dictation; and instead of the disposition of the public being to throw too much into the hands of the central power, it is rather to an excessive dislike of its action, and an exaggerated suspicion both of its means and inclinations to intrude or encroach upon local institutions. I cannot but attribute the neglect of local duties, not to ever-encroaching officialism, but to ever-increasing selfishness—the result of excessive addiction to money-making—of concession to the daily largest demands of each man's private business upon his time and energies—of a forgetfulness of the claims of all classes of society upon each other—of that want of sympathy between rich and poor mainly due to the vast operations of the new industrial economy created by steam power, which tends to accumulate great capitals in single hands and to group huge masses of workmen about particular centres of labour ....

If we could attain the best conceivable local self-government, it is probable there would be no need for central aid, counsel or interference. But it is a palpable fact—every man's experience teems with proofs of it—that we do not, except in a minority of cases, command for local government the best local materials.

8g   The State should assume an interventionist role

Pall Mall Gazette, 17 August 1869.

'The essential maxim of modern legislation is that people may in a general way be trusted to govern themselves and manage their own affairs, and that a State can do little more than render some formal and official assistance, chiefly in the removal of obstructions. There are evils that impede the current of affairs and stop the circulation. The State can do little more than clear the thoroughfare and bid all to "move on" ....' (*The Times*)

There is a helpless and muddled bewilderment about all this which would protect it from criticism if it were not typical of the imbecility of a great deal of what passes for thought upon political subjects in these days, and it embodies, no doubt in a very confused and inconsistent manner, what to us appears one of the most pernicious of modern political doctrines—the doctrine that the political function of legislation is negative, that the one great object which a legislator ought to propose to himself is the abatement of nuisance, and that the principal thing which every one requires is to be left to himself. It seems to us that these doctrines are radically false, that they are exceedingly mischievous, and that they are altogether opposed to experience. To take the last point first, nothing can be more unfaithful to fact than to represent the legislation of the last fifty years as having consisted entirely or even principally in the removal of restraints. In many directions there is far more government now than there ever was before. Look, for instance, at the legislation which has taken place in the course of the last twenty years upon matters concerned with public health. Look at the powers which have been put in the hands of railway and other public companies. Look at the Factory Acts, the Acts relating to Mines, the Acts relating to lodging houses, the Reformatory Acts, and an immense mass of other laws of which these are only a sample. Surely in all these instances Parliament has effected much more than the mere removal of these obstructions. It is much the same in other matters not immediately connected with the relief of different forms of human misery. The army, the navy, the volunteers and the militia, the universities and the different schools of all sorts of classes and adapted to all kinds of wants are all positive institutions. Does any one doubt that it is one of the most important of the duties of Parliament to make them as useful and efficient as possible? and is this consistent with the principle that all that the Legislature has to do is to act as a gigantic policeman, who is to be continually keeping the streets clear, and telling people to move on?

To us it seems that any nation which sinks into the condition of a mere police-constable removing obstructions and saying 'Move on' will both be, and deserve to become, contemptible .... It will be liable to be overthrown by any strong moral impulse which sways the minds of men as the French Revolution swayed them .... Surely this is a degraded position for a great State to be in. Nations and national governments ought ... to be the great moving and regulating powers in human life, earthly providences working out in an intelligent and practical way the designs which, as far as we can venture to attribute designs to such a being at all, must be ascribed to the Supreme Being.

8h   The growth of government quantified

Horace Mann, 'On the Cost and Organisation of the Civil Service',
Journal of the Royal Statistical Society, vol. xxxii (1869), pp. 38–60.

The Estimates for civil services in the three decennial periods

1848–9	£3,670,427
1858–9	£11,844,166
1868–9	£15,169,366

The increase here (excluding the legal and educational offices, the three revenue departments (customs, inland revenue, and post office) and the civil branches of the army and navy)... will be found to have been caused in great measure by the creation of new departments, or new branches of old departments, to carry out measures demanded by the public ....

	Amount of Estimate in 1868–69 or Increase over Estimate, &c. of 1848 £
Charity Commission	18,438
General Register Office, Ireland	18,306
Agricultural statistics (Great Britain)	14,500
Public health (Privy Council)	13,000
Factory inspection	12,356
Inspection of coal mines	10,500
Civil Service Commission	9,407
Inspectors and Commissioners of Fisheries	8,182
Cattle plague	7,743
Public Record Office	7,903
General Register Office, Scotland	7,608
Lunacy Commission	6,206
Inspection of constabulary	4,425

Public Record Office, Ireland	4,296
Inspection of alkali works	3,300
Inspection of prisons	2,400
Inspection of reformatories	2,305
Inspection of lime juice	2,000
Registration of designs	1,896
Local Government Act Office	1,223
Inspection of burial grounds	1,120
Inspection of anchors and cables	1,100
Inspection of oyster fisheries	500
	158,714

I think the conclusion generally drawn from these facts will be, that the greater portion, if not the whole, of the additional burdens on these estimates during the past twenty years, has been imposed for purposes which the public desired, and still desires, to effect .... If the public is inclined now to give up the various advantages which have been obtained in return for this additional expenditure; if we should be content with fewer public improvements, less police protection, fewer sanitary safeguards, a harsher poor law, fewer and dearer courts of justice, fewer postal facilities, and fewer and less useful schools for three-fourths of the community—then it will be easy enough to reduce the civil service estimates by abolishing several departments and attenuating others. But if the public really wants the things for which it, and not the departments, has been crying out, it can only get them by paying for them. My own belief ... is that, so far from reducing its demands for improvements by means of the State-machinery, the public, under the new regime, will considerably increase them; and that the civil service estimates will be called upon to provide for a much larger quantity of work than that which is now paid for from that source.

8i   A Conservative politician on the necessity of State intervention

Stafford Northcote, *Transactions of the National Association for the Promotion of Social Science* (1869), pp. 4–5.

... any candid person, who takes a comprehensive view of our position, must admit that in some respects the intervention of the Government is much more necessary now than it used to be in former times; and that social questions are assuming such large dimensions that they cannot be adequately dealt with except by the employment of the central administrative machinery. This arises partly from the magnitude of the operations which have to be effected, and partly from the complication of the interests which they affect, and from the increased power of classes which in former times exercised comparatively little influence over our social arrangements. The rapid increase of the population, the great development of our communications, the accumulation of our wealth, the application of science to industry, the pressure of foreign competition, and many other causes which it would be tedious to enumerate, tend to render it more and more necessary, when any important social improvement is in question, to secure the co-operation of large classes upon a large scale. This can best be done, and in some cases can only be done, through the intervention of the central Government .... It may still be true that an enlightened sense of self-interest is a powerful agent for effecting public good, but the difficulty is to bring men up to the necessary pitch of enlightenment; and, even when you have done that, you have done nothing unless you can convince them that others will act up to the common standard; for it is the first condition of co-operation that men should have faith in those who are to co-operate with them. Hence arises the demand for some kind of compulsion, and this leads to a call for Government interference. And if the interposition of Government is often needed to give effect to the principle of co-operation, it is equally often to to prevent its abuse; that is to say, to prevent the weak and helpless being made its victims, and to secure fair play to individuals.

Part Two

The viability of collectivism, 1870–95

9 The growing responsibilities of the State

In the last thirty years of the nineteenth century, the powers of the State grew rapidly. Reactions to this development in social policy were mixed. Some, like the individualist philosopher and sociologist Herbert Spencer (1820–1903), regarded it with alarm (9c); others, like the influential Fabian and strategist of the early Labour Party Sidney Webb (1859–1947), saw it as a natural and appropriate phase of community development on the broad march to socialism (9e). Alfred Marshall (1842–1924), the leading economist of his day, argued that in a mature economy the State should take the initiative to eliminate the crudities of unrestrained capitalism (9g). Though no socialist, he saw society developing a collective purpose to subdue 'individual caprice'. Professor David Ritchie (1853–1903), the Oxford philosopher later famous for his attack on the theory of natural rights, criticized Spencer's views, particularly from the utilitarian standpoint that the State could minimize the gross waste of resources which resulted from unrestrained capitalism (9h). When he wrote, in 1891, he was a member of the Fabian society, though his political views were rather liberal-radical.

Politicians used the powers of the State as weapons on their platforms. Joseph Chamberlain (1836–1914), who had risen to national prominence from the secure base of Birmingham politics as a collectivist social reformer, saw the State as the crucial agency by which misery and destitution could be conquered, and gross inequalities in society modified (9d). He retained his belief in social reform whether on the Liberal or, from 1886, on the Unionist benches. Arthur Balfour (1848–1930) shrewdly saw both a viable future for Conservatism and an effective buttress against socialism in the adoption of cautious and carefully considered social reform (9i). For all their well-publicized antagonisms and the rhetoric of their public pronouncements, the views of the two dominant statesmen of their age was not fundamentally dissimilar. W.E. Gladstone (1809–98) and Benjamin Disraeli (1804–81) both believed in the overriding importance of individual initiative; neither accepted that the State could or should contribute more than a minor part in personal advancement. Disraeli drew attention to the oft-forgotten fact that most of his 'social' legislation was permissive in character, though he was wrong to suggest that most of his Liberal opponents favoured compulsory State action (9a). Most social legislation in the 1870s, whether Liberal or Tory inspired, indicated what initiatives local authorities might take; little, except in the well-defined sphere of public health, imposed compulsory minimal provision. Gladstone was just as insistent at the end of his long career as he had been at its beginning that State action should not stifle 'the spirit of true and genuine manly independence' (9f).

The growth of government alarmed many backbench Members of Parliament. C. N. Newdegate (1816–87), a Warwickshire squire who might fairly be described as a Tory backwoodsman, deplored the increasing influence of departmental business in the work of the Commons. The Commons immersed itself in what this foxhunting Member obviously considered administrative trivia, to the detriment of 'great questions' of national policy (9b). *The Economist* ploughed on, manifesting a consistency rare in long-lived nineteenth-century journals, in its campaign against both the cost and the inefficiency of government bureaucracy (9j). In contrast to the views of D.G. Ritchie, the journal believed that government expenditure engendered greater waste than it averted.

Suggestions for further reading

See P. Smith, *Disraelian Conservatism and Social Reform* (1967), for political responses to the growing powers of the State in the 1870s. H.M. Lynd, *England in the Eighteen-Eighties* (1945), is particularly concerned with what she sees as a crucial decade in the emergence of a State with recognizably modern attitudes to social problems.

9a   The characteristic of a free people

Benjamin Disraeli, Debate on the Agricultural Holdings Bill, 24 June 1875. *Hansard* (3rd series), vol. ccxxv, col. 525.

It may be all very well for hon. and right hon. Gentlemen to treat with affected contempt the notion that our legislation should be founded on permission, but permissive legislation is the characteristic of a free people. It is easy to adopt compulsory legislation when you have to deal with those who only exist to obey; but in a free country, and especially in a country like England, you must trust to persuasion and example as the two great elements, if you wish to effect any considerable change in the manners and customs of the people .... Gentlemen opposite seem proud that on all occasions they are the advocates of compulsion in legislation. I do not envy them the lordly attributes they arrogate to themselves .... I trust that those who are sitting on this side of the House will give no encouragement to a policy which I believe to be so pernicious—that they will advocate that course upon public measures which they believe to be beneficial to the country; and that they will trust to example and persuasion to induce a free and intelligent people to adopt their views, and to follow their example.

9b   A backbench Tory deplores the changing functions of parliament

C.N. Newdegate, Debate on a Resolution to Consolidate the Departments of Commerce and Agriculture, 8 July 1879. *Hansard* (3rd series), vol. ccxlvii, cols. 1928–30.

Ten or 15 years ago the House would not have entertained such a proposal as that which was now before it. The House would have considered, and considered rightly, that the proposal involved an invasion of its functions. When he first entered Parliament, and for years afterwards, the real head of Public Departments was the House of Commons itself.... The House did not spend hour after hour, day after day, week after week, and month after month in the consideration and re-consideration of the details of every measure that came before it; but devoted itself mainly to the consideration of great questions, such as that which his hon. Friend now proposed should be devolved upon the Departments. The present state of things had suggested to him grave reflections .... He did not think it would be advantageous to combine in one Department the supervision of the interests of agriculture and commerce too closely .... He believed there was room, and ample room, for two heads of Departments, who should take charge of the interests of agriculture and commerce respectively ....
With respect to the interests of commerce, this Motion was in itself a proof that the doctrine of what has been termed that of '*laissez-faire*'—the

doctrine which prevailed in the year 1846, and for some years afterwards
...—had completely passed away.

9c   The growth of government invites slavery

Herbert Spencer, *The Man Versus the State* (1884), Penguin ed. 1969, pp.
91–102.

Let us now observe the general course of recent changes, with the
accompanying current of ideas, and see whither they are carrying us.

The blank form of an inquiry daily made is—'We have already done
this; why should we not do that?' And the regard for precedent suggested
by it, is ever pushing on regulative legislation. Having brought within
their sphere of operation more and more numerous businesses, the Acts
restricting hours of employment and dictating the treatment of workers
are now to be made applicable to shops. From inspecting lodging-houses to
limit the numbers of occupants and enforce sanitary conditions, we have
passed to inspecting all houses below a certain rent in which there are
members of more than one family, and are now passing to a kindred
inspection of all small houses .... Supplying children with food for their
minds by public agency is being followed in some cases by supplying food
for their bodies; and after the practice has been made gradually more
general, we may anticipate that the supply, now proposed to be made gratis
in the one case, will eventually be proposed to be made gratis in the other:
the argument that good bodies as well as good minds are needful to make
good citizens, being logically urged as a reason for the extension ....

The extension of this policy, causing extension of corresponding ideas,
fosters everywhere the tacit assumption that Government should step in
whenever anything is not going right. 'Surely you would not have this
misery continue!' exclaims someone, if you hint a demurrer to much that
is now being said and done. Observe what is implied by this exclamation.
It takes for granted, first, that all suffering ought to be prevented, which is
not true: much of the suffering is curative, and prevention of it is
prevention of a remedy. In the second place, it takes for granted that every
evil can be removed: the truth being that, with the existing defects of

human nature, many evils can only be thrust out of one place or form into another place or form—often being increased by the change. The exclamation also implies the unhesitating belief ... that evils of all kinds should be dealt with by the State. There does not occur the inquiry whether there are at work other agencies capable of dealing with evils, and whether the evils in question may not be among those which are best dealt with by these other agencies. And obviously, the more numerous governmental interventions become, the more confirmed does this habit of thought grow, and the more loud and perpetual the demands for intervention ....

'But why is this change described as "the coming slavery"?' is a question which many will still ask. The reply is simple. All socialism involves slavery.

What is essential to the idea of a slave? We primarily think of him as one who is owned by another.... That which fundamentally distinguishes the slave is that he labours under coercion to satisfy another's desires .... If, without option, he has to labour for the society, and receives from the general stock such portion as the society awards him, he becomes a slave to the society. Socialistic arrangements necessitate an enslavement of this kind; and towards such an enslavement many recent measures, and still more the measures advocated, are carrying us.

The policy initiated by the Industrial Dwellings Acts admits of development, and will develop. When municipal bodies turn house-builders, they inevitably lower the values of houses otherwise built, and check the supply of more. Every direction respecting modes of building and conveniences to be provided, diminishes the builder's profit, and prompts him to use his capital where the profit is not thus diminished. So, too, the owner, already finding that small houses entail much labour and many losses—already subject to troubles of inspection and interference, and to consequent costs, and having his property daily rendered a more undesirable investment, is prompted to sell; and as buyers are for like reasons deterred, he has to sell at a loss .... The multiplication of houses, and especially small houses, being increasingly checked, there must come an increasing demand upon the local authority to make up for the deficient supply. More and more the municipal or kindred body will have to build houses .... And when in towns this process has gone so far as to make the local authority the chief owner of houses, there will be a good precedent for publicly providing houses for the rural population .... Manifestly, the tendency of that which has been done, is being done, and is presently to be done, is to approach the socialistic ideal in which the community is the sole house-proprietor.

9d   The State as a social engineer

Joseph Chamberlain, speech at Warrington, 8 September 1885. Reprinted in *Manchester Guardian*, 9 September 1885.

The great problem of our civilisation is unsolved. We have to account for and grapple with the mass of misery and destitution in our midst, co-existent as it is with the evidence of abundant wealth and teeming prosperity. It is a problem which some men would put aside by reference to the eternal laws of supply and demand, to the necessity for freedom of contract and the sanctity of every private right in property. Ah, gentlemen, these phrases are the convenient cant of selfish wealth (Cheers). They are no answer to our questions (Hear, hear). I could understand the reason for timidity in dealing with this matter as long as a Government was merely the expression of the will and prejudices of a limited few, and under the circumstances there might well be reason for refusing to entrust it with greater functions and higher powers for the relief of undeserved misery and distress. But now, now when at last we have a Government of the people (loud cheers) in which all shall co-operate in order to secure every man his natural rights, his right to existence (cheers) and to a fair enjoyment of it (cheers). I shall be told tomorrow (laughter) 'this is Socialism' (A voice: 'Never mind; gives us a bit more of it'). I have learned not to be afraid of words flung in my face in place of argument. Of course, it is Socialism. The Poor-law is Socialism, the Education Act is Socialism, the great part of our municipal work is Socialism; every kindly act of legislation by which the community recognises its responsibility and obligations to its poorer members is socialistic, and it is none the worse for that (cheers). Our object is the elevation of the poor (hear, hear), of the masses of the people—a levelling up which shall do something to remove the excessive inequalities in the social condition of the people, and which is now one of the greatest dangers as well as the greatest injury to the State (Hear, hear and cheers).... I think that taxation ought to mean equality of sacrifice (hear, hear) and I do not see how this is to be obtained except by some form of graduated taxation ... which is proportioned to the superfluities of the taxpayer (Hear, hear).

9e The growth of government: a Fabian perspective

Sidney Webb, 'The Basis of Socialism: Historic', in G.B. Shaw (ed.), *Fabian Essays in Socialism* (1920 ed.), pp. 40-9.

The result of the industrial revolution, with its dissolution of medievalism amid an impetuous reaction against the bureaucratic tyranny of the past, was to leave all the new elements of society in a state of unrestrained license. Individual liberty, in the sense of freedom to privately appropriate the means of production, reached its maximum at the commencement of the [nineteenth] century....

The Utilitarian philosophy, besides aiding in the popularization of economic science, strongly influenced its early character. The tendency to *Laisser Faire*, inherited from the country and century of upheaval and revolt against authority, was fostered by Bentham's destructive criticism of all the venerable relics of the past. What is the use of it, he asked, of every shred of social institution then existing.... Few of the laws and customs—little, indeed, of the social organization of that time could stand this test.... At last it came to be carelessly accepted as the teaching both of philosophy and of experience that every man must fight for himself; and 'devil take the hindmost' became the accepted social creed of what was still believed to be a Christian nation. Utilitarianism became the Protestantism of Sociology, and 'how to make for self and family the best of both worlds' was assumed to be the duty, as it certainly was the aim, of every practical Englishman....

[But in the light of experience] England was compelled to put forth her hand and succor and protect her weaker members. Any number of Local Improvement Acts, Drainage Acts, Truck Acts, Mines Regulation Acts, Factory Acts, Public Health Acts, Adulteration Acts were passing into law.... Step by step the political power and political organization of the country have been used for industrial ends, until today the largest employer of labor is one of the ministers of the Crown (the Postmaster-General); and almost every conceivable trade is, somewhere or other, carried on by parish, municipality, or the National Government itself without the intervention of any middleman or capitalist.... The community now carries on for itself ... the post office ... coinage, surveys, the regulation of currency and note issue, the provision of weights and measures, the making, sweeping, lighting and repairing of streets, roads and bridges.... It provides for many thousands of us from birth to burial— midwifery, nursery, education, board and lodging, vaccination, medical attendance, medicine, public worship, amusements and interment. It furnishes and maintains its own musuems, parks, art galleries, libraries, concert halls, roads, streets, bridges, markets (etc.).... Every one of these functions ... were at one time left to private enterprise, and were a source of legitimate investment of capital. Step by step the community has absorbed them, wholly or partially; and the area of private exploitation has been lessened....

Besides its direct supersession of private enterprise, the State now registers, inspects, and controls nearly all the industrial functions it has not yet absorbed ... the State registers all solicitors, barristers ... newspaper proprietors ... brewers, bankers ... all insurance companies, friendly societies, endowed schools and charities, limited companies ... lodging houses, public houses ... places of worship, elementary schools and dancing rooms....

Even in the fields still abandoned to private enterprise, its operations are thus every day more closely limited, in order that the anarchic competition of private greed, which at the beginning of the Century was set up as the only beneficient principle of social action, may not utterly destroy the State. All this has been done by 'practical' men, ignorant, that is to say, of any scientific sociology believing Socialism to be the most foolish of dreams, and absolutely ignoring, as they thought, all grandiloquent claims for social reconstruction. Such is the irresistible sweep of social tendencies, that in their every act they worked to bring about the very Socialism they despised; and to destroy the Individualist faith which they still professed. They builded better than they knew.

9f Gladstone on the spirit of self-reliance

Speech on opening a new reading and recreation room at Saltney, Cheshire, 26 October 1889. A.W. Hutton and H.J. Cohen (eds), *The Speeches of W.E. Gladstone* (London, 1892), vol. x, p. 132.

We live at a time when there is a disposition to think that the Government ought to do this and that, and that the Government ought to do everything. There are things which the Government ought to do, and does not do, I have no doubt. In former periods the Government have neglected much, and possibly even now they neglect something. But there is a danger on the other side. If the Government takes into its hands that which the man ought to do for himself, it will inflict upon him greater mischiefs than all the benefits he will have received or all the advantages that will accrue from them. The essence of the whole thing is that the spirit of self-reliance, the spirit of true and genuine manly independence, should be preserved in the minds of the people, in the minds of the masses of the people, in the minds of every member of that class. If he loses his self-reliance, if he learns to live in a craven dependence upon wealthier people rather than upon himself, you may depend upon it he incurs mischiefs for which no compensation can be made.

9g Industrial maturity brings a different perspective on industrialism

Alfred Marshall, *Principles of Economics* (8th ed., 1920), Appendix A, pp. 750-2.

It has been left for our own generation to perceive all the evils which arose from the suddenness of this increase of economic freedom [during the industrial revolution]. Now first are we getting to understand the extent to which the capitalist employer, untrained to his new duties, was tempted to subordinate the wellbeing of his workpeople to his own desire for gain; now first are we learning the importance of insisting that the rich have duties as well as rights in their individual and in their collective capacity; now first is the economic problem of the new age showing itself to us as it really is. This is partly due to a wider knowledge and a growing earnestness. But however wise and virtuous our grandfathers had been, they could not have seen things as we do; for they were hurried along by urgent necessities and terrible disasters.

We must judge ourselves by a severer standard ... the nation has grown in wealth, in health, in education and in morality; and we are no longer compelled to subordinate almost every other consideration to the need of increasing the total produce of industry.

In particular this increased prosperity has made us rich and strong enough to impose new restraints on free enterprise; some temporary material loss being submitted to for the sake of a higher and ultimate greater gain....

Thus gradually we may attain to an order of social life, in which the common good overrules individual caprice, even more than it did in the days before the sway of individualism had begun.

9h   An attack on Spencer's organic view of society

D.G. Ritchie, *The Principles of State Interference* (London, 1891), pp. 49–50.

The truth is, that Society (or the State) is not an organism, because we may compare it to a beast or a man; but because it cannot be understood by the help of any lower—i.e. less complex—conceptions than that of organism. In it, as in an organism, every part is conditioned by the whole. In a mere aggregate, or heap, the units are prior to the whole; in an organism the whole is prior to the parts—i.e. they can only be understood in reference to the whole....

The history of progress is the record of a gradual diminution of *waste*. The lower the stage the greater is the waste involved in the attainment of any end.... When we come to human beings in society, the State is the chief instrument by which waste is prevented. The mere struggle for existence between individuals means waste unchecked. The State, by its action, can in many cases consciously and deliberately diminish this fearful loss; in many cases by freeing the individual from the necessity of a perpetual struggle for the mere conditions of life, it can set free individuality and so make culture possible. An ideal state would be one in which there was no waste at all of the lives, and intellects, and souls of individual men and women.

9i   A Conservative view of the legitimate functions of the State

A.J. Balfour, speech in Manchester, 16 January 1895, reported in
Manchester Guardian, 17 January 1895.

Social legislation, as I conceive it, is not merely to be distinguished from
Socialist legislation, but is its direct opposite and its most effective antidote
(Hear, hear). Socialism will never get possession of the great body of public
opinion in this country, among the working classes or among any other
classes, if those who wield the collective forces of the community show
themselves desirous in any way in their power of using those forces, so far
as they can be used with benefit to the people concerned, to ameliorate
every legitimate grievance and to put society upon a more solid basis. And
it is in order that that may be done that I am an advocate of social
legislation and that I see with satisfaction all the discussion, all the
criticism, all the investigation which are necessary and inevitable
preliminaries to any wise and sober scheme for dealing with the questions
known as social questions.... You may safely enter upon this difficult
path.... if you firmly grasp one or two great principles. One ... is that no
class is ultimately benefited by robbing any other class (Cheers). Another
... is that, though Governments and Acts of Parliament may do much,
yet, after all, it is the individual, the free individual, using his capacities to
the best advantage, working and co-operating with his fellows in freely
organised associations, which, as in the past so in the future, must do the
great share of the work of raising the standard of life and happiness and the
cultivation of prosperity.... There is a third element in our ideal. It is to
preserve those of our institutions which still have in them the sap of life and
which are still faithful to their great work for the community at large ...
the policy of the Unionist party ... is a policy which will make enterprise
secure, which will ensure liberty to every man, and which will take care
that the collective forces of the community shall not be wasted in barren
and futile attempts at destruction, but shall be directed soberly, quietly, in a
spirit of caution, but in no spirit of fear, to the amelioration and benefit of
every class of the community. (Cheers).

9j   'The Economist' continues to reject State inference

The Economist, 25 May 1895.

The increase of expenditure of the State is the one invariable element in the Budget.... No one runs any danger of being proved wrong if he assumes that next year the total expenditure will be larger than that of the year before.

If we analyse this growth of expenditure, we shall find that it is largely due to the growth of Government action in the various departments of civil life.... Little by little, and year by year, the fabric of State expenditure and State responsibility is built up like a coral island, cell on cell. Every year half-a-dozen Acts of Parliament are passed which give the State new powers and new functions, and enact that new departments and new inspectors shall supervise, and new officials carry out these powers and functions. But new departments, new inspectors, and new officials mean the expenditure of more money, and often on a most lavish scale.... All these new Bills, clauses, and sub-sections which declare that some act or other shall not be done until the consent of the Board of Trade, or the Home Office, or the Local Government Board shall have been first obtained are drafts on the National Exchequer. They are in effect orders to engage and pay so many more clerks, to print so many more pages, and to use up so much more foolscap and red-tape. Practically, you cannot spend more money without raising more taxes. Hence the creating of new duties for the State and the development of new means of interfering with individual action are in essence the imposition of new burdens on the taxpayer. The fact may not be superficially apparent, but it is none the less true.

So much for what we may call the direct economic objections to the increase of State interference. The indirect injury done to the community considered in its economic aspect—that is, as a wealth-producing and wealth-accumulating entity is hardly less serious. No unprejudiced observer can fail to have noticed that two things always accompany interference with the freedom of individual action in matters of trade and commerce—waste and inefficiency. The trade which flourishes most is the trade which is most let alone—most free to develop itself in its own way. Directly you put the pressure of State interference on an industry it begins to suffer a certain loss of vigour. In extreme cases, indeed, the industry actually shrivels and withers. And even where the interference is most scientifically employed, there is a certain injury inflicted. And this withering, or tendency towards withering, cannot but inflict an economic loss, great or small in proportion to the nature and amount of the interference which takes place. Hence the interference of the State in matters of trade and industry not only inflicts a burden on the nation, but makes the nation less able to bear the burden.... However it is looked at economically, State interference in the dominion of civil life and with the machinery of production is an evil.

10   Local government reforms

It was clear by the 1870s that the burdens placed on local administration were insupportable. The plethora of jurisdictions in sanitation and public health resulted in waste, inefficiency and unacceptable variations in practice. Disraeli's minority government had appointed a Royal Commission to inquire into the problem of sanitation in 1868. Under the Chairmanship of the Tory politician Charles B. Adderley (1814–1905), it reported in 1871 and recommended greater central direction though arguing that in doing so the sacred principle of local autonomy would remain inviolate (10a). The Liberal government's response was to establish the Local Government Board, which unified the administration of poor law and public health. For the government, James Stansfeld (1820–98) argued that local powers were strengthened rather than diminished by the change. The only opposition came from Tory backbenchers like F.W. Knight (1812–97) who feared the creeping tentacles of centralized bureaucracy (10b).

The LGB only served to throw into clearer relief the deficiencies of a local administration still run on largely Elizabethan lines by Justices of the Peace and Quarter Sessions. C.T. Ritchie's (1838–1906) Local Government Act (1888) established sixty-two administrative counties and, from the largest towns and cities, sixty county boroughs which swept away most of the older forms of local government (10c). The crucial changes were, first, that members of local government were now elected in all cases and, second, that the new authorities were equipped to perform a wider range of tasks efficiently, and with a unified budget. Just how much could be achieved was to be demonstrated by the work of the London County Council, established in 1889. The progressive majority on the Council in its early years, including Conservatives as well as Liberal-Radicals and Socialists, endorsed a large number of pioneer collectivist schemes in the fields of municipal housing, public works and education. This alarmed many contemporaries (10d), but indicated to others the potential of an efficient, democratically elected body (10f). The LCC also gave political baptisms to figures of considerable national importance in the early twentieth century. Its first Chairman, Lord Rosebery (1847–1929), was already prominent in the Liberal Party, but he was only one of two future Prime Ministers who guided the Council's early work. James Ramsay MacDonald (1866–1937) grew to prominence there, as did the dock workers' leader John Burns (1858–1943) and the Fabian and later Labour Party intellectual Sidney Webb (1859–1947).

The corollary of the 1888 local government reforms was H.H. Fowler's (1830–1911) Parish Councils Act, 1894. This established the principle of elected parish councils in place of nominations by squire and parson; it also accompanied the emergence of Rural District Councils. Liberals naturally hoped that the measure would deal a death blow to the Tory paternalism of many village communities. The House of Lords, alive to this danger, asserted itself by insisting that no parish council could spend more than the equivalent of a threepenny rate. This early example of a Tory Upper House thwarting the will of a Liberal Commons effectively foreclosed the option of powerful, independent Parish Councils desired by the Fabians among others (10e). Fowler's Act, however, permitted women to stand as candidates for the first time in local government elections. It also completed the system of local government reorganization which survived intact until 1974, and which executed revolutionary changes in social policy during that time.

Suggestions for further reading

V.D. Lipman, *Local Government Areas, 1834–1945* (London, 1949) contains some useful background analysis in addition to facts. Joseph Redlich and Francis W. Hirst, *The History of Local Government in England* (2nd ed., Introduction by B. Keith-Lucas, London, 1970), is slighter, but useful. On the London County Council see W. Eric Jackson, *Achievement: A Short History of the L.C.C.* (London, 1965).

10a The Royal Commission on Sanitation recommends greater central direction

Parliamentary Papers, 1871, vol. xxxv, pp. 15–16, 30–6.

That more active and effective sanitary local government is necessary for the well-being of this country, is clear from the comparative condition of places which have, and of those which have not, exercised their powers....

Mortality is greatly increased by want of sanitary provisions; a marked reduction of death-rate has followed the improvement of drainage and sewerage, and the supply of other obvious sanitary requirements.

Many causes of disease are preventible: and much chronic weakness, and incapacity for work are the result of sanitary negligence and want of the ordinary requisites of civilized life....

The mere money cost of public ill-health, whether it be reckoned by the necessarily increased expenditure, or by the loss of the work both of the sick and of those who wait upon them, must be estimated at many millions a year.

The subject referred to us is only a part of a still larger subject, namely, the entire system of local government throughout the country....

The principle of local self-government has been generally recognized as of the essence of our national vigour. Local administration, under central superintendance, is the distinguishing feature of our government.

The theory is, that all that can, should be done by local authority, and that public expenditure should be chiefly controlled by those who contribute to it....

But local administration has its drawbacks. The smallness of the parochial unit of area minimizes the material for public officers.

The spirit of that self-government, which Englishmen have always vindicated to themselves through every developing period of their history, has led to the growth of many discrepancies in their institutions, and to many disconnected and even conflicting laws. Imperfect local administration has been the natural result. Local administration must nevertheless be maintained, but it should be at the same time simplified, strengthened, and set in motion.

The New Statute ... should constitute, and give adequate strength to, *one Central Authority.* There should be one recognised and sufficiently powerful Minister, not to centralize administration, but on the contrary to set local life in motion—a real motive power, and an Authority to be referred to for guidance and assistance by all the Sanitary Authorities for local government throughout the country. Great is the *vis inertiae* to be overcome; the repugnance to self-taxation; the practical distrust of science; and the number of persons interested in offending against sanitary laws, even amongst those who must constitute chiefly the Local Authorities to enforce them....

... the new Central Sanitary Office ... must be very much enlarged from the present scale of the Local Government Act Office, which under the Home Office (together with the Health Department of the Privy Council,) has almost entirely conducted the sanitary government of the Kingdom. If the Sanitary Statutes are to be made of general application (and their partial and optional application is to be no longer admissible) it is obvious that neither the present office nor the present staff can be sufficient....

When stringent provisions for thorough local government are everywhere applied, and there is a Body responsible for carrying them out in every place, the Central Authority must have adequate powers to enforce the effective action of all such Local Bodies.

The Sanitary Department must be as universal and equal in its action throughout the kingdom under the proposed Minister as its co-department of the Poor Law, which has its responsible Authorities established in every parish....

This advancement of sanitary government to the full requirements of the whole kingdom must necessarily demand both a much larger and a more powerful Central Office than the present Local Government Act Office .... At the same time the coupling of poor law with sanitary administration under the same Chief will not only harmonize but economize the working of the whole system of local government....

Central inspection is mainly wanted to set local machinery at work, and see that it is in order.

The Central Authority when ... it is charged in one of its departments with the superintendence of all Sanitary Authorities, and equipped with a sufficient staff of officers, both medical and inspectorial, must nevertheless avoid taking to itself the actual work of local government. We would leave *direction* only in the Central power. It must steer clear of the rock on which the General Board of Health was wrecked; for so completely is local self government the habit and quality of Englishmen, that the country would resent any Central Authority undertaking the duties of the local executive.

The new Department will have to keep all Local Authorities and their officers in the active exercise of their own legally imposed and responsible functions; to make itself acquainted with any default and to remedy it ... to direct enquiries, medical or otherwise; to give advice and plans when requested; to sanction some of the larger proceedings of the Local Authorities; to issue provisional orders, subject to Parliamentary confirmation; to receive complaints and appeals; to issue medical regulations on emergencies and to collect medical reports.

This New Office must be more fully empowered than the Home Secretary is at present to deal with the default of any Local Authority.

10b The establishment of the Local Government Board

Hansard (3rd series), vol. ccviii, cols 78–81, 20 July 1871.

J. Stansfeld, Chief Commissioner of the Poor Law Board:
Its [the Bill's] object was to concentrate in a new Department ... the existing functions of the Privy Council with regard to health and the prevention of disease, especially the oversight of such matters as vaccination, the powers and duties of the Home Office and of the Local Government Act Office with regard to local government, and certain other powers and duties of the Home Office with reference to the registration of births, deaths, and marriages, and the collation of local taxation Returns .... It might be supposed by some that this Bill was an effort to introduce the thin end of the wedge of a centralizing system. If that were the object of the Bill or the policy of the Government, he should be the last man to propose such a measure. There was nothing in the Report of the Sanitary Commission which he admired more than that part in which they expressed their conviction of the growing importance of local government in this country. This Bill, instead of destroying, would give new force to the principle of local government in this country.

F.W. Knight: The real origin and explanation of this Bill was that it sought to place the whole local government of the country under the Poor Law Board .... now it wished to encroach on the power of the local authorities, and to bring them entirely under its control .... The action of the Government in proposing this measure was a police action, and if such a system were to go on nothing soon would be safe from Government inspection in some form or other....

10c   Local government rationalized

Hansard 3rd series, vol. cccxxiii, cols 1642–46, 19 March 1888.

C.T. Ritchie, President of the Local Government Board:
There is a real and substantial demand for a system of decentralization by which many of the duties which are now performed by Central Departments, and in some cases by Parliament, might be entrusted to County Authorities, if they were constituted in a manner which should adequately represent the public .... It is quite certain that if we were to set up a Representative Body such as is proposed for county affairs it would be impossible for us to shut our eyes to the confusion of areas within the counties, and to the number of different authorities. We propose, therefore, not only to deal with the powers and composition of the Central Governing Body in the county, but also with the powers and composition of the Local Bodies within the area .... the desire that further powers than those which are possessed by the County Authorities should be given to a Central Body in the county is much more prevalent in the country generally than the desire for a mere change in the Governing Body; and therefore it may be convenient if I, at the outset, ask the House to consider the question of the powers which we shall propose should be given to the Central County Council when it is established .... We propose ... to transfer to the new Bodies all the existing administrative powers of the Justices in respect of County Rates and financial business, County Buildings, County Bridges, the provision and management of the County Lunatic Asylums, the establishment and maintenance of Reformatory and Industrial Schools, the granting of Licences for Music and Dancing, the granting of Licences for the Sale of Intoxicating Liquors ... the division of

the county into Polling Districts for Parliamentary Elections, the cost of
the Registration of Voters, the executing the Acts relating to Explosives,
the execution of the Acts relating to the Contagious Diseases of Animals,
the Adulteration of Food and Drugs, Weights and Measures, and various
other minor matters with which I will not trouble the House. We also
propose to entrust to the County Councils certain duties with reference to
Main Roads in the counties .... We propose ... that the raising and
management of the police should be in the hands of a joint committee of
the County Council and of Quarter Sessions.

10d   The presumptions of the London County Council

'The Advance towards State Socialism', *The Economist*, 7 April 1894.

The London County Council is always asking for more rights to legislate,
and avowedly would, if it could, become a subordinate authority. It would
like to be a Parliament with Mr. Shaw Lefevre for Sovereign, with a
nominal veto. It would like to make everybody live in a house of its own
planning, and only refrains from pulling down East London because the
rebuilding turns out to be unendurably costly. It wishes to control the
lighting of private houses, for, of course, its possession of all gas works will
involve that of all electric establishments, and is highly offended because it
is not already sole owner, for private purposes as well as public, of all
supplies of water. It desires to 'moralise' all theatres and music halls, and to
be the sole licensing authority for public houses. It seeks dominion over the
river, and looks with longing eyes at the docks, the tramways, the omnibus
service, and for purposes of regulation, at all events, the mural
advertisements of London. The London School Board, in the same way,
besides regulating all details of education, down to or up to the particular
view of the Trinity to be inculcated, is anxious about the health of children
and their meals in a degree which, if sanctioned, would involve a strict
inspection of everybody's breakfast.

10e   Fabian advice on how to influence local affairs

'The Parish Councils Act: What it is and How to Work It' (Fabian Tract, 53, London, 1894), pp. 3,6,11.

In 1894 Parliament made a law, usually called the Parish Councils Act, which every working man and working woman ought to know about. It is a law for giving the working folk who live in villages the power to manage their own affairs. It is a charter of liberty which makes them citizens of their own parish and equal with the squire and the parson in its management.

Perhaps the most important thing that the Parish Council will have power to do will be to obtain land for allotments. To the agricultural laborer the possession of a bit of land near his home and at a reasonable rent means a supply of food in the shape of bacon or vegetables or flour to the value of perhaps six or seven pounds a year; it also gives him an occupation when he is out of work ... and it makes him feel a good deal more independent.

Everything depends on the men and women who are chosen .... *It is of the utmost importance that in every case the voters should elect whomever they think is the best person for the place, and no one else.* Not the wealthiest man in the parish, not the parson, unless he is a specially good man, not the man who talks most nor the man who employs most labor, but let them elect the man who will do most work of the right kind in the right spirit. The Parish Council is not meant to be a village House of Lords, to be entered for the sake of the honor it may be supposed to give. It is to be a body of thoughtful men and women, working actively and honestly for the welfare of their neighbours ....

If it is really dangerous for any working man in the parish to stand for election, it should be borne in mind that any person over twenty-one years of age who has for a year before the nomination lived within three miles of the village boundary, may be nominated and elected. In this way a working man may perhaps be found who is not under the thumb of the parson or the squire. A blacksmith or a shoemaker from the neighbouring village may sometimes be able to stand up for the laborers better than they can stand up for themselves.

10f   The London County Council pioneers in action

Sidney Webb, 'The Work of the London County Council', *Contemporary Review*, vol. lxvii (1895), pp. 147–8, 152.

We come to ... consider the Council's determination to dispense, wherever possible, with the contractor, and execute its works by engaging a staff of workmen under the supervision of its own salaried officers. This has been fiercely attacked as being palpably and obviously opposed to political economy and business experience. It is worth while to place on record the facts. The first case is that of watering and cleaning of Works let out to a contractor. The new Council perversely went into calculations which led the members to believe that the contractor was making a very good thing out of the job, and finally to decide upon engaging labour direct. There has now been over three years' experience of the new system, with the result that, whereas the contractor charged 4s 7$^1/_2$d. to 4s. 10$^1/_2$d. per square yard, the work is now done at an average cost of 3s. 2d. a square yard, everything included.

This, however, was merely a matter of hiring labour, no constructive work being involved. It is interesting to trace the stages by which the Council was driven, by force of circumstances, to its present position of builder .... The case which finally convinced three out of every four members of the Council of the desirability of executing their own works was the York Road Sewer. The engineer estimated the cost at £7000, and tenders were invited in the usual manner. Only two were sent in, one for £11,588 and the other for £11,608. The Council determined to do the work itself, with the result that a net saving of £4477 was made ....

The outcome was the establishment, in the spring of 1893, of a Works Committee to execute works required by the other committees in precisely the same manner as a contractor .... The committee requiring any work prepares its own estimate, as if tenders were going to be invited, and the Works Committee is asked whether it is prepared to undertake the work upon that estimate ....

... the Council's net demand on the London ratepayer has, in the six years of its existence, risen by $1^1/_2 d.$ in the pound, everything included .... A halfpenny for the Parks Committee, a halfpenny for the Technical Education Board, a farthing for the increase in the Fire Brigade, and another farthing to cover the growing activities of the Public Health, Asylums, Main Drainage, and other committees—this is the price which London, as a whole, is asked to pay for the beneficent revolution that has taken place in every department of its municipal life between 1889 and 1895. In those six years over 1000 acres have been added to its open spaces, over 20 per cent to the strength of its fire-watch; a vast, though incalculable, advance has been made in its sanitation; the Thames has been so far purified that whitebait is once more caught where sewage lately floated up and down with every tide; great strides have been taken towards the better housing of the London poor ... thousands of improved dwellings are nearing completion; and every slum landlord is complaining at the expenditure to which he is now put for improvements and repairs. The reign of the contractor, with its 'rings' and 'knock-outs', has been brought to an end, and trade-union wages, with a 'moral minimum', have been established in every department of the Council's service .... Finally, during the last eighteen months, 800 of its most promising boys and girls have been started up the 'Scholarship Ladder' of the Technical Education Board, and thousands of their elder brothers and sisters have been swept into evening classes. For all this the ratepayer is asked in 1894–5 to pay $1^1/_2 d.$ in the pound more than he paid in 1889–90 ... According to Lord Salisbury, the Council is a hot-bed of Socialist experiments. Yet the net increase of charge upon each Londoner, after six years of this Progressive rule, is positively less than $1 d.$ per month, everything included. Surely, never was revolution so cheap!

11 Poverty, poor law and public health

In this period the universal applicability of the 1834 Poor Law to deal with the multifarious problems of destitution was seriously questioned. By the 1890s, with the advent of empirical social surveys, notably those of Charles Booth (1840–1916) (11g), the easy assumption that poverty was caused by individual or familial shortcomings was undermined. It was also increasingly doubtful that poverty should be alleviated by individualist charities or organizations. Through writers like W.H. Mallock (1849–1923) of the Liberty and Property Defence League were re-stating this old doctrine in the 1880s (11d), their arguments did not survive the revelation of the true extent of poverty. Between 1870 and 1895 there was a decisive shift in attitude to the problem generated arguably as much by fear of the threat posed by a vast army of the poor as by humanitarian sentiment.

In the early 1870s, however, the new Local Government Board instituted a partially successful campaign to drag Poor Law Guardians back towards the rigidities of 1834. Outdoor relief was to be exceptional, and not usually available as a more palatable alternative to the workhouse (11a). Outdoor relief was given to 880,000 paupers in 1871; by 1878 this number had declined to 569,000 despite the rise in population. It proved impossible, however, to maintain this improvement during periods of prolonged depression and unemployment in the 1880s when the stringency of the previous decade was greatly, perhaps decisively, relaxed. During the worst years of the depression, and particularly in 1886, middle-class observers, frightened by the scale of poverty, were concerned to offer a lifeline to the 'respectable poor' to divorce them from the 'residuum' or from 'the dangerous classes' who seemed to threaten both property and order (see also section 12).

The 1872 Public Health Act rationalized sanitary authorities throughout the country. It made compulsory the appointment of a Medical Officer of Health by each authority (11c). This Act was the sequel to the establishment of the LGB, and was also presented by James Stansfeld as a measure to strengthen local interests rather than the reverse. It undoubtedly raised the standard of minimum provision in many areas.

Decisive steps were also taken in this period to deal with disease. Compulsory vaccination against smallpox was established by the Vaccination Act, 1871 (11b), an extension of legislation passed four years before. The taint of pauperism was removed from a range of medical services. By the Diseases Prevention Act, 1883, admission to hospital with infectious disease was no longer to pauperize the recipient of treatment. In 1885 the Medical Relief (Disqualification Removal) Act (11e) enabled those receiving medical treatment to retain voting rights in all elections, save those for Poor Law Guardians. The Cornish Liberal L.H. Courtney (1832–1918) was one of a fairly small minority who argued that this change decisively undid the vital deterrence enshrined in the principles of 1834.

More hospitals were built. After the passage of the Infectious Diseases Notification Act in 1889, larger numbers of local sanitary authorities were persuaded to erect isolation hospitals. The Isolation Hospitals Act, 1893, further attempted to bring rural areas up to the standard achieved in many towns by permitting county councils to provide hospital facilities for isolating and treating infectious disease. Local initiatives and energy remained all-important, however ; availability and standards of treatment in the 1890s varied widely.

The local medical officer of health was the vital agent in the fight against dirt and disease. His energies in persuading local authorities to take action often had a decisive effect on standards in a particular community. As the work of the Chorley MOH shows (11f), many still had to warn against hazards which had been recognized for fully fifty years. Standards of sanitary provision were in many places primitive, and the laws protecting them still partial and even tentative.

Suggestions for further reading

The works by Rose and Lambert in sections 4 and 5 remain useful. On hospital provision B. Abel-Smith, *The Hospitals, 1800–1948* (1964), is encyclopaedic and authoritative.

11a   The Local Government Board reminds Guardians of the principles of 1834

LGB Circular on Outdoor Relief, 2 December 1871, *Parliamentary Papers*, 1872, vol. xxviii, pp. 63–8.

The large increase which has within the last few years taken place in the amount of out-door relief has been regarded by the Local Government Board with much anxiety....

The cost of out-door relief in England and Wales in ... 1860 amounted to £2,862,753 whilst the out-door relief for the year 1870 amounted to £3,633,051....

The inquiries which have been made by the Board show conclusively—

1. That out-door relief is in many cases granted by the Guardians too readily and without sufficient inquiry, and that they give it also in numerous instances in which it would be more judicious to apply the workhouse test....

2. That there is a great diversity of practice in the administration of out-door relief....

The Board request you, therefore, to bring ... the following recommendations under the notice of the Guardians:

1. That out-door relief should not be granted to single able-bodied men, or to single able-bodied women, either with or without illegitimate children.

2. That out-door relief should not, except in special cases, be granted to any woman deserted by her husband during the first twelve months after the desertion, or to any able-bodied widow with one child only.

3. That in the case of any able-bodied widow with more than one child, it may be desirable to take one or more of the children into the workhouse in preference to giving out-door relief....

5. That out-door relief should be granted for a fixed period only, which should not, in any case, exceed three months.

6. That all orders to able-bodied men for relief in the Labour yard should be only given from week to week.

7. That out-door relief should not be granted in any case unless the Relieving Officer has, since the application, visited the home of the applicant, and has recorded the date of such visit in the Relief Application and Report Book....

11. That in the most populous Unions it may be expedient to appoint one or more officers to be termed 'Inspectors of Out-Relief', whose duty it would be to act as a check upon the Relieving Officers....

It is difficult to over-estimate the importance to an Union of having the Guardians well affected to the law which they administer, and nothing will tend more completely to create such a feeling than the conviction that the law, when well administered, is calculated to diminish pauperism, whilst it benefits the ratepayers and the poor....

H. Fleming, Secretary

11b   The advent of compulsory vaccination

The Vaccination Act, 1871 (34 & 35 Vic., c. 98).

V: Be it enacted that the guardians of every union and parish shall appoint and pay one or more ... 'vaccination officers'....

X: Every person who prevents any public vaccinator from taking from any child lymph as provided ... shall be liable, on summary conviction, to pay a penalty not exceeding twenty shillings.

11c   Public health legislation unified

Hansard (3rd series), vol. ccix, cols 600–1 and vol. ccxiii, cols 262–3, 16 February and 1 August 1872.

Sir Charles Adderley: The law on the subject of public health was much less defective than confused, and the amendments required, in way of addition to it, were not very many. Little more than making authorities universal and imperatively active was needed to complete the law. It was the confusion of the law that was the chief cause of a very large and unnecessary mortality, and not only of mortality, but of chronic sickness, misery and debility among the working classes, and, as recent experience had shown, among the highest classes also. The existing law, cleared of this confusion, would almost suffice .... Few knew the authorities responsible, and the authorities knew not their own responsibility, nor did the people know the penalties to which they were liable, or the duties they had to perform ... much of the existing evil calling for remedy arose from the fact that the law was scattered over so many statutes, passed irrespectively of each other, partial, contradictory, or in repetition; and he did not hesitate to say that to add to the existing statutes without consolidating them would be to increase the mischief. Nothing was more important in this, or any free country, than that its local government should be of universal recognition and efficiency. The central Executive should set it in motion, but be kept by its activity from all temptation to supersede it.

C.N. Newdegate: this Bill will break up the system of local government, and substitute for it a system of centralization, of which we may hereafter have great difficulty in getting rid .... The real framers, the real administrators of this centralized system, will be the permanent officials – men who are totally irresponsible to this House .... I can see no reason for breaking up the whole system of sanitary administration.

J. Stansfeld, President of the Local Government Board: ... The Hon. Member for North Warwickshire ... said that the Bill completely destroyed local self-government in this country .... No new centralizing power was

taken by the Bill. The only new power taken was a power to require local sanitary authorities to appoint local medical officers of health ....
There was no division of opinion, no doubt, in the mind of anyone as to the necessity of a provision of that kind.

11d Poverty results from individual failings

W.H. Mallock, 'The Functions of Wealth', *Contemporary Review*, vol. xli (1882), pp. 207–8.

The condition of the labouring classes is, within certain limits, proportionate to their faculty of desire. If they are poor, squalid and dependent, it is because they have no efficient desire to be anything else ... they may be vaguely discontented with their condition, at times they may even be exasperated by it. But exasperation at poverty is not an efficient desire for a competence. To be efficient, such a desire must have an object that is, in the first place attainable, and in the second place definite. There are many workmen who live in squalid homes, and who yet find money to spare for drink and coarse debauchery ...: They long in the abstract to have a great hoard of money, but they do not long to save so many shillings a week .... Many a collier, when times were good, was in receipt of a better income than is many a curate: but let us conceive a cluster of poor curates' dwellings and contrast it with a pit village. In the former we should find every modest improvement that was possible. We should find such riches as there were made the most of. In the latter we should find dirt and disorder; we should find every symptom of outward penury; and yet all the while, as it were, there would be money spilling itself into the gutter. The reason is, that the riches of the colliers would be in excess of their desires. They would have the power to get many luxuries; but they would be unable to conceive what luxuries to get.

11e   The stigma of pauperism removed from medical treatment

Hansard (3rd series), vol. ccxcix, cols 576, 1414–5, 1458–9, 13 and 21 July 1885.

A.J. Balfour, President of the Local Government Board: I rise ... to explain a Bill which I am about to introduce ... it is a Bill to abolish the disqualification of persons from voting for receiving medical relief .... It appeared to the Government that if they were going to abolish the disqualification in the matter of Parliamentary Elections in regard to medical relief, it would be impossible to avoid abolishing it also in the matter of other elections. The Bill, therefore, removes this disqualification not merely at elections for Parliamentary Representatives, but also at elections for burgesses, school board elections and the like. There is but one exception to that general rule. We have not thought it right to allow a man to vote in Poor Law matters – for men to deal with the funds of the Unions—who receives relief from the funds managed by the Poor Law Guardians.

L.H. Courtney: He did not oppose this Bill because it enfranchised or disfranchised more or less ... but because he earnestly believed that it would injuriously affect the character and position of the labourers in England .... The old Poor Law had greatly aggravated the natural tendency towards pauperism. A great step had been taken [in 1834] towards reforming Poor Law administration, and putting it upon sound principles, so that the nation had been enabled to escape from the slough of pauperism and to attain a healthy improvement .... He objected to the Bill because it would bring back upon us that laxity of administration in the Poor Law from which we hoped we had escaped, would lead to the revival of evils which we hoped we had got rid of, and would promote a tendency to rely on public relief from which we were slowly emancipating the public mind.

A.J. Balfour: My hon. Friend ... says it is a most dangerous lesson to teach the working classes that by the removal from them of some primary want – in other words, by the State undertaking itself to satisfy some primary want – a most dangerous result will be produced. But, if that is so, the State has already done so .... The maintenance of health and the giving of education are both primary duties, and the means of doing both are supplied by the State in case of destitution.

11f   The day-to-day tasks of the local Medical Officer of Health

Dr James A. Harris to the Chorley Town Council, 19 March 1888, Lancashire Record Office, MB Ch 6/6.

A complaint having been made to you ... on behalf of the Managers of St. George's National Schools of the nuisance arising from the present practice of emptying the contents of the pails into the Manure drags in the Town's Yard immediately adjoining the School, I take the opportunity of again bringing under your notice the unsuitability of the present system of collecting and disposing of excreta. Throughout the week vans are continually conveying to the centre of the Town from the outside districts as well as from the immediate neighbourhood of the Town's yard. These vans, filled with pails laden with excreta, are emptied not without a most malodorous stench into the manure drags which again wend their way from the centre of the town to the outlying townships, their course being easily tracked without aid of eyes. In addition the washing of the pails at the depot is a source of annoyance to the neighbourhood. I consider the whole system to be a wrong one, and that, instead of one central, two or more depots in the outskirts of the town should be secured.

Extract from Medical Officer of Health's Report, March 1889, Chorley, Lancashire Record Office, MB Ch 6/6.

In my report for 1887 I stated that Scarlet Fever had been prevalent during the last quarter of the year .... In the latter half of 1888 however a more serious epidemic of the disease broke out in various localities throughout the town and continued, varying in severity until the end of the year. Your officers recieved [sic] notice of the existence of Scarlet Fever in nearly one hundred houses in many of which there were two or more cases. It is most probable that not more than one half of the children affected have been reported to your Officers and as many slight cases recieve [sic] no medical attendance and are yet equally fruitful in propagating the infection with the more serious forms of the disease, no effectual means of combating the spread of such diseases can be instituted until compulsory notification [of] cases liable to be infectious becomes obligatory....

The question of the establishment of an Infectious Hospital has been frequently and prominently brought under your notice during the year....

When the time comes that the people generally accept the fact that Scarlet Fever is a much more deadly disease than Small Pox under the protective influence of Vaccination – and that the isolation of the sick from the healthy ... is necessary for the common weal, the question of the establishment of a Hospital for Infectious diseases will recieve [sic] a more general and favourable attention....

I subjoin a list of various Notices which have been served during the year:

To whitewash dirty houses and disinfect infected houses	76
To cleanse filthy yard & passages	60
To cleanse filthy Closets	50
To abate Nuisance from poultry kept in cellars ...	25
To ventilate, light or supply water to defective Cowsheds and farm buildings	8
To abate Nuisance from defective piggeries	6
To alter Manure receptacles contrary to By laws	3
To pave or flag yards	24
To remedy defective closet accomodation	4
To remedy defective drainage and defective Urinals	121
To alter ashpits	69
To abate excessive discharge of smoke from chimney	1
To abate other Nuisances	16

11g   Poverty subject to scientific examination

Charles Booth, *Life and Labour of the People in London* (12 vols, 1892), vol. i, pp. 28–62.

If London north of the Thames is considered as a semicircle of which the City is an enlarged centre, the part with which I am about to deal forms a quadrant, having for its radii Kingsland Road running due north, and the River Thames running due east....

The 8 classes into which I have divided these people are:

A. The lowest class of occasional labourers, loafers, and semi-criminals.

B. Casual earnings – 'very poor'.

C. Intermittent earnings }
D. Small regular earnings } together the 'poor'.

E. Regular standard earnings – above the line of poverty.

F. Higher class labour.

G. Lower middle class.

H. Upper middle class.

The divisions indicated here by 'poor' and 'very poor' are necessarily arbitrary. By the word 'poor' I mean to describe those who have a sufficiently regular though bare income, such as 18s. to 21s. per week for a moderate family, and by 'very poor' those who from any cause fall much below this standard.

A. The lowest class ... I put at 11,000 or 1¼ per cent of the population, but this is no more than a very rough estimate, as these people are beyond enumeration, and only a small proportion of them are on the School Board Visitors' books ... there is little family life among them .... Those I have attempted to count consist mostly of casual labourers or low characters, and their families, together with those in a similar way of life who pick up a living without labour of any kind. Their life is the life of savages, with vicissitudes of extreme hardship and occasional excess. Their food is of the coarsest description, and their only luxury is drink .... They render no useful service, they create no wealth: more often they destroy it. They degrade whatever they touch, and as individuals are perhaps incapable of improvement....

B. Casual earnings – very poor – add up almost exactly to 100,000 or $11^1/_4$ per cent of the whole population....

The labourers of class B do not, on the average, get as much as three days' work a week, but it is doubtful if many of them could or would work full time for long together if they had the opportunity .... The ideal of such persons is to work when they like and play when they like; these it is who are rightly called the 'leisure class' amongst the poor – leisure bounded very closely by the pressure of want, but habitual to the extent of second nature .... The earnings of the men vary with the state of trade, and drop to a few shillings a week or nothing at all in bad times .... The wives in the class mostly do some work, and those who are sober, perhaps, work more steadily than the men .... It is in all cases wretchedly paid, so that if they earn the rent they do very well.

Both boys and girls get employment without much difficulty – the girls earn enough to pay their mothers 4s. or 5s. a week if they stay at home....

C. – Intermittent earnings – numbering nearly 75,000, or about 8 per cent of the population, are more than any others the victims of competition, and on them falls with particular severity the weight of recurrent depressions of trade .... Here may perhaps be found the most proper field for systematic charitable assistance; provided always some evidence of thrift is made the pre-condition or consequence of assistance....

The irregularity of employment may show itself in the week or in the year: stevedores and waterside porters may secure only one or two days' work in a week, whereas labourers in the building trades may get only eight or nine months in the year....

D. – Small Regular Earnings, poor, are about 129,000 or nearly $14^1/_2$ per cent of the population. The men ... are the better end of the casual dock and water-side labour, those having directly or indirectly a preference for employment. It includes also a number of labourers in the gas works whose employment falls short in summer but never entirely ceases. The rest ... are men who are in regular work all the year round at a wage not exceeding 21s. a week ... factory, dock and warehouse labourers, carmen, messengers, porters etc....

Of the whole section none can be said to rise above poverty, unless by earnings of the children, nor are many to be classed as very poor. What they have comes in regularly, and except in times of sickness in the family, actual want rarely presses, unless the wife drinks....

E. – Regular Standard Earnings .... 377,000 or over 42 per cent ... the bulk of this large section can, and do, lead independent lives, and possess fairly comfortable homes....

F. – ... higher class labour, and the best paid artisans ... 121,000, or about $13^1/_2$ per cent of the population.

G. – Lower Middle Class. Shopkeepers and small employers, clerks etc .... 34,000 or nearly 4 per cent.

H. – Upper Middle Class ... the servant keeping class. They count up to 45,000, or 5 per cent....

Grouping the classes together A, B, C and D are the classes in poverty, or even in want, and add up to 314,000 or 35 per cent of the population....

12 Pensions and unemployment

Poor law provision was most exposed in two specific circumstances: during trade depressions, and in dealing with those too old to support themselves. Between 1870 and 1895 it became clear that it was no longer adequate. Two Anglican clergymen were among the earliest to advocate provision for the aged in the form of pensions. W.L. Blackley (1830–1902) was Curate of St Peter's, Southwark, in 1878 when he published his pioneer proposal for compulsory deductions from the wages of young men to establish a fund payable in later years as a pension (12a). Canon Samuel Barnett (1844–1913), a founder member of the Charity Organization Society and an enthusiast for a variety of social reforms in London's East End, advocated a scheme which separated those whom Barnett considered the worthy from the unworthy poor. He proposed pensions for the over-60s, if they had not had recourse to the poor law during their working lives (12b).

Joseph Chamberlain was the first prominent politician to announce his conversion to old age pensions, though he was unclear about details (12c). Not surprisingly, the main opposition to State pension schemes came from benefit and friendly societies who saw a lucrative source of funds threatened if governments invaded their preserve. They announced their willingness to vary their prospectuses to make their own schemes more attractive; but they insisted that nearly all the worthy already made provision for their old age, thus obviating the need for a State scheme (12d). Self-reliance remained the surest guide. The societies, however, were finding it increasingly difficult to disguise the fact that increased longevity among their members was putting them in a position of some difficulty. Larger proportions of their funds were diverted to the support of the aged. The Aberdare Commission of 1895 saw little merit in State pensions and, in harmony with many middle-class voices, urged Boards of Guardians to be more discriminating between the 'respectable aged' and those whose destitution resulted from improvident habits (12e). The Lancashire cotton famine in the 1860s had shown the impotence of orthodox methods of poor relief in the face of massive trade dislocation and unemployment. The depressions of the 1880s alarmed the entire nation, not least because of fear of a vast army of unemployed, respectable and 'debauched', threatening the social fabric. These fears crystallized during riots by the unemployed in London in February 1886, towards the end of a very severe winter during which casual outdoor work had all but ceased. The Chamberlain Circular of March 1886 (12f) was influenced by these events. It broke new ground by urging Poor Law Guardians and local authorities to provide temporary public works for the respectable unemployed to work on during the crisis, thereby lessening applications to the Guardians. The scheme was widely adopted, not only in 1886, but in subsequent depressions. It was seen as imperative, also, to divorce the respectable poor from the contagion of the casual 'loafers' who deserved no help. In 1893 a Labour Department was established within the Board of Trade to supervise and advise on conditions of labour. It also collected statistics of unemployment for the first time (12g). John Burns (1858–1943), later an unadventurous President of the Local Government Board in the Asquith Liberal Government, advocated labour exchanges as the best means of finding jobs for an increasingly educated and sophisticated workforce. He too was concerned to separate 'the labourer from the loafer' (12h). The economist J.A. Hobson (1858–1940) was the first to identify 'unemployment' as a distinct phenomenon, which government policy could affect. His article (12i) was pregnant with significance for future attitudes to unemployment, which could no longer be seen as a sporadic and unstructured visitation from God against which little defence was possible.

Suggestions for further reading

On pensions, see D. Collins, 'The Introduction of Old Age Pensions in Great Britain', *Historical Journal*, vol. viii, (1965) and B.B. Gilbert, *The Evolution of National Insurance in Great Britain* (1966). On unemployment J.F. Harris, *Unemployment and Politics, 1886–1914* (1972) is authoritative.

12a   A pioneer pensions proposal

W.L. Blackley, 'National Insurance: A Cheap, Practical, and Popular Means of Abolishing Poor Rates', *Nineteenth Century*, vol. iv (1878), pp. 834–57.

I venture to lay down as a simple axiom that to make a reasonable provision against occasional sickness and the inevitable feebleness and infirmity of old age is the duty of every man gifted with health and strength, and in a position to earn, by his daily labour, a wage from which such provision can be made....

As a matter of fact this universally admitted duty is grossly neglected by our working classes....

Surely... there should be a power, if there be a means, of at least compelling every man to bear his own share in the burden of natural providence, instead of allowing him to cast it on the shoulders of others....

If the labouring classes can make their own provision, and will do so, let them be shown how; if they can, and will not, let them be compelled....

A man in trade has a reasonable prospect of an improved condition as he advances in years; his connections extend, his business developes [sic], his earnings increase. But with the labourer these conditions are reversed. The vigorous young man of twenty can earn as high wages as he can ever expect to do in his lifetime; and, in the vast majority of cases, he has only himself to keep. The labourer of thirty-five has a wife and family in addition to support from his no larger wages, and, if he thinks of becoming provident, has to pay at a much higher rate for the benefits assured, and to pay it from a much smaller surplus than the younger man....

The labouring man *can* make his own provision; but he can only do it at a certain period of his life, namely, while he is young and unencumbered.

Unhappily for him and for our nation, this period exactly coincides with that part of his life when he is most ignorant and inexperienced....

A pound a week is, at the present time, no unreasonable estimate to make of the average earnings even of a labourer. But to put it beyond cavil, let us place the average wages of a man of twenty at fifteen shillings per week or even less. If on these wages hundreds of thousands support themselves, their wives and families, none will deny that a young bachelor can, if he will, live, and live well on nine shillings. If he would exercise just so much self-denial *for one single* year, he might, by one payment of £15, secure aid in sickness to the amount of 8s. a week till he reached seventy years of age, and a pension of 4s. weekly from that age till his death. Thus we see that there is a period in the life of every working man in which he can, if he will, render himself independent, during his whole lifetime, of parochial relief.

12b   Pensions as a reward for honest, independent toil

S. & A. Barnett, *Practicable Socialism* (1888), pp. 195–7.

The Poor Law provides relief for the destitute and medical care for the poor. By a system of outdoor relief it has won the condemnation of many who care for the poor, and see that outdoor relief robs them of their energy, their self-respect, and their homes. There is no reason, however, why the Poor Law should not be developed in more healthy ways. Pensions of 8s. or 10s. a week might be given to every citizen who had kept himself until the age of 60 without workhouse aid. If such pensions were the right of all, none would be tempted to lie to get them, nor would any be tempted to spy and bully in order to show the undesert of applicants. So long as relief is a matter of desert, and so long as the most conscientious relieving officers are liable to err, there must be mistakes both on the side of indulgence and of neglect. The one objection to out-relief, which is at present recognised by the poor, is that the system puts it in the power of the relieving officer to act as judge in matters of which he must be ignorant, so that he gives relief to the careless or crafty and passes over those who in self-respect hide their trouble. Pensions, too, it may be added, would be no more corrupting to the labourer who works for his country in the workshop than for the civil servant who works for his country at the desk, and the cost of pensions would be no greater than is the cost of infirmaries and almshouses. In one way or another the old and the poor are now kept by those who are richer, and the present method is not a cheap one.

12c   Joseph Chamberlain announces his commitment to pensions

Speech to the Birmingham Liberal Unionist Association, 21 April 1891, reported in *The Times*, 22 April 1891.

He wanted to take that opportunity of consulting them on the subject of a national provision for old age (Cheers). After more closely going into the returns, he came to the conclusion that of the working classes one in two, if he reached the age of 60, was almost certain to have to go upon the poor law for his subsistence. It was impossible that one out of two of the industrial population of the Kingdom had done anything to deserve the fate which under existing circumstances was inevitably in store for them .... He had received an immense number of letters, many suggestions, and a great deal of criticism, for which he was very grateful. Several important questions had arisen ... should the contributions be compulsory or voluntary? He thought that the working classes were not prepared for compulsion; but it must be admitted that, if there were any readiness to accept compulsion in this matter, the scheme would be at once successful, and might be carried much further than it could be carried under other circumstances (Cheers). The second point ... was that the working classes generally would prefer that if they died before 65, their contribution, or some portion, should be paid out to those they left behind them (Cheers). There would be no difficulty whatever in arranging that.... His friend Mr. John Morley ... said to carry out a scheme of national insurance against old age was worthy of a statesman and worthier of public gratitude than the winning of great victories and of decisive battles (Cheers) .... This proposal, if carried to a successful issue, would bring happiness and comfort and hope to ... hundreds of thousands of homes in this Country (Cheers).

12d   State pensions offend the friendly societies

Thomas Scanlon, 'Mr. Chamberlain's Pension Scheme: A Friendly
Society View of it', *Westminster Review*, vol. cxxxvii (1892), pp. 357–63.

All forms of State support are founded on erroneous conceptions of the
relations between the State and the individual. It is the duty of every man
to make provision for himself and for those dependent on him; and of the
State to see that no obstacles hinder his doing so. Where the State does
more, or the individual less, there is nothing but disaster in store for both.
It is cruel folly to make pauperism attractive, or to rob it of any of its
inherent terrors....

Now, putting aside altogether such empirical remedies as those of Mr.
Chamberlain, which appear to be worse than useless, the improvement of
the condition of the industrious poor can be effected in three principal
ways, and in these the State can only play a limited part.

The first requisite is, that the poor laws shall be more carefully
administered. Much can be done in this direction without any aid from
legislation. Outdoor relief ought to be discouraged. The less popular it
becomes the more humiliating it will be considered in future; and
experience has proved that there are thousands of people who would on no
account enter the workhouse, but who think it no humiliation whatever to
accept parish relief outside the workhouse.

The second requisite is, that the relations between capital and labour
shall be so altered as to permit of the labourer reaping a larger reward for
his services than he has hitherto been able to do. The aim ought to be to
make labour less dependent on capital, instead of being as at present almost
entirely at its mercy .... By removing the taxes on industry and unlocking
the vast stores of wealth which lie buried in uncultivated lands, and by
placing the transfer of land on the same footing as that of other kinds of
property, the demands for labour would be enormously increased, and
a higher standard of wages and comfort would be the result.

The third great factor in bringing about desired change is the encouragement of private enterprise, individual and co-operative. The savings banks are doing excellent work, and so are the Industrial Insurance Companies and Friendly Societies....

... considering that insurance for death has become almost universal, and that provision for old age is in need of some stimulating influence to recommend it to the insuring public, it ought not to be difficult for the leading societies to try the experiment of popularizing the one through the other by means of new tables, which should provide for death or for a pension after sixty five, whichever should happen first. At all events, if the friendly societies, with their superior organisation and unique means of reaching the people, find it impossible to make such a scheme succeed, there is not much hope that any other agency will be found equal to the task.

We must teach [the masses] to walk erect in the path of independence and self-reliance instead of making them lame and presenting them with a crutch.

12e   A Royal Commission rejects old age pensions

Parliamentary Papers, 1895, vol. xiv, pp. 83–5

The evidence on Friendly Societies, the Post Office Savings Bank, and other like agencies, has shown remarkably the great development of habits of thrift and providence among the working classes, and has satisfied us of the general ability of those who are in any regular employment to make direct or indirect provision for old age as well as for sickness and other contingencies beyond the every-day needs of life. The various thrift organisations which have been developed during the past 60 years have without doubt contributed largely to the relative diminution of pauperism in proportion to population which has been in progress during that period....

We are of opinion that no fundamental alterations are needed in the existing system of poor law relief as it affects the aged, and that it would be undesirable to interfere either by Statute or order with the discretion now vested in the guardians ... since it is in our view of essential importance that guardians should have power to deal on its merits with each individual case. At the same time we are convinced that there is a strong feeling that in the administration of relief there should be a greater discrimination between the respectable aged who become destitute and those whose destitution is directly the consequence of their own misconduct; and we recommend that boards of guardians, in dealing with applications for relief, should inquire with special care into the antecedents of destitute persons whose physical faculties have failed by reason of age and infirmity and that outdoor relief should in such cases be given to those who are shown to have been of good character, thrifty according to their opportunities, and generally independent in early life, and who are not living under conditions of health or surrounding circumstances which make it evident that the relief given should be indoor relief.

12f The Chamberlain Circular on unemployment

Parliamentary Papers, 1886, vol. xxxvi, pp. 179–81, Letter to Boards of Guardians, 15 March 1886.

The inquiries which have been recently undertaken by the Local Government Board unfortunately confirm the prevailing impression as to the existence of exceptional distress amongst the working classes....

They are convinced that in the ranks of those who do not ordinarily seek poor law relief there is evidence of much and increasing privation, and if the depression in trade continues it is to be feared that large numbers of persons usually in regular employment will be reduced to the greatest straits....

The spirit of independence which leads so many of the working classes to make great personal sacrifices rather than incur the stigma of pauperism, is one which deserves very great sympathy and respect, and which it is the duty and interest of the community to maintain by all the means at its disposal.

Any relaxation of the general rule at present obtaining, which requires as a condition of relief to able bodied male persons ... the acceptance of an order for admission to the workhouse, or the performance of an adequate task of work as a labour test, would be most disastrous, as tending directly to restore the condition of things which, before the reform of the poor laws, destroyed the independence of the labouring classes and increased the poor rate until it became an almost insupportable burden....

The ... Board have no doubt that the powers which the guardians possess are fully sufficient to enable them to deal with ordinary pauperism, and to meet the demand for relief from the classes who usually seek it....

But these provisions do not in all cases meet the emergency. The labour test is usually stone breaking or oakum picking. This work, which is selected as offering the least competition with other labour, presses hardly upon the skilled artizans, and, in some cases, their proficiency in their special trades may be prejudiced by such employment....

What is required ... is—

1. Work which will not involve the stigma of pauperism:
2. Work which all can perform, whatever may have been their previous avocations.
3. Work which does not compete with that of other labourers at present in employment;

And, lastly, work which is not likely to interfere with the resumption of regular employment in their own trades by those who seek it.

The Board have no power to enforce the adoption of any particular proposals, and the object of this circular is to bring the subject generally under the notice of boards of guardians and other local authorities.

In districts where exceptional distress prevails, the Board recommend that the guardians should confer with the local authorities, and endeavour to arrange with the latter for the execution of works on which unskilled labour may be immediately employed.

These works may be of the following kinds, among others:—

a) Spade husbandry on sewage farms.
b) Laying out of open spaces, recreation grounds, new cemeteries, or disused burial grounds.
c) Cleansing of streets not usually undertaken by local authorities.
d) Laying out and paving of new streets etc.
e) Paving of unpaved streets, and making of footpaths in country roads:
f) Providing or extending sewerage works and works of water supply....

... the men employed should be engaged on the recommendation of the guardians as persons whom, owing to precarious condition and circumstances, it is undesirable to send to the workhouse, or to treat as subjects for pauper relief, and ... the wages paid should be something less than the wages ordinarily paid for similar work, in order to prevent imposture, and to leave the strongest temptations to those who avail themselves of this opportunity to return as soon as possible to their previous occupations....

12g   The establishment of the Labour Department

Memorandum from the Board of Trade, 18 April 1893, Parliamentary Papers, 1893–4, vol. lxxxii, p. 365.

The work of collecting, digesting and publishing statistical and other information bearing on questions relating to the conditions of labour, will in future be entrusted to a separate branch of the Board of Trade. This branch will take over the work of the present Commercial Department at the Board of Trade, and will consist of three distinct departments – commercial, labour, and statistical....

The special staff in the central office of the Labour Department ... will consist of a commissioner for labour ... a chief labour correspondent, three additional labour correspondents (one of whom will be a lady), and about thirty clerks of all grades.

12h   Labour exchanges advocated

John Burns, *The Unemployed* (Fabian Tract, 47, London, 1893), pp. 4–18.

The unemployed labourer today is not a replica of the out-of-work of a few years back .... His predecessor was a patient, long-suffering animal, accepting his position as beast of burden with a fatalistic taciturnity, looking upon his enforced idleness as inevitable, and with blind submission enduring his lot....

The extension of the franchise, education, trade unionism, Socialist propaganda, the broad and rising Labor movement have altered all this. The unemployed worker of to-day is of different stuff. He has a grievance, and he thinks he has a remedy .... His eyes are now open, and Samson of labor has pulled from them the bandage that class rule, apathy, and his own ignorance had placed upon him....

The only way ... to obtain reliable labor statistics is to establish in every district council, parish, or vestry area a completely equipped Labor Bureau, situated in the Town Hall. There the unemployed should be able to register themselves, and the trade unions should be urged to regularly post or file, for official use if necessary, their numbers out of employment .... The bureau should be the medium of communication between the men seeking work and the employers, and at the same time eliminate the loafer, to whom little consideration should be shown .... I contend, as a Socialist ... that until the differentiation of the labourer from the loafer takes place, the unemployed question can never be properly discussed and dealt with .... The gentleman who gets up to look for work at mid-day, and prays that he may not find it, is undeserving of pity....

We are passing through a transition period. *Laisser faire* has been abandoned, and for the first time in the history of the human race the working people possess universally the power through elective institutions to embody in law their economic and material desires. Concurrently with the growth of personal independence is the desire for State aid and municipal effort when individual action is futile. The unemployment movement embodies the growing desire for useful healthy lives. It is breaking up, and must ... give place to the organised and collective domination by the people of their social life through municipal administration and political development.

12i   A leading economist recognizes unemployment as a long-term structural problem

J.A. Hobson, 'The Economic Cause of Unemployment', *Contemporary Review*, vol. lxvii (1895), pp. 758–60.

Under-consumption is the economic cause of unemployment. The only remedy which goes to the root of the evil is a raising of the standard of consumption to the point which shall fully utilise the producing-power, after making due allowance for such present 'saving' as is economically needed to provide for further increase of consumption in the future. If the above analysis is correct, this remedy can only be made operative by a line of policy which shall affect the ownership of increased consuming power....

A more natural distribution of consuming-power, under which the power to consume shall be accompanied by the desire to consume – not, as now, severed from it – is the only possible remedial policy.

Towards this policy, parties of social progress are slowly gravitating .... The policy of progressive consumption has two direct lines of advance which may here be briefly indicated.

The surplus of consuming-power in the hands of the rich may be 'unearned' by its owners, but it is not 'unearned'. Part of it – for example, the growing value of town lands – is earned by public effort, and forms a property designed for public consumption in the support of wholesome public life. Our civic and, in general, our public life is narrow, meagre, inefficient and undignified in comparison with what it ought to be, if the wealth due to public effort was wisely and economically laid out in the public service. Taxation, or State assumption on equitable terms, of properties whose increased values are due to public activity and public need, to be administered in the supply of common wants and the enrichment of the common life, is likely to be of material assistance in raising the general standard of consumption. The adoption of progressive taxation of accumulated wealth through the Death Duties is based on an instinctive recognition that this assertion of a public claim is both just and expedient. The same is true of the progressive income-tax, so adjusted as to secure for purposes of public use that portion of the income of the well-to-do which otherwise would materially assist to swell the excess of accumulated forms of capital .... The other line of advance is the organised pressure of the working classes for an increasing proportion of the natural income, which they will use in raising their standard of consumption. By effective trade organisation they may raise wages, by co-operation of consumers they may expend their wages more economically, by organised use of the franchise they may secure such equality of educational and economic opportunities as will remove or abate the dangers of ignorance and destitution, which at present bar the progress of the rear-guard of labour....

... if the principle be once firmly grasped that a demand for commodities is the only ultimate demand for the use of land, labour, and capital, then the existence of 'unemployed' producing-power is proof that increased consumption is possible without a reduction in the present income of any class of the community....

The recognition of 'unemployment' as the labour aspect of a wider economic problem − viz., the excess of productive power over the requirements of current consumption − enables us for the first time to establish a sound practical standard for the test of proposed remedies and palliatives. No reform will be of the least avail in securing a net increase of employment unless it can be shown to increase the proportion of the general income of the community that is applied in demand for commodities. Unemployment means underconsumption ; and advocates of land reforms, bimetallism, labour colonies, or other remedies for industrial distress must show how their respective schemes will operate in raising the standard of consumption before they can establish any just claim to public consideration.

13 Housing

Private enterprise did not find it profitable to provide adequate housing for the working classes. Investment was channelled into factories and the suburban and country villas to which factory owners repaired at the end of the working day. The gross excess of demand over supply of cheap rented accommodation resulted in the horribly verminous and insanitary tenements which alarmed observers in the 1870s and 1880s. In London the problems of overcrowding were particularly acute. The need for action had been recognized since the 1840s, though effective measures were few. In 1851 the Earl of Shaftesbury (1801–85) introduced the pioneering Labouring Classes Lodging Houses Act which attempted, largely unsuccessfully, to raise money for the erection or lease of houses for the use of the poor. The Acts of 1868 and 1875 promoted by the Liberal W.M. Torrens (1813–94) and by Richard Cross (1823–1914) for the Conservatives both accepted the principle that houses must be kept in good repair; the Cross Act enabled demolition of grossly unsatisfactory property to be effected and solid dwellings erected in their place. The Cross Act, however, was permissive only (13b) and met with mixed success at best. Joseph Chamberlain used it in Birmingham, but more to clear the city centre for prestige buildings than to re-house the poor. Other authorities were deterred by the cost and only ten of the eighty-seven entitled to make use of it had actually done so by 1881. Many observers pointed out that those dispossessed when their houses were pulled down could not afford the rent on better property, and so merely moved into other overcrowded property. The problem was just shifted a mile or two away (13 c & f).

Housing, then, posed a stiff test for individual enterprise. Octavia Hill's (1838–1912) famous benevolent despotism in London undoubtedly improved matters for a few, though she was insistent that due business practice be observed. No one was permitted to get behind with the rent (13a). The author of *The Bitter Cry of Outcast London* entered a passionate plea for State direction of a housing policy (13c); but the old Earl of Shaftesbury presented the standard individualist answer—that State aid enfeebled those it was designed to support (13d). Recognizing that London was the main battleground, and drawing on the influence of eugenic studies, the economist Alfred Marshall (1842–1924) proposed to deter immigration of the shiftless poor to the capital by the operation of a strict, inquisitorial inspection (13e). A Royal Commission was established to investigate the housing crisis. It included such influential figures as the Prince of Wales (1841–1910), the Marquis of Salisbury (1830–1903), Archbishop Manning (1808–92) and Richard Cross, but was unable to recommend any decisive initiative that the State should undertake (13f). Local authorities were exhorted to be more active, and cheap workmen's train fares were recommended to enable the poor to live away from the overcrowded centres of big cities. The Commission's recommendations, however, skirted the essential issues.

An expository and codifying Housing Act was passed in 1885, and the Housing of the Working Classes Act became law under Salisbury's Conservative government in 1890. This legislation, although important, was hardly the landmark that some historians have suggested. Local authorities' powers to demolish insanitary property were strengthened and it was made rather easier for them to erect small new developments. The overall lack of central direction, however, persisted. The State exhorted, but refused to insist. The permissive principle remained supreme.

Suggestions for further reading

For an outstanding account of the housing crisis in London see G. Stedman Jones, *Outcast London* (1971). More general, and variable, discussions of a still under-researched field are E. Gauldie, *Cruel Habitations: A History of Working Class Housing, 1780–1918* (1974) and J.N. Tarn, *Five Per-Cent Philanthropy* (1974).

13a   Teaching the poor the virtues of a good home

Octavia Hill, 'Blank Court or Landlords and Tenants', *Macmillan's Magazine*, vol. xxiv (1871), pp. 456–9.

It was near the end of 1869 that I first heard that a good many houses in Blank Court were to be disposed of. Eventually ... six ten-roomed houses were bought by the Countess of Ducie, and five more by another lady, and placed partially under my care. I was especially glad to obtain some influence here, as I knew this place to be one of the worst in Marylebone; its inhabitants were mainly costermongers and small hawkers, and were almost the poorest class of those amongst our population who have any settled home ... when unruly and hopeless tenants were sent away from other houses in the district, I had often heard that they had gone to Blank Court....

In many of the houses the dustbins were utterly unapproachable, and cabbage leaves, stale fish, and every sort of dirt were lying in the passages and on the stairs; in some the back kitchen had been used as a dustbin and had not been emptied for years; ... in some the kitchen stairs were inches thick with dirt, which was so hardened that a shovel had to be used to get it off; in some there was hardly any water to be had .... At night it was still worse .... It was then that I saw the houses in their most dreadful aspect. I well remember wet, foggy, Monday nights, when I turned down the dingy Court, past the brilliantly lighted public house at the corner ... and dived into the dark, yawning passage ways. The front doors stood open day and night, and as I felt my way down the kitchen stairs, broken and rounded by the hardened mud upon them, the foul smells which the heavy, foggy air would not allow to rise, met me as I descended, and the plaster rattled down with a hollow sound as I groped along. It was truly appalling to think that there were human beings who lived habitually in such an atmosphere, with such surroundings....

On what principles was I to rule these people? On the same that I had already tried ... with success in other places ... firstly, to demand a strict fulfilment of their duties to me,—one of the chief of which would be the punctual payment of rent; and secondly, to endeavour to be so unfailingly just and patient, that they should learn to trust the rule that was over them.

... I would make a few improvements at once—such, for example, as the laying on of water and repairing of dustbins, but, for the most part, improvements should be made by degrees, as the people became more capable of valuing and not abusing them. I would have the rooms distempered, and thoroughly cleansed, as they became vacant, and then they should be offered to the more cleanly of the tenants. I would have such repairs as were not immediately needed, used as a means of giving work to the men in times of distress .... I would have the landlady's portion of the house—i.e. the stairs and passages—at once repaired and distempered, and they should be regularly scrubbed, and, as far as possible, made models of cleanliness, for I knew, from former experience, that the example of this would, in time, silently spread itself to the rooms themselves, and that payment for this work would give me some hold over the elder girls. I would collect savings personally, not trust to their being taken to distant banks or savings clubs. And, finally, I knew that I should learn to feel these people as my friends, and so should instinctively feel the same respect for their privacy and their independence, and should treat them with the same courtesy that I should show towards other personal friends. There would be no interference, no entering their rooms uninvited, no offer of money or the necessaries of life. But when occasion presented itself, I should give them any help I could, such as I might offer without insult to other friends—sympathy in their distresses; advice, help, and counsel in their difficulties; introductions that might be of use to them; means of education; visits to the country; a lent book when not able to work; a bunch of flowers brought on purpose; an invitation to any entertainment, in a room built at the back of my own house, which would be likely to give them pleasure. I am convinced that one of the evils of much that is done for the poor, springs from the want of delicacy felt, and courtesy shown, towards them, and that we cannot beneficially help them in any spirit different to that in which we help those who are better off. The help may differ in amount, because their needs are greater. It should not differ in kind.

13b   The genesis of the Artisans Dwelling Act

Memorandum to Cabinet by R.A. Cross, 28 January 1875. Public Record Office, PRO 30/6/72, pp. 235–6.

'That which is really wanted ... is some easy and effective process by which, under proper restrictions, local sanitary authorities can purchase and obtain possession of waste spaces, vacant sites and dilapidated buildings of large towns, with power to dispose of them to others who would be willing to repurchase such property and build thereon ... a class of houses suited to the requirements and limited means of the labouring class.

There is ... good reason for believing that with increased facilities for obtaining possession of dilapidated and notoriously unwholesome property, as well as of property in which conflicting interests are concerned, there would soon arise a class of investors, actuated as much by sound commercial principle as by benevolent considerations, who would be willing to engage in judicious building schemes for the better housing of the poor ... ' (Report on the Sanitary Condition of the City of London, 1872–3).

The proposed procedure is as follows:

The medical officer, of his own accord or set in motion by 20 ratepayers, makes to the local authority a representation that a certain district is unhealthy from the construction and arrangement of the buildings ... the local authority ... if satisfied of its truth and of the practicability of applying a remedy, due regard being had to the local resources, are to pass a resolution that the district is unhealthy and to make a scheme for its improvement.

The scheme will provide generally for the re-arrangement and re-construction of the district, and especially for the erection and permanent appropriation of buildings and dwellings for as many persons of the labouring class as will be displaced....

... though the Bill makes it compulsory on the local authority to consider the report of the medical officer, it does not also compel them to proceed to make a scheme, if there be difficulty on financial grounds. But if they do make a scheme and it be passed into law, it will become obligatory upon them without delay to proceed to carry it out. For this purpose compulsory powers are given.

13c State initiatives necessary to aid the destitute

(?) W.C. Preston, *The Bitter Cry of Outcast London* (1883), 1970 ed., pp. 6, 15–19.

Few who will read these pages have any conception of what these pestilential human rookeries are, where tens of thousands are crowded together amidst horrors which call to mind what we have heard of the middle passage of the slave ship....

The child-misery that one beholds is the most heart-rending and appalling element in these discoveries; and of this not least is the misery inherited from the vice of drunken and dissolute parents .... From the beginning of their life they are utterly neglected; their bodies and rags are alive with vermin; they are subjected to the most cruel treatment; many of them have never seen a green field, and do not know what it is to go beyond the streets immediately around them, and they often pass the whole day without a morsel of food....

That something needs to be done for this pitiable outcast population must be evident to all who have read these particulars as to their condition—at least, to all who believe them. We are quite prepared for incredulity. Even what we have indicated seems all too terrible to be true .... Incredulity is not the only difficulty in the way of stirring up Christian people to help. Despair of success in any such undertaking may paralyse many. We shall be pointed to the fact that without State interference nothing effectual can be accomplished upon any large scale. And *it is* a fact. These wretched people must live somewhere. They must live near the centres where their work lies. They cannot afford to go out by train or tram into the suburbs; and how, with their poor emaciated, starved bodies, can they be expected—in addition to working twelve hours or more, for a shilling, or less—to walk three or four miles each way to take and fetch? It is notorious that the Artizans Dwellings Act has, in some respects, made matters worse for them. Large spaces have been cleared of fever-breeding rookeries, to make way for the building of decent habitations, but the rents of these are far beyond the means of the abject poor. They are driven to crowd more closely together in the few stifling places still left to them; and so Dives makes a richer harvest out of their misery, buying up property condemned as unfit for habitation, and turning it into a goldmine because the poor must have shelter somewhere, even though it be the shelter of a living tomb.

The State must make short work of this iniquitous traffic, and secure for the poorest the rights of citizenship; the right to live in something better than fever dens; the right to live as something better than the uncleanest of brute beasts. This must be done before the Christian missionary can have much chance with them.

13d   Private initiative must find a solution

Earl of Shaftesbury, 'The Mischief of State Aid', *Nineteenth Century*, vol. xiv (1883), pp. 934–5.

The sudden manifestation of public feeling in regard to the domiciliary condition of large portions of the working classes in our cities and great towns, and specially in London, is one of the healthiest signs of modern times. It is strange that this feeling has lain so long dormant, for the disclosure of the evil was made more than forty years ago, and ever since that date, the efforts of individuals, companies and associations have been unremitting to proclaim the mischief, to devise remedies, and, in some instances, to apply them....

The 'Society for Improving the Condition of the Labouring Classes' ... had in view the erection of model dwellings for all the varieties and grades of industrial life; it desired to show, in the buildings that it raised, what was necessary for the comfort, health, and decency of the inmates, and also the lowest figure at which the structures could be provided, and the rents imposed, consistently with a moderate, though fair, return of interest on the capital expended....

There is a loud cry, from many quarters, for the Government of the country to undertake this mighty question; and any one who sets himself against such an opinion is likely to incur much rebuke and condemnation. Be it so. But if the State is to be summoned not only to provide houses for the labouring classes, but also to supply such dwellings at nominal rents, it will, while doing something on behalf of their physical condition, utterly destroy their moral energies. It will, in fact, be an official proclamation that, without any efforts of their own, certain portions of the people shall enter into the enjoyment of many good things, altogether at the expense of others. The State is bound, in a case such as this, to give every facility by law and enabling statutes; but the work itself should be founded, and proceed, on voluntary effort, for which there is in the country an adequate amount of wealth, zeal, and intelligence.

13e   State powers should be used to control immigration to cities

Alfred Marshall, 'The Housing of the London Poor', *Contemporary Review*, vol. xlv (1884), pp. 224–31.

Doubtless many of the poor things that crouch for hire at the doors of London workshops are descended from vigorous ancestors, and owe their degradation partly to misfortune and partly to the taste for drink that misfortune at once begets under the joyless London sky. But a great many more of them have a taint of vice in their history. The descendants of the dissolute are naturally weak, and especially those of the dissolute in large towns. It is appalling to think how many of the poor of London are descendants of the dissolute.

Thus there are large numbers of people with poor physique and a feeble will, with no enterprise, no courage, no hope, and scarcely any self-respect, whom misery drives to work for lower wages than the same work gets in the country....

The population of London is already migratory in a large measure. One out of five of those now living who were born in London has already gone elsewhere. Of those who are now in London more than a third were born elsewhere .... Of these immigrants a great part do no good to themselves or others by coming to London ; and there would be no hardship in deterring the worst of them from coming by insisting on strict regulations as to their manner of living here.

It would be possible to do this, by a just discrimination, without pressing too severely on the old inhabitants, if Mr. Llewellyn Davies' proposal as to inspection were acted on. According to this ... specially bad districts would be 'proclaimed'; they would be inspected by a large staff of officers in a rigorous, uncompromising way .... If it got to be known that these officers would enforce the letter of the law rigidly and without mercy on all new-comers, a good many shiftless people who now come to London would stay where they are, or be induced to go straight to the New World, where the shiftless become shiftful....

Other means must be made for those who cannot or will not work. Probably this will never be done satisfactorily till we have braced ourselves to say that being without the means of livelihood must be treated, not as a crime, but as a cause for uncompromising inspection and inquiry. So long as we shrink from the little pain that this would give, we are forced to be too kind to the undeserving, and too unkind to the unfortunate....

13f   A Royal Commission fails to grasp the housing nettle

Parliamentary Papers, 1884–5, vol. xxx, pp. 23–4, 40, 60.

... demolitions made by owners have for their main purpose the improvement of the value of the property .... This is seen in the case of the great demolitions which take place in consequence of the warehouses of the City of London spreading over the adjoining parish of St. Luke's and driving on the poor northwards to already crowded districts. Rookeries are destroyed, greatly to the sanitary and social benefit of the neighbourhood, but no kind of habitation for the poor has been substituted. This is the extreme instance of everything being sacrificed to the improvement of the property....

There are also the demolitions which take place under Mr. Torrens's and Sir Richard Cross's Acts. Such demolitions are undertaken in the interest of public health and welfare. The houses so removed are generally in a hopelessly bad condition, and the number thus pulled down is very small compared to the number which on every ground ought to be removed. Nevertheless a good deal of hardship is caused by this class of displacement. The overcrowded state of Spitalfields is attributed to a great measure of such clearances, and the rise of rent, which had doubled in the Mint district, is largely owing to demolitions of the same kind.

Your Majesty's Commissioners are clearly of opinion that there has been a failure in administration rather than in legislation, although the latter is no doubt capable of improvement. What at the present time is specially required is some motive power, and probably there can be no stronger motive power than public opinion....

Evidence has been given showing that the inadequacy of the water supply in the poorer quarters of the metropolis and the great towns is the cause of much unhealthiness and misery in the dwellings of the working classes, and ... [we] recommend that the water supply should, as a general rule, be in the hands of the local authority....

Your Majesty's Commissioners also recommend that it shall be declared by statute to be the duty of the local authority to put in force such powers as they are by law entrusted with, so as to ensure that no premises shall be allowed to exist in an insanitary state.

14 Education

The 1870 Education Act was designed to fill the gaps left by the voluntary system and, once the school boards which it established began their work, it became clear that a compulsory system of elementary education was both feasible and desirable. Education, as the inspector Dr Clutterbuck observed (14a), could teach even the children of depraved parents a proper sense of duty and independence, thus offering the prospect of reduced poor-rate expenditure. It was, indeed, the State's duty to moralize children if parents would not.

Compulsory education was a live political issue. The Conservative Government, in power from 1874 to 1880, was particularly concerned to preserve the status and influence of voluntary Church schools against the incursions of rate-supported Board schools. These latter were seen as a major threat to traditional, Tory, controls in the countryside. The 1876 Education Act, promoted by Viscount Sandon (1831–1900) brought compulsion a stage nearer by establishing school attendance committees which enforced the child-labour laws and could make by-laws for compulsory attendance as did school boards. The government emphasized the important role of the voluntary schools in any move towards compulsion (14b). Numbers of school attenders continued to grow in the 1870s, paving the way for the incoming Liberal Government to decree mandatory school attendance for children of up to ten years in 1880 (14c). The Vice-President of the Committee of the Council on Education, A.J. Mundella (1825–97), saw this as a rationalizing exercise, enunciating no new principle. Ensuring that recalcitrant parents sent their children to school rather than adding to the family budget by working proved to be a difficult task, however, and various inspectors urged local authorities to appoint vigorous school attendance officers who would make evasion more difficult (14e).

Many Liberals, Mundella included, were aware that a compulsory, but not free, education system was anomalous. In addition, the 2d. or 3d. a week fee was sufficient disincentive to many parents, particularly as evasion of the 1880 regulations was possible with little fear of prosecution. It was the Conservative Government, however, which established free elementary education by the Fee Grant Act of 1891. This was a calculated move to preserve the voluntary schools which would be at risk if fees were abolished and education expenditure became purely a charge upon the rates — the scheme favoured by most Liberals. Rate-payers providing cash for elementary schools were unlikely to preserve that independence for voluntary schools which the Tories saw as vital to their long-term prosperity. The 1891 Act provided government grants which schools might accept. Not all schools became free institutions; though after 1891 the opportunity for free education was available to nearly all children. The Conservative and Anglican Press was proved right in its confident assertion that no Tory Government would allow free education without preserving the interests of the voluntary schools (14f & g). The Act was, in part, an exercise to outflank more dangerous Liberal proposals before the next election.

During this period the grant system for schools was modified. The rigidities of the Revised Code were somewhat relaxed. Appropriate standards in the '3Rs' had still to be reached and deductions from the grant were ordered for failure to reach them (14d), but in 1890 a simplified system was introduced whereby payments were made for regular attendance, as before, and if the inspector was generally satisfied with the work presented. No longer need the 'Rs' be separately inspected. There was thus scope for introducing a wider range of subjects into the curriculum. Rather more imaginative teaching methods, if not exactly encouraged, were at least possible. These trends were accentuated by further revisions of the Code in 1893 and 1895, passed on the initiative of the Vice-President of the Committee of Council A.H.D. Acland (1847–1926). In 1893, also, the school leaving age was raised from ten to eleven.

For the most part, elementary school instruction remained dull and fact-orientated. By 1895, however, there was some scope for better things.

Suggestions for further reading

The Sutherland pamphlet (see Section 6) and B. Simon, *Education and the Labour Movement, 1870–1920* (1965) are reliable starting points.

14a   'Extinguishing the pauper spirit'

4th Report of the Local Government Board, *Parliamentary Papers*, 1875, vol. xxxi, pp. 205–19: The Education of Pauper Children in the Western District, by Rev. Dr Clutterbuck.

I ask, first, what is the aim we should propose to ourselves in the education of the children of the poor, of those, that is, who have to earn their bread by labour? ...

The poor man's child has to acquire, in a comparatively short time, such mechanical and mental power as shall best enable it to become self-supporting .... We must, therefore, consider as of prime importance for the pauper child that kind of training which tends to direct self-preservation, and that kind of knowledge which shall secure to him the power of becoming self-supporting. It is to the extinguishing of the pauper spirit by the creation of a rightful sense of self-respect that we must look forward in all our schemes for the amelioration of the poor man's lot....

From a Medical Officer:

'Dear Sir,

The present system of workhouse education does not, in my opinion, eradicate or modify hereditary taint; for when orphan children enter workhouse schools they are mixed with children of depraved parents, and when illness overcomes them they share the sick wards with adult paupers, most of whom are the refuse and scum of the country, and women of the worst characters, who only enter the workhouse for a short time with their children, fresh from the haunts of vice and crime, to which they will speedily return, but not till they have contaminated their other companions with ophthalmia and other loathsome bodily disease, and fill their minds with not less loathsome ideas and thoughts.'

The removal of the children from the workhouse, or the rescue of the children from the influence of their parents and other adults, is one of the most urgently needed legislative reforms. To institute ... legal safeguards against such fearful abuse of parental rights is, I hesitate not to say, the duty and wisdom of the legislature. Workhouse schools, exposed as they must be to this abuse, are doomed, unless some stringent remedy can be devised .... I know of no remedy short of legal intervention between a worthless parent and her child. I know a nation cannot be coerced into morality by Act of Parliament, but Acts of Parliament can and do neutralize the baleful effects of wrong already done .... It is a paramount duty of the State to protect the innocent and weak from the power of the vicious.

14b   The objectives of the Tory 1876 Education Act

Viscount Sandon's Memorandum to Cabinet, Public Record Office, PRO 30/6/72, pp. 191–2, 4 November 1875.

1. To simplify the existing conflicting Acts respecting the employment and education of children....

2. To require from all children before they go to labour, either proficiency in elementary reading, writing, and arithmetic, or regular attendance for some years at an efficient school.

3. To secure that moral teaching should be provided in the Public Elementary Schools, as well as Elementary Religious teaching for those who do not repel it; a full conscience clause being everywhere insisted upon.

4. To check the unnecessary increase of School Boards, and prepare the way for the extinction of unnecessary ones, holding fast to the avowed original intention of the Act, that it was to supplement, not to supplant the existing Voluntary System.

It cannot be too often repeated that School Boards, though politically harmless and often highly necessary in large towns, are of the worst political effect in small communities when they afford the platform and notoriety specially needed by the political Dissenting Ministers (many of them, to my mind, the most active and effective revolutionary agents of the day), and also to provide a ready machinery for lowering the legitimate and useful influence of the leading personages of the place....

5. To preserve the Voluntary School System — as being much less costly than that of the Boards; as having important social influence in the

country; as offering a better security for moral and religious teaching; and as being indirectly a great and legitimate source of strength to the Church.

6. To avoid the creation of fresh local bodies, and to concentrate duties as much as possible on existing ones.

7. To avoid the machinery and vexation of direct compulsory attendance at school (unless adopted by the free choice of a locality), for the children of the industrious poor, and to work by indirect compulsion and the offer of advantages for school attendances and success, instead of by penalties and attendance officers.

8. To sweep into schools, without remorse, neglected children of school age, neither at work nor under instruction ....

9. To maintain in all cases the right of the parent to choose the school, where there can be a choice of schools.

14c   The advent of compulsory education

A.J. Mundella, House of Commons, 2 August 1880. *Hansard* (3rd series), vol. ccliv, cols 1966–8.

In 1870 the number of children on our school registers was 1,693,000. In 1874 it had risen to 2,497,000, and in 1879 ... the numbers were 3,710,000, showing an actual increase in numbers of children in elementary schools of 2,017,000 or 119 per cent of the numbers in 1870. The average numbers of attendances is also interesting. In fact, the average attendance is a better test of the real progress of this country than school places. In 1870 it was 1,152,000, in 1874 it was 1,679,000, and in 1879 it was 2,595,000, showing an increase in average attendance of 1,443,000, or 125 per cent increase .... In 1870 there were 1,878,000 places in our elementary schools in England and Wales. In 1874 there were 2,872,000 ... and in 1879 it had risen to 4,142,000 ... the accommodation has increased 121 per cent. The accommodation has not increased faster than the number of children. The rate of grant in 1870 was 9s. 11$\frac{1}{4}$d. per head; in 1874 it was 12s. 5d. per head; and in 1879 it was 15s. 5$\frac{1}{2}$d. per head, being an increase in grant of 56 per cent. My last is the percentage of population on the school registers. In 1870 it was only 7·7 per cent; in 1874 it was 10·6 per cent; and in 1879, 14·7 per cent .... The growth in the number of attendances in our elementary schools has proved, beyond all doubt, the necessity for, and the efficiency of, compulsion .... I think I might without risk or exaggeration, say there are still from 400,000 to 500,000 children who ought to be brought into these schools ....

At the time of the passing of the Act of 1870, only half the population was under bye-laws [for attendance at school], and the increase from 12,000,000 to 18,000,000 has been very gradual. It may be said that something like 200,000 children a year have been added by means of compulsion to our schools .... We are still getting children into our schools who appear wholly neglected, who are wholly ignorant, and who are absolutely untaught, at ages at which they ought to have made a reasonable and respectable attendance. Of course, this must be expected, as long as 5,000,000 or 6,000,000 of the population are not under bye-laws.

A.J. Mundella to Mr Leader, 28 June 1880. Mundella Papers, Sheffield University Library.

Tonight we have introduced in the Lords two Bills .... One is for a Commission dealing with the Endowed Schools of Scotland. The other is of considerable importance for England — it establishes *bye-laws* throughout the Kingdom. It harmonizes the labour Acts and Factory Acts with the Education Acts, will make Compulsion general, and enable us to sweep away a whole net-work of *complicated machinery and a mass of red tape* which have inflicted immense labour upon Teachers and Educational Authorities generally.

14d   School inspection at the grass roots

Inspection of Burley Road School, Leeds, 14 December 1881. Leeds City Archives. Leeds School Board 14/1.

Boys' School The boys have as usual passed a very good Examination. There is some weakness of Spelling of the fourth and fifth Standards, otherwise the Standard work was most creditable, and this remark especially applies to the writing and Arithmetic of the second and third standards. In these standards out of 82 boys presented in Arithmetic there were no failures. The Grammar and Geography have been intelligently taught, especially in the lower Standards. Literature which was taken as a specific subject was not very successful. In the fourth Standard the poetry was not well repeated, and the letters were meagre. The upper Standards did better in this subject, the paraphrasing in the fifth Standard being superior to the Composition in the Sixth. The Physical Geography papers generally were well done. The Discipline deserves praise and the Singing is good.

Girls' School It is much to be regretted that no permenant Mistress was appointed to this School until the beginning of January. As a consequence the attainments have suffered, but the present Mistress seems to have worked very hard and conscientiously since her appointment. In the second, third and fourth Standards the Spelling needs attention, and in the two former Standards the Arithmetic is backward. On the other hand the Writing is well formed. The elder girls read well, and do their sums well .... The Domestic Economy papers were good on the whole. The needlework was well done in the upper Stages and fairly well in the lower ones. The Discipline is good.

Infants' School The State of this School continues to be very far from satisfactory. Out of 43 examined in the first Standard, 17 fail in Reading, 28 in writing, and 23 in Arithmetic. In the preparatory Class Reading is decidedly bad, Writing is not in good style, and number not well known. The phonic system of Reading is professedly taught here, but this teaching is not given to all the youngest children, and the next Class do not know the phonic sounds properly. The kindergarten Exercises as at present given cannot be said to be justified by the results. The needlework worked on the day of Inspection was unsatisfactory. I regret to add that some of the children are not by any means so obedient as they should be. The Mistress suffered in health during the year, and the teaching Staff is by no means strong. Steps will I hope be taken by the Board to make this which used to be the model Kindergarten School really efficient.

My Lords are compelled to order a deduction of one tenth from the Grant to the Infants' School for faults of instruction (Article 32(b)).

14e The difficulties of enforcing compulsory education

Report of S.G. Tremenheere on Schools in the Kendal District, Parliamentary Papers, 1884, vol. xxiv, pp. 415–19.

ON ATTENDANCE

Compared with the whole of England and Wales these figures [of attendance in Cumberland and Westmorland] are extremely good .... However, it is impossible to rest content with the condition of affairs .... In particular, the action, if such a term can be used, of the school attendance committees for the union of Whitehaven is open to grave criticism. In their district only 16·4 per cent of the population is enrolled on the books, and of these only 65·6 in every hundred are daily at school. They ought to have 1,000 more names on the registers, and 1,600 more scholars in average attendance .... I found that for the town population of 20,000 only part of one man's time was engaged for attendance work; that their country officer had not once entered some of the schools under his charge during the preceeding 12 months; that from neither officer did his employers require any account of either his time or his results; and that no school census had been taken since the committee commenced ... their functions. Moreover, I ascertained that it was an established rule of the authority that no parent should be prosecuted unless he had received a warning during the preceeding month; thus enabling a parent, provided he sent his child to school with fair regularity every alternate month, to escape with no severer penalty than six warnings per annum ....

One of the chief causes of absenteeism appears to me to be either apathy or want of method on the part of the local authorities.

To meet this I would strongly urge (a) that each local authority throughout the Kingdom be *required to report annually* to the Education Department ... ; (b) that every local authority be required to appoint one or more attendance officers at the discretion of the Department; (c) that every attendance officer report periodically, say once a quarter ... for the expenditure of his time and showing the results of his efforts; (d) that teachers be *bound* to send in ... lists of irregular children; (e) that a census of schoolable children be taken by each local authority at least every three years.

14f   Fears over free elementary education

The Times, 31 January 1890.

Assuming that free education is to come ... in what form is it to come? Is it to come in the shape of an extinguisher upon voluntary schools? ... it is tolerably certain that the present Parliament will not sanction free education in any form which seems calculated to injure the denominational schools. Speaking at Nottingham last November, Lord Salisbury was explicit enough ... 'The gift of free or assisted education', he observed, 'must be so conducted as not to diminish in the slightest degree the guarantee that we now possess for religious liberty as expressed by the voluntary schools. If it is to suppress the denominational schools, free education would not be a blessing but a curse ....'

The voluntary schools are immensely valuable as auxiliaries to our State schools, and, although their efficiency occasionally leaves something to be desired, nothing must be done wantonly to lose to the taxpayer the large sum which is annually collected in subscriptions. There is much to be said for settling the question of free education during the present Parliament, since the composition of that Parliament is such as to guarantee that the reform shall be introduced upon an equitable basis.

14g   Tactical withdrawal to secure Church influence on education

'Free Education', *Church Quarterly Review*, vol. xxx (1890), pp. 172–77.

We have no hesitation in saying that ... the advocates of free schools have entirely failed to make out their case ... Parental responsibility is not felt too strongly at the present day, and we very much regret anything that has a tendency still further to weaken it; we fear that free schools may have this effect. Then in days when Socialistic theories are in the air, we regret any steps that seem to rest upon the idea that those who can be made to pay by law may be mulcted to any extent for the benefit of the poorer members of the community, when these can command a majority in Parliament; and we fear that there is a savour of this view in the principle of free schools. But beyond this we are inclined to believe that people do not prize that which costs them nothing; and though they may eagerly grasp at a boon of the kind when it is first offered them, they soon cease to value it and look upon it as a right, and in no way as a privilege, and consequently make less of the advantages thus provided for them than they would do if they had to make some sacrifice to obtain them ....

Churchmen have to consider what is the wisest course for them to pursue. The question before them is not whether they prefer free schools or schools where the parents pay a suitable fee for the education of their children, but whether they will try to come to terms with the present Government, who are anxious to deal fairly with them, or fall back upon a *non possumus*, and run the risk of having to face proposals for free schools made by a Government determined to ruin their schools, and probably to confiscate them.

We confess that, much as we dislike free education, and convinced as we are that it will fail to secure the benefits expected from it by its advocates, whilst it will probably be the parent of expected and unexpected evils to the community, we dare not recommend the more venturous course. Religious education is, in our opinion, the all-important point in debate, and we feel that all other considerations are light in the balance when weighed against this. It is obviously as possible to secure definite religious teaching in schools where no fees are paid as in schools where they are required. And if we can obtain Parliamentary guarantees that justify us in believing that our voluntary schools can be maintained in their integrity, we think it is wiser to submit to a force that we cannot resist, and to come to a concordat now, rather than to trust to an unknown future, with the great probabilities that at no distant day all for which we most care in popular education will be entirely destroyed.

15 Land Reform

Land Reform is the great forgotten issue of nineteenth-century history. Yet it does not deserve to be. It was a live issue in the 1840s, when Cobden and Bright, logically but inexpediently, argued that a nation professing free trade in all other commodities should not shore up redundant aristocratic privilege by retaining the outmoded paraphernalia of entail, strict settlement and primogeniture. These restricted covenants prevented the benefits of free trade from being realized. The new Domesday Survey of landownership in 1873 revealed that one-half of the enclosed land of England was owned by not more than 2,250 families.

The 1880s witnessed the fiercest controversy over land reform. Against a background of dramatic agricultural depression in the south and east of England, Disraeli remarked that the land question ranked equally with Ireland as the decisive issues in the 1880 election. A great need was felt to extend ownership to a large number of tenant-farmers. Others wished to make the ownership of a small plot of land a realistic prospect for the urban worker. The extension of ownership was an important plank of the Liberal party platform in the 1885 election, and Jesse Collings (1831–1920) believed that his slogan of 'three acres and a cow' had helped to swing the newly enfranchised rural voters to the Liberals. Collings was particularly concerned to promote ownership schemes by State intervention in the form of cheap loans (15d). Joseph Chamberlain, whose castigation of the aristocracy as a class who 'toil not neither do they spin' was famous, wished to reverse the trend of rural depopulation while loosening the hold of the great landowners by selective taxation (15e). Henry George, Philadelphia lawyer (1839–97), had a more drastic solution. His 'single tax' policy came close to land nationalization as it involved the State's taking away all the economic rent in the form of taxation (15a). His book *Progress and Poverty*, first published in the United States in 1879, was very popular in Britain, and required some careful rebuttals. John Rae's (1845–1915) attack concentrated on the improving and benevolent aristocrats who injected capital into the land during periods of depression, thus keeping many on the land who would otherwise have been forced to leave (15c). Given the history of the Highland Clearances, however, his example—the Duke of Sutherland—could have been more happily chosen.

Successive governments did enact legislation, though radicals argued that it failed to attack the basic structural problems. The Agricultural Holdings Act, 1883, amended weaker legislation of 1875 and secured to tenants compensation at the termination of their leases for improvements made during their tenancy (15b). The Tory Government of 1886–92, sensitive to public opinion, and ever willing to promote compromise legislation in the hope of forestalling more radical measures, passed an Allotments Act in 1887 and a Smallholdings Act in 1892. These neatly avoided the ultimate horror of compulsory purchase while providing some modest extensions in the range of landownership. Certain tenants were able to make use of State-aided purchase schemes.

The land question was successfully met, partly by skilled manoeuvres and partly by Gladstone's grasping of the Irish nettle in 1886. This effectively split the anti-aristocratic forces and imprisoned Chamberlain within the Liberal-Unionist ranks. Ironically, then, the landed aristocracy, whom Cobden and Bright believed had been rendered redundant by the Industrial Revolution, survived all assaults to enter the twentieth century almost unscathed by legislation while other institutions were subject to much more radical reform.

Suggestions for further reading

Roy Douglas, *Land, People and Politics, 1878–1952* (1976) provides a useful, if lightweight, summary of the main issues. See also F.M.L. Thompson, 'Land and Politics in England in the Nineteenth Century', *Transactions of the Royal Historical Society*, vol. xv (1965) and H.J. Perkin, 'Land Reform and Class Conflict in Victorian Britain', in J. Butt and I.F. Clarke, *The Victorians and Social Protest* (1973).

15a   The single-tax attack on landlords

Henry George, *Progress and Poverty* (1884 ed.), pp. 8, 253, 313–14.

The association of poverty with progress is the great enigma of our times. It is the central fact from which spring industrial, social and political difficulties that perplex the world, and with which statesmanship and philanthropy and education grapple in vain....

We have traced the unequal distribution of wealth which is the curse and menace of modern civilisation to the institution of private property in land. We have seen that as long as this institution exists no increase in productive power can permanently benefit the masses; but, on the contrary, must tend to still further depress their condition....

There is but one way to remove an evil—and that is, to remove its cause. Poverty deepens as wealth increases, and wages are forced down while productive power grows, because land, which is the source of all wealth and the field of all labour, is monopolised. To extirpate poverty, to make wages what justice commands they should be, the full earnings of the labourer, we must therefore substitute for the individual ownership of land a common ownership....

We must make land common property....

I do not propose either to purchase or to confiscate private property in land. The first would be unjust; the second needless. Let the individuals who now hold it still retain, if they want to, possession of what they are pleased to call *their* land....Let them buy and sell, and bequeath and devise it. We may safely leave them the shell, if we take the kernel. It is not necessary to confiscate land; it is only necessary to confiscate rent....

We already take some rent in taxation. We have only to make some changes in our modes of taxation to take it all.

What I...propose as the simple yet sovereign remedy, which will raise wages, increase the earnings of capital, extirpate pauperism, abolish poverty, give remunerative employment to whoever wishes it, afford free scope to human powers, lessen crime, elevate morals, and taste, and intelligence, purify government, and carry civilisation to yet nobler heights, is—*to appropriate rent by taxation.*

In this way the State may become the universal landlord without calling herself so, and without assuming a single new function. In form, the ownership of land would remain just as now. No owner of land need be dispossessed....For, rent being taken by the State in taxes, land, no matter in whose hand it stood, or in what parcels it was held, would be really common property, and every member of the community would participate in the advantages of its ownership.

Now, inasmuch as the taxation of rent or land values, must necessarily be increased just as we abolish other taxes, we may put the proposition into practical form by proposing—

To abolish all taxation save that upon land values.

15b   Owner-occupation the bastion against revolution

G. Shaw Lefevre, 'The Agricultural Holdings Act, 1883', *Nineteenth Century*, vol. xiv (1883), pp. 692–4.

It is probable...that we are approaching a period when tenancy will not be the all-prevailing condition of cultivation of land in England, and that ownership will be combined with occupation to a far larger extent....Ownership is the best form of security which can be given to the cultivator; and it may be confidently stated that the highest kinds of cultivation, those requiring most application of capital, can be carried out under the stimulus of security which ownership alone can give.

The future condition, then, of landownership in England and of its relation to tenancy and the cultivation of land, and whether reform will take the direction of a social revolution, or will assume the gradual process which is characteristic of English progress, will depend upon the extent to which landowners themselves appreciate the forces around them, and read the lessons of the past and the present....

...it may seem almost old-fashioned to suggest that the principle of individual property in land is worth a struggle, and that measures leading naturally to the multiplication of owners and to bringing them within reach of all the incentive of ownership, will be the best means of giving encouragement to industry and thrift, and the safest rampart against revolutionary movements. If we are not prepared to arrive at this end...by admitting the tenants to a co-partnership with their landlords in their holdings, let us at least adopt legislative measures which will have these objects in view, and which will not savour of either socialism or confiscation.

15c   Land nationalization plans attacked

John Rae, *Contemporary Socialism* (1884), pp. 480–3.

So far as I am able to judge, there is only one respect in which the pecuniary interest of the landlord appears to be unfavourable to an extension of cultivation. There is probably a considerable quantity of land that might be cultivated with advantage to the community generally by labourers who expected nothing from it but the equivalent of ordinary wages, and which is at present suffered to lie waste, because its produce would be insufficient to yield anything more than wages and would afford nothing to the capitalist farmer as profit or to the landlord as rent...but here again, one may deal with waste ground...without resorting to any revolutionary schemes of general land nationalisation. Of course much land is kept in an inferior condition...but the same result would happen under the nationalisation plan, through want of capital on the part of the tenants. Mr. George does not propose to supply any of the necessary capital out of public funds...so that the occupier would be no better situated under the State than he would be under an embarrassed landlord... In either case he would improve as far as his means allowed, and he would improve no further. But if by nationalisation of land we get rid of the embarrassed landlord, we lose at the same time the wealthy one, and the tenants of the latter would be decidedly worse off under the State which only drew rents, but laid out no expenses. The community, too, and the general cultivation of the country would be greatly the losers. Mr. George has probably little conception of the amount of money an improving landlord thinks it necessary to invest in maintaining or increasing the productive capacity of his land. A convenient illustration of it is furnished by the evidence of Sir Arnold Kemball, commissioner of the Duke of Sutherland, before the recent Crofters' Commission. Sir Arnold gave in an abstract of the revenue and expenditure on the Sutherland estates for the thirty years 1853–1882, and it appears that the total revenue for that period was £1,039,748, and the total expenditure ...was £1,285,122, or a quarter of a million more than the entire rental. Here, then, is a dilemma for Mr. George: With equally liberal management of the land on the part of the

State, how is he to endow widows and pay the taxes of the *bourgeoisie* out of the rents? And without such liberal management how is he to promote the spread of cultivation better than the present owners?

15d   Giving the land to the people who work it

Jesse Collings, 'Occupying Ownership', *Fortnightly Review*, vol. xli (1884), pp. 258–63.

The question of the land affects so vitally the welfare of human beings that it cannot be left to 'freedom of contract', but requires State interference to preserve the natural rights of the people....

The principle...is that of State aid given through the agency of local authorities. The State...would advance money on loan at low interest, say 3 per cent, to the local authorities for the purpose of enabling tenants and others to purchase farms, and for labourers and others to acquire land in suitable quantities....The security would be the land itself supplemented by the local rates....With a view of meeting the wants of labourers and a smaller class of cultivators, the local authorities should be further empowered to purchase farms and estates, and divide them into holdings of from 1 acre to 20 or 30 acres each...

In England every difficulty is placed in the way of the labourer...and the very idea of possessing property in land is strange to him....For him, so far as the land is concerned, the lower rounds [sic] of the social ladder have been deliberately broken away, and it is almost impossible for him to ascend. There is no career open to him in an occupation which he understands and loves, and so it comes to pass that the only outlet for the most able and enterprising is to get away from the land, to emigrate, or to migrate into the towns....Let the labourer once know, however, that if he can save from £12 to £20 he can become the owner of a couple of acres of land and have enough left to work it; let him also know that by further savings – his own or jointly with others – he can add to his possessions, and that by still further care and thrift he might have a house – a home of his own from which no one can evict him – and a magical advance would

set in, in the habits, aims, modes of thought, in independence of character
— in short in the whole social status — of our rural population, such as
sermons on sobriety, homilies on thrift, and tracts against early
marriages...are powerless to secure.

15e   Joseph Chamberlain tilts at landowning privileges

Speech at Birmingham, 29 January 1885 in H.W. Lucy (ed.), *Speeches of
the Rt. Hon. Joseph Chamberlain* (1885), pp. 119–21.

During the last twenty years there has been a more extraordinary advance
in the prosperity of the country; wealth has increased, manufactures have
developed, invention has prospered and our exports and imports have
doubled and trebled....During the whole of this time there have been
constantly in receipt of parish relief nearly one million of persons; and
probably at the very least one million more have been on the verge of
pauperism. During the same time 800,000 people have left the land. They
have been forced to emigrate or driven into the towns....

I have two objects in view. In the first place I want to see the burden of
taxation is distributed according to the ability of the tax payer, and in the
second place I want to increase the production of the land, and I want to
multiply small owners and tenants. All this clamour about confiscation
and blackmail and plunder is so much dust raised by men who are
interested in maintaining the present system, and who are either too
prejudiced to read my proposals or too stupid to understand them....If it be
blackmail to propose that the rich should pay taxation in equal proportion
to the poor, what word is strong enough to describe the present system,
under which the poor pay more than the rich? If it be confiscation to
suggest that land may be acquired at a fair value for public purposes, what
language will fitly describe the operations of those who have wrongfully
appropriated the common land, and have extended their boundaries at the
expense of their poorer neighbours too weak and too ignorant to resist
them? If it be plunder to require the restitution of this illgotten property, I
should like to know what we are to say to those who perpetrated the

original act of appropriation. The fact is, there are some people who have no conception of any property at all except the property of private owners like themselves; and the public purse, the public right, the public land, and public endowments are so many abstractions unworthy of care or of protection. Well, that is not my view. I hold that the sanctity of public property is greater even than that of private property, and that if it has been lost, or wasted, or stolen, some equivalent must be found for it, and some compensation may be fairly exacted from the wrongdoer.

16 Self-help and charity

There were no dramatic developments in self-help in the last quarter of the nineteenth century. The challenge of State provision had to be met, however, by evidence that voluntary agencies were able to cope. Steps were taken to improve reliability in the management of friendly societies, in whom probably 8,000,000 people had some financial stake. A Royal Commission on Friendly and Benefit Building Societies made four reports between 1871 and 1874, and recommended that societies should be persuaded to manage their affairs more efficiently. They should be valued every five years, and should make use of precisely calculated actuarial tables. The Commission stopped short of recommending compulsory registration of societies. Its Chairman, Stafford Northcote (1818–87), was firmly of the view that contributors must be left to exercise their own judgments about the probity of a society (16a). He retained this view when, as Chancellor of the Exchequer in Disraeli's government, he piloted the Friendly Societies Act through parliament in 1875. This Act established the office of Chief Registrar of Friendly Societies, and the post was filled by the Secretary to the Royal Commission, John Ludlow (1821–1911). Ludlow was well known for his interest in social questions, having been involved in the Christian Socialist movement, and also a founder of the London Working Man's College in 1854. Ludlow's main complaint was that his office had neither the staff nor the resources to provide the central supervision the Act called for (16b).

Self-help societies faced a testing time in the last quarter of the century. Building societies, in particular, were hampered by economic uncertainties, and the challenge of State pension schemes loomed on the horizon. Funds were not in serious danger of drying up, however, since falling prices left a margin for savings from most of those who were in work.

For those who could not, or would not, help themselves, charity, the poor law, or a combination of both, were available. There were vast numbers of charitable agencies, soup kitchens and the like; but pre-eminent was the Charity Organization Society, founded in 1869. This Society quickly developed the philosophy that charity of itself had limited value. The type of relief provided should vary according to the particular circumstances of the individual, and it should enable recipients thereafter to be independent. The Society, therefore, under the able but inflexible leadership of Charles Stewart Loch (1849–1923), deplored loafers who resisted attempts to improve them and indiscriminate alms-giving in almost equal proportions (16c). It aimed at nothing less than the moral reformation of those who fell into poverty, and a heavy debt of obligation was extracted from those who received its assistance. For those who refused assistance with COS strings attached, Loch and his influential associates had no time. They epitomized both the virtues and the vices of the individualist ethic. They took enormous pains to discover the true state of poverty, and in so doing laid the foundations of the case-work approach to poverty relief, but they found it extremely hard to accept that destitution was the result of factors other than personal shortcomings. The Nottingham delegate at the 1886 General Meeting spoke for most members when he poured scorn on public-works schemes of relief (16d) and Frederick Temple (1821–1902), Bishop of London, an enthusiastic social reformer, evinced a certain corporate arrogance in his assumption that the COS should be permitted to direct the charitable effort of the entire metropolis. The Society attracted a large number of able and dedicated workers, but its efforts were blinkered by an unbending individualism. It opposed all schemes which gave a greater role to the State, and, while remaining extremely influential, it was beginning to swim against the tide by the end of the period.

Suggestions for further reading

The Gosden book (section 7) remains useful. For the COS see the account of Loch's grandson, C.L. Mowat, *The Charity Organisation Society, 1869–1913* (1961).

16a Rigid controls of friendly societies rejected

Stafford Northcote to S. Estcourt, 11 November 1874. British Library, Department of Manuscripts, Add. MSS. 50052, ff. 52–3.

My leading idea is, that we should leave all kinds of societies to work as freely as possible, and the people to exercise their own judgement as to embarking in any of them, provided we can secure to every man a fair opportunity of ascertaining what manner of society he is about to invest in, and can educate him sufficiently to enable him to discern between the good and the bad. For this he requires easily accessible information as to the actual affairs of any Society, and this we propose to give him by means of local (county) registration. It may be a rather expensive system for the State; but if we can afford to establish it we shall put it within the power of those who are really interested to obtain all the particulars for forming a judgement as to the solvency of any given society. Then will they be able to use the information so as to form a correct judgement? I think that by publishing standard tables, and by prescribing forms of account for general use, we shall give men of ordinary intelligence and fair education the means of doing so. If John Hodge cannot be expected to see through all the intricacies of the accounts himself, there will be those who will be able and willing to help him....

16b   A commentary on the working of the 1875 Friendly Societies Act

Report of the Chief Registrar of Friendly Societies, 1885. *Parliamentary Papers*, 1886, vol. lxi, pp. 11–12.

In its main features ... the Chief Registrar ... believes the Act of 1875 requires no amendment. In retaining the voluntary character of registration, in abstaining from making any certification of an actuarial character, or the adoption of any particular tables compulsory, in allowing Friendly Societies generally to choose their own tribunal for the settlement of disputes, inside or outside of their own body, in withholding from the Registrar all power of interference on his own motion with the management of societies, the Chief Registrar believes that true principles have been followed....

The weakness of the Act ... does not lie in its principles, but in the absence of that which was expressly recommended by the Friendly Societies Commissioners, viz, 'local machinery under central control' .... The Friendly Societies Registry Office in each county is simply a head without limbs. As respects England and Wales, it is hopelessly absurd to expect a small office in London, with a staff of 17 all told, copyists included, to exercise any searching practical oversight over 25,000 different bodies from Land's End to Berwick-upon-Tweed .... What is needed ... is officers under the control of the central office, spread over the country in sufficient numbers to be able to look after the working of societies in their districts, were it only for the purpose of getting in returns and valuations, and supplying information as to the existence of societies.

16c   Charles Loch's charitable principles

C.S. Loch, 'Some Necessary Reforms in Charitable Work', *Charity Organisation Reporter,*' vol. xi (3 August 1882), p. 238.

... it is my belief that certain principles have now been ascertained. They are these: That all charity should be administered in reference to the wants of the individual; and ... consequently all wholesale or periodic distributions of alms are injurious. Their tendency is to create pauperism, to weaken the motives for exertion, to reduce wages and thus injure the labourer most vitally, viz., by the deterioration of his sole capital, his labour. That a wholesale or indiscriminate supply of the necessaries of life is especially injurious ... to be beneficent, charity should assist adequately i.e. so as to produce self-help in the recipient. That with some obvious exceptions, all charitable work stands or falls by this list. That to learn how the recipient can be assisted, and whether Charity or Poor Law should aid him, a knowledge and a skilled consideration of his circumstances are necessary. That the aim of charitable persons should be to utilise the means at their disposal and the charitable resources of the community in supplying to the individual what will work to his social cure. That for this purpose co-operation between alms givers and alms-administrators is absolutely necessary. That these principles afford a fair basis for the organisation of charity and the charities, and is a fit substitute for the indiscriminate alms giving and the arbitrary restrictions which now so often prevail.

16d   The need for structural assistance to the destitute

17th Annual Meeting of the Charity Organisation Society, 18 January 1886, *Charity Organisation Review*, vol. ii (1886), pp. 52–3, 60.

Bishop of London (Rev. Frederick Temple): I think there is very great reason to fear that a very large number of people consider that they are fulfilling the commands of charity by simply giving such assistance as they can easily afford to the most importunate applicants they come across. In doing this they do no real good to the receiver, but simply find a relief for their own feelings.

True charity is of necessity a much deeper thing morally, and a much more difficult thing physically, imposing a duty which can be discharged, it may be, by not giving money at all. If it is to be discharged rightly, it must take the form of giving thought as well as money, taking care that what money is given shall be given in such a manner as to be of real benefit, and in a place like the metropolis it is of the gravest importance to do this because of its enormous size, and also because of the enormous complexity of the agencies employed for the purpose of charitable relief. The charities of London are almost innumerable …. Some of them do a certain amount of useful work, but I am sorry to say that a very great many of them are very little more than the refuge of imposters, who have failed elsewhere to get assistance. Hence, it is of very great importance, if charity is to be rightly administered, that all the various agencies should have the means of coming into right relations with each other….

The Charity Organisation Society aims at helping cases, if possible, in such a way as to make the benefit permanent. It always endeavours, if it can, to give a man such help as will enable him to be afterwards independent of charity altogether …. It is certainly the duty of the public at large to support the Society to see that the charity entrusted to it shall be administered in such a way as to be real charity, and that it shall not degrade while it aids. One great source of degradation always is the facility with which those who apply for relief are able, unless great care is taken, to obtain relief from a greater variety of relievers—charitable societies, charitable funds, charitable individuals—and by these means to obtain relief quite out of all proportion to their needs. The result of this always is that people who deserve to be assisted do not get assistance, because it is exhausted upon those who get a great deal more than they ought....

Mr. R. Simon (Nottingham) said that.... In this town it had been stated in the winter of 1884 that 16,000 men were out of employ. A registry of the unemployed, when instituted, however, showed a different result, for the 16,000 shrank to 1,100, many of whom were admittedly loafers, and scores of whom preferred, as they had a perfect right to do, to be out of work rather than go in at the reduced wages of £2 a week. In December, 1884, the town had an exceptional population—40,000 people had been added to 186,000 in a few years, many of whom were connected with the building trade, which fell off. There was a large population with no settled connections in the town in which they happened to be, and they found themselves suddenly and inevitably thrown out of work. The Socialists seized the opportunity, and held a meeting, attended largely by the idle, and by some of the destitute, marched to the Corporation, and found a committee more than willing to meet them half-way. Five hundred men were set on to turn a hill into a valley, at 12s. per week each, in order to form a building site. Benevolent people said what a fine thing it was to prevent men from being pauperised. A week after another 500 men wanted to be employed. There was not another hill handy, but the second batch would not be denied, and so the first batch were put on half-time; the second batch went to work on the same hill, and the earnings were reduced to 6s. 4d. a week. Thus within a fortnight all pretence of adequate relief had vanished—the pretence of adequate employment had never existed—it was only an excuse to provide the men with wages.

Some of the men were originally hard working, no doubt, but they had every inducement to keep the hill up as long as they could. The hill thus made slow progress in being levelled. The number of men at work increased to 1,400, and when at last the hill disappeared some £7,000 or £8,000 of the ratepayers' money had disappeared with it, having accomplished a task which, in the ordinary manner, would have cost £2,000 or £3,000. When the relief works were stopped, and there was nothing more to do, these 1,400 men, upon whom were more or less dependent 3,600 women and children, were suddenly thrown out of work again. They met, and declared they were starving, and 500 of them went to the guardians and demanded relief. They were received politely and firmly, and offered the house or work in the labour yard, and twenty-seven of them accepted the offer of working in the labour yard. That experience conclusively showed the hollowness of the demand for employment by the corporation. Works promoted for the purpose of paying wages were an insidious revival of the old poor-law in its worst form. When the proposal was made again this year ... it met with no support.

Part Three

The birth-pangs of welfarism, 1895–1914

17   Collectivist perspectives

The idea that the State both could and should evolve a social policy aimed at improving standards of living for its citizens took root in the first decade of the twentieth century. The revelation of the depth and scale of poverty by Booth, Rowntree and others, the depressions which killed the notion that an unregulated economy would thrive and a regulated one falter, the fact that over 60 per cent of adult males had the vote after 1884, all these played their part in redefining the role of the State. Many of the leading theorists of State intervention were on the progressive wing of the Liberal party. L.T. Hobhouse (1864–1929), a Professor of Sociology, argued that the State should ensure the means of maintaining civilized living standards, from which base men would the more readily help themselves and their families to independence and even prosperity (17e). Winston Churchill (1874–1965), who had left the Tory party in 1904 over the free trade issue, was more of a practical politician and argued that the Liberal party was the only organization which could ensure both progress and democratic advance. Though he denied any antithesis between individualism and collectivism, he recognized that the complexity of early twentieth-century society demanded more State intervention (17b).

J.A. Hobson (1858–1940), the leading theoretician of progressive Liberalism, argued strongly that the party should accept social reconstruction. Writing as the conflict with the House of Lords reached a crisis, he argued that it was the duty of the State to ensure social justice. Only thus could the individual liberties which Liberals had traditionally prized continue to flourish. Old *laissez-faire* individualism was dead (17d).

The extent to which social reconstruction could go, of course, divided the progressives. Leo Chiozza Money (1870–1944) saw salvation only in State ownership of the means of production (17a). This view also commended itself to the Fabian novelist H.G. Wells (1866–1946) who saw Socialism as a scientific creed, with social policy based on rational planning to evolve 'a comprehensive design for all the social activities of man' (17c).

The reaction of those Conservatives outside the backwoods inhabited by the Tory peers was essentially pragmatic. They had learned much from the intelligent and generally underpraised leadership of Salisbury (1830–1903), and consequently ruled out little on principle. Salisbury's son, Lord Hugh Cecil (1869–1956), accepted the principle of State intervention, while subjecting its various manifestations in practice to cool appraisal. In particular, moves to redistribute income were challenged (17f). Thinking Conservatives were anxious, during the long period of opposition after 1905, not to miss the collectivist tide and be stranded up the creek of unreconstructed individualism. Though many State initiatives in social policy were not electorally popular, the Tory party could ill afford to appear anachronistic—a fate it only narrowly averted during the constitutional crisis of 1909–11.

The Liberal journal, the *Nation*, charted the progress of State intervention in various areas of public life by 1913 (17g). Its editor, Henry Massingham (1860–1924), looked forward to its continued development, leading to further public ownership and the emergence of a planned economy. Though the leading thinkers were included to advocate a greater degree of planning than the Liberal government would accept, there is no doubt that by 1914 it had been accepted that the State should have a major role in the formulation and execution of a coherent social policy.

Suggestion for further reading

D. Read, *Edwardian England* (1972), chapter 3, provides a useful introduction to the mass of literature on this topic.

17a   The necessity for public ownership

L.C. Money, *Riches and Poverty* (10th ed., 1911), pp. 255–6, 343–4

It has long been recognized that certain services can only be effectually and efficiently performed under one management. Railways, tramways, water-service, lighting and so forth have come to be looked upon as 'natural monopolies' .... Indeed, it is apparent to the most unthinking that between two points A and B there can only be one best route for a railway, and that, therefore, railway service between points A and B should be a monopoly. Similarly it would be an obvious absurdity to construct two sewers in one road, competing with each other for the removal of refuse, or for one or two gas managements to run mains in the same streets. In these and many other cases it is clearly recognized that economy of labour is consistent with monopoly alone .... An overwhelming weight of opinion has decided that public ownership must go with monopoly, wherever monopoly is shown to be necessary ....

To deal with causes we must strike at the Error of Distribution by gradually substituting public ownership for private ownership of the means of production. In no other way can we secure for each worker in the hive the full reward of his labour. So long as between the worker and his just wage stands the private landlord and the private capitalist, so long will poverty remain, and not poverty alone, but the moral degradations which inevitably arise from the devotion of labour to the service of waste. So long as the masses of the people are denied the fruit of their own labour, so long will our civilization be a false veneer, and our every noble thoroughfare be flanked by purlieus of shame.

17b   The growing collectivist impulse

W.S. Churchill, speech at St Andrew's Hall, Glasgow, 11 October 1906, in *Liberalism and the Social Problem*, pp. 78–80.

Liberalism supplies at once the higher impulse and the practicable path; it appeals to persons by sentiments of generosity and humanity; it proceeds by courses of moderation. By gradual steps, by steady effort from day to day, from year to year, Liberalism enlists hundreds of thousands upon the side of progress and popular democratic reform whom militant Socialism would drive into violent Tory reaction. That is why the Tory Party hate us. That is why they, too, direct their attacks upon the great organisation of the Liberal Party, because they know it is through the agency of Liberalism that society will be able in the course of time to slide forward, almost painlessly—for the world is changing very fast—on to a more even and more equal foundation. That is the mission that lies before Liberalism. The cause of the Liberal Party is the cause of the left-out millions; and because we believe that there is in all the world no other instrument of equal potency and efficacy available at the present time for the purposes of social amelioration, we are bound in duty and in honour to guard it from all attacks, whether they arise from violence or from reaction.

... It is not possible to draw a hard-and-fast line between individualism and collectivism. You cannot draw it either in theory or in practice. That is where the Socialist makes a mistake. No man can be a collectivist alone or an individualist alone. He must be both an individualist and a collectivist. The nature of man is a dual nature. The character of the organisation of human society is dual. Man is at once a unique being and a gregarious animal. For some purposes he must be collectivist, for others he is, and he will for all time remain, an individualist. Collectively we have an Army and a Navy and a Civil Service; collectively we have a Post Office, and a police, and a Government; collectively we light our streets and supply ourselves with water; collectively we indulge increasingly in all the necessities of communication. But we do not make love collectively, and the ladies do not marry us collectively, and we do not eat collectively and we do not die collectively, and it is not collectively that we face the sorrows and the hopes, the winnings and the losings of this world of accident and storm.

No view of society can possibly be complete which does not comprise within its scope both collectivist organisation and individual incentive. The whole tendency of civilisation is, however, towards the multiplication of the collective functions of society. The ever-growing complications of civilisation create for us new services which have to be undertaken by the State, and create for us an expansion of the existing services.

17c   A socialist looks forward to a planned economy

H.G. Wells, *New Worlds for Old* (1908), pp. 22–3, 305–7.

The fundamental idea upon which Socialism rests is the same fundamental idea as that upon which all real scientific work is carried out. It is the denial that chance impulse and individual will and happening constitute the only possible methods by which things may be done in the world. It is an assertion that things are in their nature orderly, that things may be computed, may be calculated upon and forseen .... The Socialist has just the same faith in the order, the knowableness of things and the power of men in co-operation to overcome chance; but to him, dealing as he does with the social affairs of men, it takes the form not of schemes for collective research but for collective action and the creation of a comprehensive design for all the social activities of man. While Science gathers knowledge, Socialism in an entirely harmonious spirit criticizes and develops a general plan of social life. Each seeks to replace disorder by order ....

There are four distinct systems of public service which could very conveniently be organized under collective ownership and control now ... There is first the need of public educational machinery, and by education I mean not simply elementary education, but the equally vital need for great colleges not only to teach ... but also to enlarge learning and sustain philosophical and literary work. A civilized community is impossible without great public libraries, public museums, public art schools, without public honour and support for contemporary thought and literature ....

Then next there is the need and opportunity of organizing the whole community in relation to health, the collective development of hospitals, medical aid, public sanitation, child welfare, into one great loyal and efficient public service.

A third system of interests ... lies in the complex interdependent developments of transit and housing, questions that lock up inextricably with the problem of replanning our local government areas. Here, too, the whole world is beginning to realize more and more clearly that private enterprise is wasteful and socially disastrous, that collective control, collective management ... give the only way of escape from an endless drifting entanglement and congestion of our mobile modern population.

The fourth department of economic activity in which collectivism is developing ... is in connection with the more generalized forms of public trading, and especially with the production, handling and supply of food and minerals .... It must be manifest that State initiative has altogether out-distanced the possibilities of private effort, and that the next step to the public authority instructing men how to farm, prepare food, run dairies, manage mines and distribute minerals, is to cut out the pedagogic middleman and undertake the work itself.

17d   A new role for the State in modern society

J.A. Hobson, *The Crisis of Liberalism* (1909), pp. xi–xii, 92–3.

The real crisis of Liberalism lies … in the intellectual and moral ability to accept and execute a positive progressive policy which involves a new conception of the functions of the State.

It is true that no sudden reversal of policy is required: the old individualism has long since been replaced by various enlargements of public activity. But hitherto these interferences and novel functions of the State have been mostly unconnected actions of an opportunist character: no avowed principle or system has underlain them ….

Our crisis consists in the substitution of an organic for an opportunist policy, the adoption of a vigorous, definite, positive policy of social reconstruction, involving important modifications in the legal and economic institutions of private property and private industry …. The full implications of this movement may not be clearly grasped, but Liberalism is now formally committed to a task which certainly involves a new conception of the State in its relation to the individual life and to private enterprise. That conception is not Socialism, in any accredited meaning of that term, though implying a considerable amount of increased public ownership and control of industry. From the standpoint which best presents its continuity with earlier Liberalism, it appears as a fuller appreciation and realisation of individual liberty contained in the provision of equal opportunities for self-development. But to this individual standpoint must be joined a just appreciation of the social, viz., the insistence that these claims or rights of self-development be adjusted to the sovereignty of social welfare.

The negative conception of Liberalism, as a definite mission for the removal of certain political and economic shackles upon personal liberty, is not merely philosophically defective but historically false. The Liberals of this country as a party never committed themselves either to the theory or the policy of this narrow *laissez faire* individualism; they never conceived liberty as something limited in quantity or purely negative in character. But it is true that they tended to lay an excessive emphasis upon the aspect of liberty which consists in the absence of restraint, as compared with the other aspect which consists in presence of opportunity; and it is this tendency, still lingering in the mind of the Liberal Party, that today checks its energy and blurs its vision.

Liberalism will probably retain its distinction from Socialism, in taking for its chief test of policy the freedom of the individual citizen rather than the strength of the State .... But it will justify itself by ... great enlargements of its liberative functions. In seeking to realise liberty for the individual citizen as 'equality of opportunity' it will recognise that, as the area and nature of opportunities are continually shifting, so the old limited conception of the task of Liberalism must always advance. Each generation of Liberals will be required to translate a new set of needs and aspirations into facts.

17e Does State action blunt individual enterprise?

L.T. Hobhouse, *Liberalism* (1911), pp. 154–64.

If the State does for the individual what he ought to do for himself what will be the effect on character, initiative, enterprise? It is a question now not of freedom, but of responsibility ... and in respect of which opinion has undergone a remarkable change .... On all sides we find the State making active provision for the poorer classes, and not by any means for the destitute alone. We find it educating the children, providing medical inspection, authorizing the feeding of the necessitous at the expense of the ratepayers, helping them to obtain employment through free Labour Exchanges, seeking to organize the labour market with a view to the mitigation of unemployment, and providing old age pensions for all whose incomes fall below thirteen shillings a week, without exacting any contribution. Now, in all this, we may well ask, is the State going forward blindly on the paths of broad and genèrous but unconsidered charity? Is it and can it remain indifferent to the effect on individual initiative and personal or parental responsibility? Or may we suppose that the wiser heads are well aware of what they are about, have looked at the matter on all sides, and are guided by a reasonable conception of the duty of the State and the responsibilities of the individual?

We said ... that it was the function of the State to secure the conditions upon which mind and character may develop themselves. Similarly we may say now that the function of the State is to secure conditions upon which its citizens are able to win by their own efforts all that is necessary to a full civic efficiency. It is not for the State to feed, house, or clothe them. It is for the State to take care that the economic conditions are such that the normal man who is not defective in mind or body or will can by useful labour feed, house, and clothe himself and his family. The 'right to work' and the right to a 'living wage' are just as valid as the rights of person or property. That is to say, they are integral conditions of a good social order ....

If this view of the duty of the State and the right of the workman is coming to prevail, it is owing partly to an enhanced sense of common responsibility, and partly to the teaching of experience .... He owes the State the duty of industriously working for himself and his family .... On the other hand society owes to him the means of maintaining a civilized standard of life, and this debt is not adequately discharged by leaving him to secure such wages as he can in the higgling of the market.

17f   Tory reaction to the growing powers of the State

Hugh Cecil, *Conservatism* (1912), pp. 195–8.

It is ... important to emphasise that a policy of State interference is not, as such, alien from Conservatism. The questions that arise as to the respective spheres of the State and the individual cannot, in short, be answered by Conservatives with any general answer. The only proposition of a general character that can be laid down is that the State must not treat individuals unjustly, that is, must not inflict upon them any undeserved injury. This condition granted, any scheme for enlarging the function of the State must be judged by Conservatives merely on its merits without reference to any general formula, but from a standpoint prudently distrustful of the untried, and preferring to develop what exists rather than to demolish and reconstruct. Conservative social reform need not, therefore, proceed on purely individualist lines. There is no antithesis between Conservatism and Socialism, or even between Conservatism and Liberalism. Subject to the counsels of prudence and to a preference for what exists and has been tried over the unknown, Conservatives have no difficulty in welcoming the social activity of the State. The point which principally distinguishes their attitude from that of other political parties is a rigorous adherence to justice. This involves resistance to any measure which would impoverish classes or individuals by depriving them of all or even of a considerable fraction of what they possess. It is so plain that to take what one man has and give it to another is unjust, even though the first man be rich and the second poor, that it is surprising that legislative measures which consist essentially in such transfers should ever be advocated or defended .... To carry out ... the enrichment of the poor by impoverishment of the rich, even if it were practically an efficient policy, would not be just. But in fact, such a measure would be as unworkable as it is immoral. The apprehension of confiscation would oblige people to export or to conceal their wealth, and the uncertainty whether the accumulations of wealth in the future would be respected, would be fatal to the enterprise and confidence that enable commerce and industry to prosper .... Conservatives thus support measures of social reform as cordially as any political school but more scrupulously than some.

17g 'The Reality of Social Progress'

Nation, 8 November 1913.

... We have recovered a belief in the power and the duty of government as a powerful adjutant in the work of social progress, which was conspicuously lacking a generation ago.

The Trade Boards Act and Coal Mines Acts, and the new proposals for a state-fixed minimum for agricultural labor, illustrated better than anything else the new and almost revolutionary faith in the power of public policy to cure poverty, put down overcrowding and insanitary housing, provide against sickness, old age, disablement and other powerful emergencies of working class life. The paralysing fears of business men and politicians, as to any effective control of industrial conditions and the public expenditure required for such improvements, are yielding before a wiser understanding of the economy of efficient workers and of the adaptability of business enterprise. Full security of regular employment is as yet very far from being attained. But unemployment insurance, the process of decasualization, advisory committees in touch with school authorities, and the whole policy of Labor Exchanges, are making substantial advances to security. Education, Housing, Insurance, Town-planning, not to mention the less conspicuous but important labor of Guilds of Help and Social Welfare Councils, are moving, not in two or three, but in scores of ways, for the actual improvement of the conditions of working class life. There is a new reality in the term Public Health, and the results of the campaign against tuberculosis come home in reduced death-rates, the enlarging faith in preventive and corrective powers of medical science sustain our general confidence in progress.

Hardly less instructive is the evidence of activity in the development of the natural resources and the general industry of the nation .... It means that in spite of all suspicions of bureaucracy and of all preferences for purely private enterprise, the collective life of the whole people is beginning to seek a larger and more varied expression .... It seems quite evident to us that in a few years' time our railways and our mineral resources, most of the houses in our villages, and in the outlying, residential sections of our towns, will have passed from private into public possession.

18 The concept of national efficiency

Arguably, the single most important precondition for the spate of social reforms between 1905 and 1914 was fear of the consequences of an unfit and debilitated population. The revelations of Booth and Rowntree, and even more the physical condition of the working men who offered themselves for service in the Boer War between 1899 and 1902 alarmed many influential people. Fears were expressed for the future of the British Empire if its stock in the Mother Country had sunk so low. In this way, the causes of Imperialism and Social Reform came to be linked.

Arnold White (1848–1925), no deep thinker, but a polemicist of some skill, had considerable success with his *Efficiency and Empire* which voiced Darwinian fears about the poor physical condition of the British working man (18a). The theme was taken up by Maj.-Gen. Sir Frederick Maurice (1841–1912) who testified to the poor quality of army recruits (18b). His evidence that only two of every five men who offered themselves for recruitment were considered fit soldiers two years later excited much fevered comment. Thomas Horsfall (1841–1932), the Manchester educational reformer and town planner, was one of the first to argue that compulsory national service would improve the national stock. Conscription would reveal the full extent of the 'deterioration' problem, so that appropriate remedies could be applied (18c). Horsfall's major concern was to improve the condition of the working classes, but many others who advocated national service did so in the belief that the efficacy of the Empire depended on a drilled and disciplined soldiery. The early failures in South Africa strengthened this view.

The widespread concern aroused by these writings led to the establishment in December 1903 of an Inter-Departmental Committee of Home and Education Departments and the Local Government Board to determine from the available evidence the extent of the problem, and to propose solutions. The Committee met under the Chairmanship of Almeric Fitzroy (1851–1935), Secretary to the Privy Council. The dreadfully low standards of health in many large cities was fully confirmed by many inspectors, including Dr Alfred Eichholz, Medical Inspector for the London borough of Lambeth. The Committee found no evidence of progressive physical deterioration (18d); but it made many far-reaching recommendations, particularly affecting the welfare of children. These included school medical inspections, free school meals for the destitute and training in mothercraft. Many of the major Liberal Government reforms stem directly from the conclusions of this Conservative-appointed committee.

Suggestions for further reading

G. R. Searle, *The Quest for National Efficiency* (1971) and B. Semmel, *Imperialism and Social Reform* (1960), though neither is comprehensive.

18a   A woeful workforce

Arnold White, *Efficiency and Empire* (1901), pp. 100–3.

Increase in numbers is commonly regarded as a sign of national progress, and as evidence of the soundness of the State. Recent growth of population in the United Kingdom, however, is actually a symptom of political decline. A vast population has been created by the factory and industrial systems, the majority of which is incapable of bearing arms.

Spectacled school-children hungry, strumous, and epileptic, grow into consumptive bridegrooms and scrofulous brides, and are assured beforehand of the blessing of the Church, the aid of the compassionate, and such solace as hospitals provided wholesale by unknown donors can supply. If a voice be raised in protest against the unhealthy perversion of the command, 'Be ye fruitful and multiply' it is drowned in a chorus of sickly emotion....

In the Manchester district 11,000 men offered themselves for war service between the outbreak of hostilities in October 1899 and July 1900. Of this number 8000 were found to be physically unfit to carry a rifle and stand the fatigues of discipline. Of the 3000 who were accepted only 1200 attained the moderate standard of muscular power and chest measurement required by the military authorities. In other words, two out of every three men willing to bear arms in the Manchester district are virtually invalids.

18b   Inadequate recruits to defend the nation

Maj.-Gen. Sir Frederick Maurice, 'National Health: A Soldier's Study', *Contemporary Review*, vol. lxxxiii (1903), pp.41–56.

During nearly the last seven years it has been one of my duties about once a month to visit the Herbert Hospital for the purpose of sanctioning the discharge from the Army of men who had been brought forward by a 'Medical Board' as no longer fit for H. M. Service. I very soon found that an alarming proportion of these men had involved the State in considerable expense, but had given no return ... out of every five men who wish to enlist and primarily offer themselves for enlistment you will find that by the end of two years' service there are only two men remaining in the Army as effective soldiers .... Surely ... it is worth while to enquire whether there are not removable causes which tend to produce this appalling disproportion between the willing and the physically competent, and what in the Army we briefly call 'the fit'. But there is another consideration which to my mind is even more serious. Whatever steps are taken by increasing the inducements to enlistment or by any form of pressure, compulsory or otherwise, to raise the standard of the Army either in numbers or physique seem to me to be only like more careful methods of extracting cream from milk. The more carefully you skim the milk the poorer is the residue of skimmed milk. I think it is safe to say that no nation was ever yet for any long time great and free when the army it put into the field no longer represented its own virility and manhood....

Does my ugly figure of the five to two imply that the class from which we have hitherto drawn the bulk of its defenders is from some cause or causes ceasing to supply the numbers of healthy men that it used to do, or at all events to such an extent suffering in its virility that it cannot now supply them? There are certain factors in our modern life that may tend in that direction: the continuous rush of the people from the country districts into the towns, the disappearance of the class of Yeomen, the general depression of the agricultural districts, the fact—to which Mr. Booth so strongly testifies—that it is capacity or skill alone which in some form or other commands or ever can command an adequate wage in the towns; and therefore the enormously strong presumption that neither the unskilled labourer who has been tempted into the towns, nor the hereditary townsman who, after two or three generations, has deteriorated in physical vigour, will be able to rear a healthy family.

18c   Conscription as an ameliorating factor

T. C. Horsfall, *The Relation of National Service to the Welfare of the Community* (Manchester, 1904), pp. 28–32.

The establishment of general military service in this country would do much towards ensuring the improvements in the state of our towns, in the position of our working classes....

1. The annual examination of all our young men who reached the age for military service would give to everyone information, which no one at present possesses, respecting the true condition of our people....

2. A system of general service would show that a large number of young men were physically unfit to bear arms .... Who that knows how common kindness and good feeling are among English people will doubt that ... a very large proportion of the hale and well-to-do members of the Service would have the desire for social reform ... created in them by simple knowledge of the evil case of their fellow-countrymen, greatly strengthened by the feeling of comradeship which would be created by common service.

3. If all boys of all classes knew that they must ... so train their bodies as to enable them to become stalwart defenders of their country ... a new strong feeling of love towards the common country would soon be created, which would make all classes more willing to bear burdens of service for its good when they returned to civil life.

4. General service could not fail to improve the position of the working class as a whole greatly .... Most of these men ... would be physically unfit for service, though some ... would be fit, and the large proportion of rejec-

tions among them would compel the community to improve the conditions under which they lived, and to prevent, by good physical training in
schools, by continuation classes, by the feeding of hungry children, and the
discouragement of drinking the creation of any more poor creatures of the
kind. By these measures, and the training in common action which all
who served in the army would receive, the power of the working classes to
work together for ends desired by them, and the knowledge possessed by
them respecting the conditions necessary for their welfare, would be very
greatly increased.

18d   Generalized physical degeneracy denied

Report of the Inter-Departmental Committee on Physical Deterioration,
Cmnd. 2175, 1904, pp. 13-14.

It may be as well to state at once that the impressions gathered from the
great majority of the witnesses examined do not support the belief that
there is any general progressive physical deterioration.

The evidence of Dr. Eichholz contains a summary ... so admirably
epitomising the results of a comprehensive survey of the whole subject,
that the Committee cannot do better than reproduce it ... :-

1. I draw a clear distinction between physical degeneracy on the one
hand and inherited retrogressive deterioration on the other.

2. With regard to physical degeneracy, the children frequenting the
poorer schools of London and the large towns betray a most serious
condition of affairs, calling for ameliorative and arrestive measures, the
most impressive features being the apathy of parents as regards the school,
the lack of parental care of children, the poor physique, powers of
endurance, and educational attainments of the children attending school.

3. Nevertheless, even in the poorer districts there exist schools of a type
above the lowest, which show a marked upward and improving tendency,
physically and educationally—though the rate of improvement would be
capable of considerable acceleration under suitable measures.

4. In the better districts of the towns there exist public elementary

schools frequented by children not merely equal but often superior in physique and attainments to rural children....

5. While there are, unfortunately, very abundant signs of physical defect traceable to neglect, poverty and ignorance, it is not possible to obtain any satisfactory or conclusive evidence of hereditary physical deterioration—that is to say, deterioration of a gradual retrogressive permanent nature, affecting one generation more acutely than the previous....

6. In every case of alleged progressive hereditary deterioration among the children frequenting an elementary school, it is found that the neighbourhood has suffered by the migration of the better artisan class, or by the influx of worse population from elsewhere.

7. Other than the well-known specifically hereditary diseases which *affect poor and well-to-do alike*, there appears to be very little real evidence on the pre-natal side to account for the widespread physical degeneracy among the poorer population. There is, accordingly, every reason to anticipate RAPID amelioration of physique so soon as improvement occurs in external conditions, particularly as regards food, clothing, overcrowding, cleanliness, drunkenness, and the spread of common practical knowledge of home management.

8. In fact, all evidence points to *active, rapid improvement, bodily and mental, in the worst districts*, so soon as they are exposed to better circumstances, even the weaker children recovering at a later age from the evil effects of infant life.

9. Compulsory school attendance, the more rigorous scheduling of children of school age, and the abolition of school fees in elementary schools, have swept into the schools an annually increasing proportion of children during the last thirty years. These circumstances are largely responsible for focussing public notice on the severer cases of physical impairment.

19 A fairer State: redistributive taxation

If large schemes of social reform were to be put in hand, it was obvious that they must be financed. Many progressives around the turn of the century accepted that taxation could, in a limited sense, redistribute wealth for the greater good of society at large. Herbert Samuel (1870–1963), later to be an influential figure as the Liberal party declined, and its leader from 1931–5, argued in 1902 that State expenditure on education, housing and poverty relief benefited not only the immediate recipients but the whole community by ensuring a more efficient and contented workforce (19a). His mentor, J. A. Hobson, however, had come to accept redistributive taxation not on grounds of social welfare, but because it offered a solution to the underconsumption of economic resources.

The Liberal party came to power in December 1905 with a political philosophy much less clearly articulated than its subsequent achievements in the field of social welfare might indicate. Its legislation, however, combined with the need to counter an assumed German arms race, made increased government expenditure inevitable. As a Treasury Memorandum (19c) indicated, a higher level of taxation on large incomes was considered the most expedient method of raising the revenue. Those taxed would complain, but they would still pay. David Lloyd George (1863–1945) followed this line of reasoning as Chancellor of the Exchequer from 1908 to 1915, and his famous 1909 Budget introduced the Super-Tax for the first time (19d). To raise the £16,000,000 necessary to finance old-age pensions and the battleship programme, Lloyd George also increased death duties (first introduced by Sir William Harcourt, 1827–1904, in 1894), introduced new revenue duties on land, new taxes on petrol and cars—still very much the playthings of the rich—and higher rates on tobacco and spirits. The budget was avowedly redistributive, and gained the guarded approval of Socialists like Philip Snowden (1864–1937) for being so (19e). Predictably, and intentionally, it roused the House of Lords to fury. The Lords' rejection of the budget precipitated the constitutional crisis which it took two general elections in 1910 and a Parliament Act in 1911 to resolve.

Most Conservatives had a natural dislike of redistributive taxation. Not only were many of them rich, but they argued—and still argue—that the device was both unfair and led to diminution of effort by the talented, whose efforts are crucial to the nation's well-being. Tory reaction to the problem was mixed. Joseph Chamberlain, fertile as ever, offered one possible solution. The policy of imperial preference and tariff reform, which he advocated with characteristic vigour from 1903 onwards, could finance welfare schemes without recourse to higher rates of direct taxation (19b). His solution got over one huge Tory dislike—direct taxation—but it raised another. Try as he might, Chamberlain could not shake off the taunt that trade restrictions would load the workman's budget with higher food prices. The Liberal spectre of the 'dear loaf' proved a decisive vote-winner in 1906. Many Tories refused to accept tariff reform, and some were prepared to countenance limited redistributive taxation in order to finance welfare schemes.

Suggestions for further reading

H. V. Emy, *Liberals, Radicals and Social Politics, 1892–1914* (1973) is useful on Liberal taxation ideas. On the Tory dilemma, see Julian Amery, *Joseph Chamberlain and the Tariff Reform Campaign* (2 vols, 1969).

19a   Improved services benefit all classes

Herbert Samuel, *Liberalism* (1902), pp. 183–4

It is little better than robbery, we are sometimes told, to tax men merely according to their ability to pay. The State renders certain services; it is those who benefit by the services who ought to bear the cost of them. To take money from one class in order to spend it on another is obviously wrong. 'Why', says a man of the middle class 'should I be rated in order to provide Board Schools which my children will never enter, to maintain free libraries which I shall never use, to improve districts in which I do not live, or to relieve a destitution into which I am not likely to fall? ...'

Liberals answer that all national expenditure which is wise benefits the nation...

A grant, for example, is made for establishing technical schools for artizans. Is it the artizans who are to be considered the beneficiaries and who ought to be taxed for the purposes of the grant? They receive, it is true, a training free of cost, and through their greater skill are able to earn higher wages. Clearly they benefit. But then the employers also benefit; they are provided with more skilful workmen and are able to make higher profits. And surely the public at large benefit as well, for the goods they need are better made and are perhaps lowered in price, and the national trade, in which all classes are interested, is maintained and encouraged. Who can tell to which of the three the advantage is greatest, and what proportion of the cost, on the principle of benefit, each of them should bear?

Let the man of means who objects to see his rates and taxes spent on schemes of social improvement and thinks he gains no advantage in return, consider what would be the effect on his own daily life, and on his wider interests if that expenditure were stopped .... Is he an employer of labour? His work-people would be of a low type, inefficient and careless, and if he is competing in business with the manufacturers of Germany and the United States, he would find himself heavily handicapped. Is he a householder? The servants in his home, the nurses of his children, would be drawn from an ignorant and degraded class. A consumer, the goods he bought would be dear or badly made. A citizen, he would be out-voted by a discontented, ill-informed and perhaps revolutionary electorate ... he would speedily find in how many ways his own welfare was dependent on the welfare of the poorer classes, and how large was the benefit he had indirectly gained from the efforts of the State to raise the people. He would soon be compelled to confess that he also drew no small advantage from public expenditure on social reform.

19b   Protection may provide the funds for social reform

Joseph Chamberlain, speech to the Conservative Constitutional Club, 26
June 1903, in Julian Amery, *Joseph Chamberlain and the Tariff Reform
Campaign* (1969), pp. 267–8.

When I am told that our prosperity is bound up with free imports, I ask ...
what is our prosperity? Is it the fact, as we are told on the high authority of
Sir Henry Campbell-Bannerman, is it the fact that 12,000,000 of our
people, more than one fourth of our whole population, are always on the
verge of starvation? Is that a proof of the blessings of free imports?
.... The greatest boon that could be conferred upon the working people
of this country was such a reform as would ensure every industrious man
full and constant employment at fair wages. Do free imports secure this
result? ...

You know I have suggested ... that inasmuch as any alteration of our
fiscal system must necessarily largely increase the sums received in the shape
of indirect taxation, a portion of these sums, at any rate, should be applied
in order to provide old-age pensions for the poor. (Hear, hear)

Thereupon I am told that this is a most immoral proposition—that it is a
discreditable attempt to bribe the working classes of this country. That
criticism is hasty, and it is harsh. Those who make it have altogether
forgotten my past in this matter. I entered upon an investigation of the
subject many years ago; it has always been near to my heart. I believe that
such a system would be of immense advantage to the people. I have earnestly desired to make it successful .... As long as we depend so much on
our direct taxation, as long as there is an inclination to put every increased
expense on this direct taxation, I say it would be very unfair to think even
of old-age pensions if we were to put an enormous increase on the payers
of income tax, many of whom are already sufficiently straitened in the
condition of life in which they find themselves (Cheers) .... Was it not
natural when ... I thought it was probable that large sums might be at the
disposal of any future Chancellor of the Exchequer, that I should put in a

word for my favourite hobby, if you like to call it so, and that I should
ask the working classes ... to consider whether it would not be better for
them to take the money which is theirs in the shape of a deferred payment
and a provision for their old age rather than in the shape of an
immediate advantage?... That is a matter which will come later. When
we have the money then will be the time to say what we shall do with it;
and if the working classes refuse to take my advice, if they prefer this
immediate advantage, why it stands to reason that if, for instance, they
are called upon to pay 3*d*. a week additional on the cost of their bread, they
may be fully, entirely relieved by a reduction of a similar amount in the
cost of their tea, their sugar, or even of their tobacco. (Hear, hear.) In
this case, what is taken out of one pocket would be put back into the other.
There is no working man in the kingdom ... who need fear under the
system I propose that without his good will his cost of living will be
increased by a single farthing .... I believe there never was a grosser
imposture than the cry of the dear loaf.

19c   A civil servant deploys the case for progressive direct taxation

Treasury memorandum, 26 February 1907. Public Record Office,
CAB/37/87/22.

The present Government have recognized the pressing need for social
reforms which must entail heavy expenditure. No one now expects that
reductions of existing expenditure will provide the necessary means ....
The time has gone by when it was possible to look to indirect taxes,
such as those on beer and spirits, to supply the want of funds. The country
refuses any longer to drink itself out of its financial straits. Unless the
whole system of our taxation is to be recast, the solution must be found
in the increase of direct taxation....

The only feasible remedy, consistent with the maintenance of the
present system for the general income tax, is the supertax on large incomes.
The objections that can be urged against such a tax are undoubtedly
imposing   in   appearance.   The   expert   Department   pronounces
unhesitatingly against it. No precedent can be adduced from the practice of

any other country for such a degree of taxation on large incomes as would be required if the supertax is to make a serious contribution to revenue. The supertax would be levied on net income, while the general tax is levied on gross income, so that an entirely novel principle of assessment has to be introduced. Our business system is so complex ... that a complete system of check would be impossible to devise, and the opportunities of evasion would be manifold.

Yet if we are content to inaugurate a supertax on a small and manageable scale, hoping thereby to gain the knowledge and to establish the machinery for its extension when necessary, it is far from certain that these objections are insuperable. We may contemplate, as a beginning, a supertax applicable only to incomes of £5,000 and upwards, the number of which is estimated not to exceed 10,000. The rate of supertax might be limited to 3*d.* in the £ on incomes between £5,000 and (say) £20,000, with an additional 3*d.* on any excess over £20,000.

The objections to supertax are mainly based upon the assumption that the people subject to the tax will regard it as unjust, and will do all in their power to evade it. This idea does not appear to take sufficiently into account the disposition of an Englishman to respect the law because it is the law. It also ignores the fact that the supertax is imposed as a measure of justice. The persons subject to it would be all people of educated intelligence, fully qualified to appreciate the reasons which make it equitable that they should contribute to the Income Tax in a higher proportion than those who are less fortunate. If the supertax in the beginning be fixed at such a moderate rate as has been suggested, there seems little reason to suppose that people of position and reputation will incur the risks of evasion in order to escape a burden which they cannot deny to be justly their due.

19d   Lloyd George introduces supertax

D. Lloyd George, *The People's Budget* (1909), pp. 22–9.

The rate of income tax under the present law is absolutely uniform upon all incomes in excess of £2,000 a year.... The introduction of a complete scheme of graduation, applicable to all incomes ... would require an entire reconstruction of the administrative machinery of the tax, including in all probability the abandonment to a very large extent of the principle of collection at the source upon which the productivity of the tax so largely depends. It would create for the administrative Department a series of problems which, if not insoluble, could at any rate scarcely hope to obtain a satisfactory solution in a year when other taxation of a novel character must necessarily claim a large part of its attentions.

The imposition of a super-tax, however, upon large incomes ... is a more practicable proposition, and it is upon this basis that I intend to proceed....

While ... I propose to limit the tax to incomes exceeding £5,000, I propose to levy it upon the amount by which such incomes exceed £3,000, and at the rate of 6*d.* in the £ upon the amount of such excess. An income of £5,001 will thus pay in supertax 6*d.* in the £ on £2,001, the equivalent of an addition to the existing income tax of rather less than $2^{1}/_{2}d.$ in the £, and an income of £6,000 the equivalent of an additional 3*d.*

The equivalent of an extra 4*d.* (of total income tax of 1*s.* 6*d.* in the £) will only be reached when the total income amounts to £9,000 and of 5*d.* not until the total income reaches £18,000.

19e   Socialist reaction to the people's Budget

Philip Snowden, 'The Budget', *Socialist Review*, vol. iii (1909), pp. 254–6.

The purpose of Socialism being to get social wealth for social use, it follows that any proposal which will secure some portion of social wealth for social use is in accord with Socialist principles. There are two ways by which that purpose can be pursued: by transferring particular industries or services to the public, and by taking, by taxation, portions of the social wealth which individuals appropriate as rent, interest, and profit....

This budget ... to a greater extent than any former Budget, applies the Socialist idea that taxation should appropriate socially created wealth .... This is the feature of the Budget which justifies Socialist support. In each of the four proposals for increased direct taxation ... we have the taxation imposed because of the special nature of the particular form of property.

The four proposals to which I refer are the Super Tax, the Estate Duties, the Licence Duties, and the Land Taxes. The Super Tax is the practical recognition of the obligation of the rich to contribute in proportion to their means to the cost of dealing with the poverty in the community. The same remark applies to the Estate Duties. The very satisfactory increases in the rates imposed on the larger estates made by Mr. Asquith two years ago and by Mr. Lloyd George in this Budget are evidence of the growth of the opinion that great wealth must contribute more generously towards public services. The proposed increases in the liquor licences are pure instances of the taxation of social values....

The taxes on undeveloped land and upon reversions are also of the nature of the taxation of social values for public use. These taxes are selected to help to satisfy the Chancellor's need because the form of values to be taxed is declared to be socially created. This is distinctly Socialistic in both theory and practice....

A Budget must be judged not only by the test of how it raises the money, but by how it proposes to spend it. Apart from the increases in the Navy expenditure, Socialists may regard the destination of the taxation with every satisfaction. Two-thirds of it goes to Old Age Pensions; a considerable sum to the scheme of road improvements; and the surplus, which will probably be considerable, to a National Development Fund, which is a proposal full of great possibilities.

20 Education and children

Education beyond the elementary level envisaged by the 1870 Act became a live, and highly controversial, issue in this period. Certain school boards had begun to offer courses of more than an elementary nature in 'Higher Grade Schools'. In addition, technical education was provided by some county councils under the Technical Instruction Act of 1889. The Royal Commission which met under the chairmanship of the Oxford jurist James Bryce (1838–1922) wished to expand opportunities in secondary and technical education, since greater specialist skills were necessary to meet the economic challenge of the United States and Germany. Alarmed by the patchwork nature of secondary education provision, the Commission recommended centralized supervision (20a).

The voluntary schools, overwhelmingly the responsibility of the Church of England, were unable to compete with the greater resources of the city board schools and also looked to centralized supervision for their protection. In addition, they probably suffered the more from the vagaries of the pupil–teacher system, where too often facts were taught without understanding (20b). Although they still taught more than half the elementary school pupils, they were losing ground and nonconformists looked forward with glee to the time when they would be swallowed up everywhere but in the remoter rural areas. The 1902 Education Act resolved the voluntarists' problem, by giving them additional financial protection from public funds.

The true architect of the Act, R.L. Morant (1863–1920), an official in the Education Department, had waged a successful battle against the legality of the Higher Grade Schools, since they did not offer strictly elementary education. With the status of these prize blooms of the school board garden in doubt, Morant could move to drafting an Act which both rationalized the provision of secondary education, as advocated by Bryce, and preserved the voluntary schools. The 1902 Act dismantled the school boards, and established the recognizably modern pattern by which county councils became the education authorities for both primary and secondary education (20c). These councils also funded the voluntary schools, since while Church authorities provided the buildings, current expenses were met from the rates. By a crucial concession, voluntary schools retained their control over the appointment of teachers. The schools had already been supported from taxes in many cases, so to this extent nonconformist and progressive howls of anguish over a 'Church on the rates' were misplaced (20d). This concealed, however, a deeper anguish. Nonconformists had hoped to see the back of voluntaryism, and felt disadvantaged by it, particularly in areas where the only school was a voluntary one.

No Liberal Government could have passed an Act so offensive to the nonconformists, and in 1906 an attempt was made to redress the balance which was thwarted by the House of Lords. Some progressives, however, notably Sidney Webb, applauded the Act on grounds of rationality and efficiency. Under the able direction of Morant, Permanent Secretary of the Board of Education from 1903, provision of secondary education proceeded at a sedate pace. The wider availability of 'free-place' secondary education after 1907 enabled more poor children to get a better schooling, but the bias towards middle-class children was very marked (20g). In Leicester, a city of 227,000 people in 1901, only 953 children attended State secondary schools in 1910.

The recommendations of the Committee on Physical Deterioration led directly to the Education (Provision of Meals) Act in 1906. It was hardly a Liberal measure, having been introduced initially by the newly elected Labour MP for Westhoughton, the Carpenters' leader William T. Wilson (1855–1921). It permitted local authorities to provide meals for children in elementary schools, which could be paid for either by parents, by private enterprise, or by a half-penny rate. No treasury money was made available until 1914, by which time only cautious moves had been made by most councils. The measure was much more modest than Wilson had intended, but it still raised the ire of individualists and private benefactors like Sir Arthur Clay (1842–1928) who believed that it would weaken that spirit of self-reliance which was essential for real progress (20e). These years also witnessed the beginnings of an effective system of school medical inspection, smuggled into the regulations by Morant, and the passing of a Children Act (8 Edw. VII c. 67) in 1908 which codified existing legislation on children's rights, and extended protection available to them from parental neglect and the full rigours of the adult law (20f).

Suggestions for further reading

J. Lawson and H. Silver, *A Social History of Education in England* (1973), chapter 10, supplements the Simon volume cited in section 14. On welfare services for children see B.B. Gilbert, *The Evolution of National Insurance in Britain* (1966), chapter 3.

20a   The need to rationalize the provision of secondary education

The Bryce Commission Report on Secondary Education, *Parliamentary Papers*, 1895, vol. xliii, pp. 17–18, 256–61.

... there is one feature in the growing concern of the State with education which must not be here overlooked. The growth has not been either continuous or coherent; i.e. it does not represent a series of logical or even connected sequences .... Each [agency] has remained in its working isolated and unconnected with the rest. The problems which Secondary Education presents have been approached from different sides at different times, and with different views and aims. The Charity Commissioners have had little to do with the Education Department and still less with the Service and Art Department. Even the Borough Councils have, to a large extent, acted independently of the school boards .... This isolation and this independence, if they seem to witness to the rich variety of our educational life, and to the active spirit which pervades it, will nevertheless prepare the observer to expect the usual results of dispersed and unconnected forces, needless competition between the different agencies, and a frequent overlapping of effort, with much consequent waste of money, of time, and of labour....

Recommendations

So far from desiring that Secondary Education should be a matter for a Department of State to control, we propose to leave the initiative in public action to local authorities .... We conceive, in short, that some central authority is required, not in order to control, but rather to supervise the Secondary Education of the country, not to override or supersede local action, but to endeavour to bring about among the various agencies which provide that education a harmony and co-operation which are now wanting....

The central authority ought to consist of a Department of the Executive

Government, presided over by a Minister responsible to Parliament....

The Central Office may, when it considers that a statement shows the provision of Secondary Education in any area to be defective, require the Local Authority for that area to take steps for making a due provision, and obtain from time to time from the Local Authority an account of the action it has taken for that purpose, and may, if it deems that action insufficient, continue to require further action, until the provisions made appear to it to be satisfactory.

20b The deficiencies of the pupil–teacher system

Diocesan Inspector's Report to the Bishop of Durham on the work of Church schools, Durham Record Office, EP/Wi 92.

I have sometimes felt that more has been done in the way of ensuring sound teaching for the future by ten minutes' conversation with the Teachers than by an hour's examination of the children. May I point out that here lies the best field of valuable and lasting works on the part of the clergy? Too often the Clergy may be found regularly making themselves responsible for a definite portion of the syllabus of one particular class, but not in touch with the religious teaching of the rest of the School. In the great majority of cases certificated Teachers need little assistance .... But the great army of Uncertificated and Pupil Teachers—how much trouble they would be saved, and how much more valuable would their work be, if they were in the habit of consulting with one who should be an expert in religious teaching. A Teacher, for instance, has the Miracle of 'The Feeding of the Five Thousand' marked down on the syllabus. On the inspection day a few questions elicit the fact that the only moral lessons drawn from the narrative are (a) always say grace before meat (b) never waste anything. A chat after the examination made it clear that the children have not forgotten, for they have never been taught any further spiritual lessons in connexion with the miracle.

20c   A defence of the 1902 Education Act

A.J. Balfour, speech to Liberal Unionists in Manchester, 14 October 1902, reported in *The Times*, 15 October 1902

... the existing educational system is chaotic, is ineffectual, is utterly behind the age, makes us the laughing stock of every advanced nation in Europe and America (cheers) ... there is at this moment in England no public authority which is capable of supplying secondary education in its true sense, and when you come to that higher primary education which has been illegally carried on by the Board schools, though I heartily sympathise with the objects they had in view (hear, hear), when you come to deal with them ... under the existing system, between the corporation on one side and the Board schools on the other, you have inevitable overlapping .... And when ... I come to that primary education which is the necessity of every class in the community and to which we justly desire every man in the land from the highest to the lowest to subject his children, what do we find? Under the existing system we find Board schools which are in no relation either to the voluntary schools on the one side, or to the secondary schools and higher technical schools on the other, and we find the voluntary schools, educating, remember more than half the children of this country (cheers) we find them in many cases starved for want of funds and incapable of carrying out to perfection, at all events, the greatest duties entrusted to them by the community ....

And what is our solution? ... in substance it is ... that we should put all the branches of education of which I have spoken under the control and supervision of those great public assemblies, the borough councils and the county councils of the country. That is the central principle of the Bill .... We want those great municipal and county authorities to co-ordinate the higher with the lower education, to provide secondary education and higher elementary education without overlapping .... We want this municipal and county authority to provide the machinery for training teachers, and we want it to control all the schools so far as secular education is concerned.

20d   The 1902 proposals condemned

Meeting of Londoners called by the London Progressive Education Council, 14 October 1902, reported in *The Times*, 15 October 1902.

Principal Fairbairn ... moved the following resolution: 'That this meeting of citizens of London declares its adhesion to the principle of efficient, free, and unsectarian education in schools maintained at the public expense and managed by the directly-elected representatives of the people; and calls upon all friends of education to use every effort to ensure the withdrawal of the Education Bill now before Parliament.' He said that the essence of this Bill was that it was unjust, not simply to Nonconformists, but to English citizens; and if the Government dared to carry through a Bill based on injustice, it was a thing that England would not stand. (Cheers). If there was to be education, the people must first find the means, and they must stand fast to the old English principle that those who found the means must hold the purse-strings. This Bill was an adroit attempt to give private schools public support and to retain instruction under the public authority, but leave the denomination to appoint the teacher and manage the religious affairs of the school. He would ask a plain question—'Can you have secular instruction through an ecclesiastical instructor without its being ecclesiastically tainted or tinged?' (Hear, hear)

20e   The debilitating effects of free school meals

Sir Arthur Clay, 'The Feeding of School Children', in J. St L. Strachey, *The Manufacture of Paupers* (1906), pp. 15–19.

The demand that the State should assume the duty of feeding schoolchildren has of late been persistently urged …. The demand is supported by the assertion that large numbers of school-children are 'underfed' and are thus incapacitated from receiving instruction….

There is no generally accepted definition of the word 'underfed' …. If, however, the term is taken as synonymous with 'hunger' the sensational figures published and constantly quoted by public speakers are grossly exaggerated …. It is malnutrition, not hunger, that is so frequent a cause of child distress, and this trouble is by no means confined to the children in the elementary schools. The evil is not quantitative but qualitative. The mischief begins at birth, and the only effectual cure is the better instruction of mothers in the judicious feeding of their children….

There can be no reasonable doubt that if a system of State-aided feeding is once adopted, the complete maintenance of children by the public, with all the far-reaching and radical changes which it involves, can only be a matter of time. At present there is no sign that this country desires so vast an alteration in its social system, and such public support as is given to this measure is, for the most part, given in ignorance of the consequences certain to follow upon its acceptance. Apart, however, from this danger, the immediate result would be a heavy addition to the burden under which rate and tax payers are now labouring. The cost of school meals, possibly moderate at first, would rapidly become very large. The proffered supply is certain to create a continually increasing demand….

The financial burden … is, however, by no means the most serious objection to this measure …. To feed a child is to give relief to its parents, and the effect must be to undermine their independence and self-reliance, and to give to their children an object-lesson in the evasion of responsibility which will never be forgotten, and which will bear fruit when they in their turn become parents.

20f   The Children's Charter explained

'The Children Act—What it is and Does', *Liberal Monthly*, vol. iv
(February 1909), p. 5.

1. Little children who are put out to nurse away from their parents will
be more fully looked after by the local authorities, and the law for
preventing the abuses of baby-farming is strengthened in many
particulars.

2. Among the 'Homes' supported by charitable subscriptions in which
orphan children are kept, it is believed that there are a few in which grave
evils prevail. There is at present no power for any one to enter these places
to see what is going on except with a magistrate's warrant. The Children
Act sets up a system of inspection.

3. Over 1,000 little children are burnt to death every year through
unguarded fires, and an even larger number are seriously injured. In
future, parents must have guards on their grates, or must take other
precautions for the safety of their children, or they will be liable to a fine if
death or serious injury occurs.

4. Many hundreds of infants, again, are overlaid in bed by drunken
parents. There will be a penalty in such cases also....

7. Children up to the age of fourteen will not be allowed to be in any
part of a public-house used as a drinking bar or mainly for the
consumption of alcoholic liquor.

8. It is forbidden to give alcohol to children under the age of five,
anywhere, except in the case of illness.

9. Tobacconists are not allowed to sell cigarettes or cigarette papers to
children apparently under the age of sixteen....

12. If the children are sent to school in a verminous condition power is
given to the school authority to have them cleansed....

14. Tens of thousands of children are brought before the magistrates
every year, mostly charged with quite petty offences. The Act requires that
these children shall be kept quite separate from older offenders and that
their cases shall be heard by a 'Juvenile Court', sitting at different time or
place from the ordinary Court.

15. Parents will be required to attend the Court when their children are charged, and they may be required to pay the fine if they have not looked after their children properly.

16. The imprisonment of children in the ordinary gaols is abolished.

17. The death sentence on children is abolished.

20g   The progress of secondary education in one city

General Report on the Public Secondary Schools in the County Borough of Leicester, Leicestershire Record Office, 19D 59/VII.148.

There are four Schools working under the Regulations of the Board, and all are now under the control of the Authority.

The numbers in the Schools ... were

	Boys	Girls	Pupil–Teachers
Wyggeston Grammar School for Boys	585	—	—
Wyggeston Grammar School for Girls	—	484	—
Alderman Newton's School	280	—	—
The Newarke Secondary School	88	200	1 male 67 female
Total	**953**	**684**	**68**

The proportion of ex-Elementary School children was as follows:—

	Per cent
Wyggeston Grammar School for Boys	48
Wyggeston Grammar School for Girls	44
Alderman Newton's School	98
The Newarke Secondary School	98

The following were the proportions of Free Scholars:—

	Per cent
Wyggeston Grammar School for Boys	31
Wyggeston Grammar School for Girls	21
Alderman Newton's School	32
The Newarke Secondary School	50

The competition for Scholarships is keen; 897 candidates presented themselves at the last examination for 100 places. At the Wyggeston Grammar School for Boys, 168 competed for 30 places; at the Wyggeston Grammar School for Girls, 405 for 17; at Alderman Newton's School, 180 for 23; and at the Newarke Secondary School 144 for 30.

Report on Newarke Secondary School, Leicester
Class in Life from which Pupils are drawn

	Percentage		Percentage
Professional	9	Public Service	10
Farmer	1	Domestic Service	2
Wholesale Traders	12	Artisans	22
Retail Traders and Contractors	24	Labourers	1
Clerks and Commercial Agents	19		

Finance
From the accounts last submitted, which owing to a necessary change in the financial year cover a period of 20 months, it appears that the cost per head of maintenance works out at slightly under £13 a year.

Nearly half the cost is defrayed by grants from the Board of Education; one moiety of the remainder is met by the income from fees and the grant from the County Authority, the other constitutes a cost to the rates, amounting in all to a trifle over £1,000 a year....

/Subject Reports/
History
The History course extends over four years. In the first three years the whole of English History from the invasion of Caesar to modern times is covered. Continental History, so far as it affects England, is also studied, and attention is given to the expansion of England, to political reform, and to commercial and industrial developments.

In the fourth year a special period is studied in more detail, together with the corresponding period of European History. The growth of the Constitution is also taken in this year.

The lessons heard were carefully prepared and well delivered, in one or two cases they partook, perhaps, a little too much of the lecture type—still in all cases many apt questions were asked, and well answered by pupils, whose interest was evidently secured....

The interest of the History teaching would be increased if occasionally illustrative extracts were read in class from books inaccessible as a rule to the pupils.

The History teaching is on sound lines, and good work is being done.

21 Housing and land reform

There were important developments in housing at this time though few of them were the result of government policy. One crucial factor was the growth of a public transport system, particularly around big cities. This enabled clerks, better-paid artisans and others to live a few miles from their place of work and commute. In the first decade of the twentieth century the geography of large cities was dramatically altered by suburban drift, as builders found it profitable to provide houses on cheaper land away from city centres (21a). In general, large centres benefited most; and many of them were able greatly to alleviate the housing crises which had blighted them in the 1880s and 1890s. Some of the more adventurous, like Sheffield, felt restricted by the cautious loans policy of the Local Government Board, which was poorly adapted to a period of housing boom (21b).

The benefits of this boom were not universal, however. In the north-east, including Newcastle, conditions were still appalling, with overcrowding figures in Northumberland and Durham between four and five times worse than the national average (21c). A large problem here was the system of tenure for colliers' cottages, which gave neither mine owners nor coal workers incentive to change. Many miners paid no rent for the tied-hovels in which they had lived most of their lives.

John Burns (1858–1943) at least recognized the problems. The Housing and Town Planning Act, for which he claimed so much (21d), achieved very little, however. The slum-clearance clauses of the 1890 Act were made binding on local authorities; authorities were urged, on the shining examples of suburbs like Bournville in Birmingham and the Hampstead Garden Suburb, to plan new developments with airy and liberally spaced accommodation. The Act was badly timed; the boom came to an end in 1910, with builders scared by the increased land duties of the previous year's budget. Local authorities as a consequence were slow to respond. By the end of 1913, fewer than 200,000 houses had been made habitable under the Act, and only just over 1,000 new dwellings had been built. Indeed, overcrowding was actually on the increase again in 1914. Nor was much town planning achieved. The real breakthrough in housing policy was not to come until 1919, when local authorities were forced to supply their own houses to remedy the deficiency, and were given government funds to enable them to do so. Until then, the inadequacies of private enterprise were being savagely exposed by overcrowding and death-rate statistics (21e).

Land reform had always been close to the heart of David Lloyd George (1863–1945), who grew up close to what he saw as landlord-exploitation. However much they alarmed traditionalist Liberals like the Lord Chancellor, R.B.S. Haldane (1856–1928), Lloyd George saw his land proposals as important vote winners when an unpopular Liberal Government faced the electorate again, as it was expected to in 1915. His aim was to prevent rural depopulation by providing, from government funds, an adequate supply both of allotments and of labourers' cottages. An all-powerful Ministry of Lands was to be charged with the task of tilting the balance decisively in favour of the tenant and the smaller rural interests (21f). The outbreak of war killed the scheme; land reform, when it came in the 1920s, owed much more to market forces and much less to government initiative than Lloyd George either expected or desired.

Suggestions for further reading

The works by Gauldie and Tarn cited in section 13 remain relevant.

21a Suburban drift

'Greater Birmingham', *Birmingham Daily Mail*, 26 November 1903.

Until a comparatively recent date, Acock's Green and Olton enjoyed at least one characteristic in common with their more aristocratic neighbour, Solihull. They were able, so to speak, to keep themselves to themselves. A railway service, suited to the few rather than the many, kept them select, and the absence of any other popular means of conveyance adapted to the multitude, enabled both places to set at defiance the advancing tide from a great town. Here and there a new residence made its appearance ... but for the most part they were of that stamp which carried with it the superior respectability of the semi-detached villa. Of small house property, beyond a few cottages, there was little or none .... For the business folk who had found a home at 'the Green', this was an eminently happy state of affairs. All the delights of a pretty rural district were at their command, within four miles of the centre of Birmingham .... It was admirable—but, obviously, it could not last for ever. Away across the meadows the urban tide of bricks and mortar was creeping stealthily ever onwards; it swept through Sparkbrook to Greet, through Small Heath to Hay Mills, until to-day, on two sides, it menaces the existence of 'the village'. What is more, a new life has crept into Acock's Green itself. In ten years the place has doubled the number of its inhabitants .... On all sides the builders have either begun, or are about to begin, operations. The small house has come, and it has come to stay.... .

With the influx of the small householder the inevitable change is coming over the social condition of Acock's Green .... Those of the more wealthy residents who have loved the place for its quiet exclusiveness and pleasant detachment are moving further out. The establishment of a factory on the outskirts of the district, and the springing up of rows of houses of the cheaper type, are to them a disagreeable reminder of what the near future has in store. So, like the Arab, they are folding their tents and stealing silently away in the direction of Knowle or Solihull, when the octopus tentacles of expanding Birmingham are as yet in the distance. Silently and without any show of ostentation a little revolution is in progress .... One does not mean to imply that all the better-class people are leaving Acock's Green .... But, generally speaking, the tendency is towards the smaller house—the house adapted to the means of the family man of limited income who likes to live just outside the artisan belt encircling the city.

21b   Municipal housing enterprise baulked by the Local Government Board

Letter from the Town Clerk of Sheffield to other Town Clerks, 7 November 1906. Copy in Cumbria Record Office (Carlisle) SMB/Wo, 1906–7, pp. 27–8.

I am directed by the Sheffield City Council to request you to bring before your Council the question of the desirability of greater powers being conferred on municipalities with respect to the acquisition of lands in the outskirts of their areas, without being subject to some of the restrictions imposed by the Local Government Board on the granting of sanctions for loans for purchase moneys, and without being required to declare at the time of the purchase to what municipal purpose the lands acquired shall ultimately be devoted.

The Sheffield Council have purchased an estate of 42 acres by private treaty, in a district which they consider suitable for the purposes of the Housing of the Working Classes Acts. The Local Government Board, however, refused to sanction a loan for the purchase money, and have recently, on a further application being made to them, repeated their refusal.

The position, therefore, is that a Local Authority representing a population of nearly half a million, are checked in a matter of purely local interest, as to which they are best fitted to decide, by the decision of the Board, who are acting on the report of an Inspector who spent only a few hours in the district.

The policy of the Board, whether intentionally or not, is to prevent municipalities from buying suitable lands in their suburbs at a time when prices are reasonable, and to compel them to wait until, by the natural growth of the population, and the introduction of improvements by the municipality—such as the construction of new roads and sewers and the provision of tramways—the value of the land has been greatly increased, and then they may buy at an increased price, the increase being entirely due to the municipalities' own action.

My Council feel that the time has come when united action on the part of the municipalities should be taken with a view to secure the passing of remedial legislation. They accordingly direct me to ask you to lay this communication before your Council, and to express the hope that they will adopt a resolution urging the passing of legislation authorising Municipal Authorities to acquire lands when they find suitable opportunities of doing so, and to have the adequate powers of borrowing the necessary purchase moneys, without at the time having to declare for what purpose the lands shall be used....

21c   Poor quality colliery housing in the north-east

Report by L.W. Darra Mair to the Local Government Board on the Sanitary Circumstances of Whickham Urban District. Durham Record Office PH92/1, pp. 7–16.

At the Census of 1901 the number of inhabited houses in the Whickham Urban District was 2,524; and they were occupied by 2,567 families .... Of these 2,567 tenements, 2,243 or nearly 89 per cent were 'small' tenements ... of fewer than five rooms each....

The proportion of persons ... living more than two per room, and classed by the Census Commissioners as 'overcrowded' ... is very large indeed ... as high as 38 per cent of the total population of the district....

In England and Wales as a whole, the proportion of 'overcrowded' persons to the total population was but 8·20 per cent....

Now it is the case that there is in existence in Northumberland and Durham, at all events in so far as the coal industry is concerned, an arrangement in regard to house accommodation .... By this arrangement, most of the heads of families employed in and about the coal mines are provided with accommodation by their employers, rent-free, or, in the absence of such house accommodation, with a rent-allowance in the shape of an addition to their wages....

The very fact that proprietors of collieries are known to be responsible for the provision of houses for their workmen must interfere with the

building of houses by private enterprise. Anybody who builds houses ...
would not be attracted to a place in which he knew that other persons had
built houses or might build houses, let or to be let for no rent at all....

In the second place it seems but natural that colliery owners should seek
not to build more houses than are absolutely necessary, seeing that they
receive no rent for them; and also not to lay out more capital than is
absolutely necessary on the houses which they do build. As a consequence
houses have been built with as few rooms as possible....

No better example of the factors above referred to could, perhaps, be
found than the case of the Marley Hill houses, which brought about this
inquiry. These dwellings, which are all 'rent-free' are rows of back-to-
back houses, without, of course, means of through ventilation.

The lower 'living' room is entered directly from the air outside, and is
used as a kitchen, the living room, the washing room, and generally also as
a bedroom; while the upper room is a low room with an attic ceiling,
without fireplace, with a small window level with the floor, and
approached from the room below by a step ladder....

Most of these houses are of two rooms each occupied by a large number
of persons ... sometimes by as many as eight, nine, ten or even twelve
persons each....

Both masters and men are ... interested, from different motives, in
hindering the closure of bad houses; and thus both may also be said to be
interested in hindering attempts, on anything like an adequate scale, to
improve the sanitary condition of dwellings lest such attempts lead to
closure....

21d   The Housing and Town Planning Act, 1909

Hansard (4th series), vol. clxxxviii, cols 949–52, 960–1, 12 May 1908.

John Burns, President of the Local Government Board:
The Bill aims in broad outlines at, and hopes to secure, the home healthy, the house beautiful, the town pleasant, the city dignified, and the suburb salubrious. It seeks, and hopes to secure, more homes, better houses, prettier streets, so that the character of a great people, in towns and cities and in villages, can be still further improved and strengthened by the conditions under which they live .... On its housing side the Bill seeks to abolish, reconstruct, and prevent the slum. It asks ... the House of Commons to do something to efface the ghettos of meanness, the Alsatias of squalor that can be found in many parts of the United Kingdom .... It seeks to improve the health of the people by raising the character of the house and the home, and by extended inspection, supervision, direction, and guidance of central control to help local authorities to do more than they now do. The need for this Bill I must justify by a few facts, and I trust not many figures. Increasingly the British people are becoming ... a town people; what is more, they are becoming more and more a great town people. Thirty-five per cent of our population live in towns of over 100,000 in size, and in the short space of sixty years ... we have seen this, that where sixty years ago 75 per cent of the people lived in rural areas, only 25 per cent now so live....

Taking the general population with the general death-rate, we find that the general death-rate in back-to-back houses is 135 as against 100 in the ordinary cottage; in zymotic diseases it is 155 as against 100; and in diarrhoea it is 182 as against 100 .... In London wherever you find density per room there you find infant mortality; wherever you find overcrowding it produces disease to an extent that we ought to terminate.

The existing Housing Acts enable local authorities to provide houses for the working classes, either in the shape of lodging houses or separate dwellings with half an acre of land attached to them, but Part III of the existing legislation is adoptive only, and can only be adopted in rural districts with the consent of the county council. The Act has only been adopted in nine or ten rural districts. That is something the country ought to be ashamed of, ... and we seek to rectify it by the superior powers we give in this Bill .... We propose to make Part III of the Housing Act universally applicable without adoption, so that it will be in force in all urban areas and in rural areas it will be possible to build new cottages and houses without having to go to the county council for consent. We also think they should have power to acquire land compulsorily for the purpose of housing....

21e   The failures of the private enterprise

Annual Report of the Whitehaven Medical Officer of Health, 1913, Cumbria Record Office (Carlisle) SMB/Wh, pp. 13–14.

I pointed out in my Annual Report for 1912 that it was not so much the existance [sic] of houses which were in themselves unfit for human habitation that we had to deal with, but the deplorable overcrowding of houses on area, and said that, in my opinion, the only way to remedy this was to take the numerous courts one by one, removing houses which were 'obstructive' and making such improvements and alterations in the remaining houses as they required .... This process necessarily reduces the number of available houses and imposes on the Town Council the obligation of providing houses to take the place of those demolished or absorbed. Everyone now admits that private enterprise has failed to meet the difficulty—not that private enterprise was ever expected to build houses to accommodate people turned out of homes unfit for human habitation, but there had been some hope that if a sufficient number of rather better class houses was erected on the more open available sites there would be a gradual moving up, those able and willing to pay the rents demanded taking the new houses, leaving the houses they had vacated to be occupied

by people who had previously lived in poorer houses, so that the worst ...
might be closed and demolished without any portion of the population
being left houseless, but this hope has been abandoned. In these
circumstances it behoved the Town Council themselves to carry out their
statutory and moral obligation to prohibit the occupation of houses that
were unfit for human habitation. In order to do this they must provide
more houses.

21f   Liberal land reform proposals

Lloyd George, speech at Swindon, 22 October 1913, reported in *The
Times*, 23 October 1913.

There is a great deficiency in the number of houses. You are 120,000 short
in the rural areas and there are thousands who leave the rural districts, not
merely because of wages, but because they cannot get houses to go to. And
this is very true of young married couples. We have therefore decided ...
that it ought to be dealt with as an urgent problem .... There are two ways
of dealing with it. One is leaving it to the local authorities. (Much
laughter). I see you have settled that; and I do not mind telling you we
agree with you .... We have, therefore, come to the conclusion that the
central government have got to do it. We propose, therefore, to get a
schedule of all these districts; find out what the shortage is, what houses are
required; and we propose to build them ourselves (Loud cheers)....

Why Commissioners? [to administer the scheme] I will tell you why. It
is an idea we got from the landlords. (Laughter) When they enclosed the
commons they did it through Commissioners, and those Commissioners
did the work they were set to do so neatly, so thoroughly, that we decided
that Commissioners having deprived the people of their interest in the land,
Commissioners are just the people to restore the land to the people. (Cheers)
It is a great undertaking ... it is one that may involve us in a struggle with
great interests. We are accustomed to that. We have beaten interests
before, and we will do it again. But it is a task which, when accomplished,
will bring Britain in our judgment a long march nearer the dawn. I believe
it will have the effect, not merely of filling the countryside with a happy,

contented peasantry, but it will do more than that. It will free towns from
the nightmare of unemployment and sweating slums. Then we shall have a
motherland ... that its children can rejoice in, and one that the Empire to
the ends of the earth can be proud of. (Prolonged cheers)

Summary of Proposals

A Ministry of Lands to be set up

All the existing functions of the Board of Agriculture to be transferred to
the Ministry of Lands....

The Ministry of Lands ... to have control and supervision of land
generally—small holdings, land purchase, disputes between landlord and
tenant, powers of reclamation, afforestation, and development of
uncultivated land....

Powers of the Commissioners:

The revision of eviction notices, with power to award ... compensation
and exemplary damages in cases of 'capricious eviction'.

The authority to treat 'wanton' notices to quit as null and of no effect.

In case of sale to order the seller to compensate the farmer for
improvements and to give him substantial compensation for disturbance....

The ability to acquire derelict and uncultivated land and to afforest,
reclaim, or to equip it with a view to cultivation.

The revision of the hours of labour.

Power to fix the price of land when compulsorily acquired for any public
purpose.

Housing:

The provision of cottages to be undertaken by the Central Government.

An economic rent for cottages to be charged.

The Insurance Reserve Fund to be used for the building of cottages.

22 Poverty, poor law and public health

This was the decisive period for the break-up of the poor law. Though the Guardians were not to be finally swept away until 1929, most of the decisive initiatives in social welfare in this period by-passed poor law administration, and even the firmest adherents of the philosophy of 1834 were convinced that radical reform was necessary.

Seebohm Rowntree's (1871–1954) study of York (22a) provided decisive evidence that poverty on the scale revealed by Booth was not confined to the metropolis; and his conclusions, buttressed by superior methodology, pointed incontrovertibly in the same direction. Though Charity Organization Society adherents like Helen Bosanquet (1848–1923) still stressed the importance of family inspiration and inveighed against incautious categorization (22b) it was clear that social and economic factors far beyond the control of individuals or families were the main causes of poverty.

Attacks on the rigidities of poor law provision were being generated from within, particularly in London. Will Crooks, (1852–1921) Labour MP for Woolwich from 1903–18, used his position as Chairman of the Poplar Board of Guardians from 1897 to introduce dramatic dietary improvements, and to stimulate greater expenditure on the poor. Rate-payers were invited to see the problem from the viewpoint of the pauper; and successive Conservative Presidents of the Local Government Board, Henry Chaplain (1840–1923) and Walter Long (1854–1924) urged improved 'Poplar' standards on Guardians elsewhere (22c). Expenditure on poor relief increased from £11·5m in 1901 to £14m in 1906. Improved standards of life for the poor could be discerned, but the process was a slow one and they remained horribly exposed to an unfavourable economic climate. In this period also infant mortality levels began to fall, though in many areas, including the north-east, they remained very high (22e). Medical men were not agreed on the reasons for improvement, though less overcrowding and more information about mothercraft undoubtedly had their effects.

The outgoing Conservative Government appointed the famous Royal Commission on the Poor Laws in 1905. It became the most exhaustive study yet made of the poverty issue, and was not to report until early in 1909. Closely questioned, the permanent head of the Poor Law Division, James Stewart Davy (1848–1915), a stern critic of increased expenditure, maintained that the principles of 1834 were still applicable in 1906 (22d). His view had little support, even though the Commission included influential COS members like C.S. Loch, Octavia Hill and Helen Bosanquet as well as known critics like Charles Booth, Beatrice Webb (1858–1943) and George Lansbury (1859–1940), a friend and colleague of Will Crooks on the Poplar Guardians.

The masses of evidence collected did not lead to a unified view. The Majority Report (22f) stressed the importance of continued voluntary effort and private charity to work effectively with new public assistance committees. As might be expected with so much COS influence, the Report looked to a proper fusion of individual and institutional elements to solve the poverty problem. The Minority Report (22g) was masterminded by Beatrice Webb, but signed also by Lansbury, the Carpenters' Union leader Frederick Chandler (1849–1937) and the Chairman of the Central Committee on the Unemployed, later to be Bishop of Birmingham, Rev. Russell Wakefield (1854–1933). It advocated that all poor law functions be transferred to specialist county council committees, and also recommended the establishment of employment exchanges and structured public works schemes to alleviate unemployment.

Largely because of the didactic method and propagandist fervour of the Webbs, attention has been focused rather on the distinctions between the two Reports, usually to the detriment of the majority conclusions. It should be noted, therefore, that both were agreed that the poor law should be broken up. Both also agreed on the need to provide more rational and less wasteful services under proper control. Though Lloyd George, as a shrewd politician, would not hitch his 'ambulance wagon' to either scheme, the death knell of the 1834 system had been truly sounded by 1914.

Suggestions for further reading

In addition to Rose (section 4), sample the flavour of Webbite partisanship in B. Webb, *Our Partnership* (1948). More massive is S. and B. Webb, *English Local Government* (1929), vols viii and ix.

22a   Rowntree's classifications of poverty

B.S. Rowntree, *Poverty: A Study of Town Life* (1901), pp. 271, 295–8.

Families regarded as living in poverty were grouped under two heads:

a) Families whose total earnings were insufficient to obtain the minimum necessaries for the maintenance of merely physical efficiency. Poverty falling under this head was described as 'primary' poverty.

b) Families whose total earnings would have been sufficient for the maintenance of merely physical efficiency were it not that some portion of it was absorbed by other expenditure, either useful or wasteful. Poverty falling under this head was described as 'secondary' poverty....

For a family of father, mother, and three children, the minimum weekly expenditure upon which physical efficiency can be maintained in York is 21s.8d., made up as follows:

Food	12s.9d.
Rent (say)	4s.0d.
Clothing, light, fuel	4s.11d.

The number of persons whose earnings are so low that they cannot meet the expenditure necessary for the above standard of living, stringent to severity though it is, and bare of all creature comforts, was shown to be no less than 7230, or almost exactly 10 per cent of the total population of the city. These persons, then, represent those who are in 'primary' poverty....

20,302, or 27·84 per cent of the total population, were returned as living in poverty. Subtracting those whose poverty is 'primary' we arrive at the number living in 'secondary' poverty viz 13,072, or 17·93 per cent of the total population.

Budget...

Labourer. Wages (average for thirteen weeks), 15s.

The family consists of a father, aged 25, mother 25, and three children all under 4. The father is a labourer and works irregularly, as he often

complains of being ill. During the thirteen weeks this budget was being
kept the mother earned, on the average, about 2s.6d. per week. All the
children look ill and rickety, and are very small and poorly developed, the
two youngest being unable to walk. They possess little vitality. Mr. and
Mrs. S. live in a house with four rooms, which faces east, and gets little
sun, as it is situated in a narrow passage with a high wall on the opposite
side. The living room contains comfortable furniture; there are lace
curtains in the window, and many ornaments adorn the walls. The rent of
the house is 3s.10^1/$_2$d. weekly, the rates being paid by the landlord. Mrs. S.
is tidy in person, and the house and children are spotlessly clean. The food
is bought in small quantities. Mrs. S. buys hot suppers sometimes of fried
fish and potatoes, or sausages and potatoes. The children eat little at meal
times, but have sweet biscuits given them between meals. The family is
heavily in debt. The protein in this family's diet only amounts to one-half
of the standard requirements, and the total energy value shows a deficiency
of 32 per cent.

Statement of Income and Expenditure for Thirteen Weeks:

Income:

Wages, thirteen weeks at 15s.	£ 9.	15.	0
Mrs. S.	1.	13.	5

Expenditure:

Food, including beverages	5.	6.	0^1/$_2$
Rent and rates	2.	10.	4
Coal	0.	11.	8
Oil	0.	1.	10^1/$_2$
Soap etc.	0.	4.	1
Sundries	0.	5.	0^1/$_2$
Back rent	1.	6.	0
Sick Club	0.	4.	7
Life Insurance	0.	3.	0
Clothing	0.	15.	0
Papers	0.	0	9
	£11.	8.	5

22b   The importance of terminology as an incentive to effort

Helen Bosanquet, *The Strength of the People* (1902), pp. 331–2, 339.

... We have allowed to grow up amongst us the conception of ... [a] class, to which we apply a great variety of names, all tending to the degradation of those concerned. We call it the Residuum, the Poor, the Submerged, the Proletariat, the Abyss; and we call its homes Slums, and Ghettos, and Mean Streets....

Now, it may be said that it matters little what we call these people ....
But I think that this is a grave mistake .... To have classified a man as belonging to the poor, or the residuum, or the submerged, means that we no longer expect from him the qualities of independence and responsibility which we assume as a matter of course in all others; and by this view of him, combined with our careless policy of relief and charity, we go far to annihilate in reality the qualities which we have already denied him in imagination. A man is one of the poor, then we must feed his children and provide for his old age, and leave him with nothing but his own immediate wants to think of; he belongs to the residuum, then we cannot expect him to be a good workman even in his own degree; he is one of the submerged, then we deny him all manliness, and expect no effort on his part to raise himself above the waves....

...what I protest against is the tendency to create a great degraded class, to which all belong automatically whose incomes fall below a certain level ... or to which all belong who live in a certain geographical district. Any analysis conscientiously undertaken of those whose incomes fall below an arbitrarily chosen 'Poverty Line' ... shows at once how utterly misleading these pseudo-classifications may be. The individual families comprised in them are as diverse in their qualities, their ideals, their mode of life, as if they had been drawn from all ranks of society....

... when all is said and done which well-wishers can say or do, it still remains true that the strength of the people lies in its own conscious efforts to face difficulties and overcome them .... Any class or any individual which is neither unconscious of difficulties, or unable to make the effort to master them must stagnate and ultimately deteriorate .... The real solution will rest in the hands, or rather the minds, of the people most nearly affected. If they cannot be made to care for it and seek for it, it can never be given to them from outside.

22c Improving dietary standards in the workhouse

George Haw, *From Workhouse to Westminster: The Life Story of Will Crooks, M.P.* (1917), pp. 114–16.

First he developed the system of bread-breaking in the workhouse, in order to get better and cheaper bread than was being supplied under contract from outside. Under the direction of one or two skilled bakers, the work provided many of the inmates with pleasant and useful occupation. They made all the bread required in the workhouse for both officers and inmates, all the bread required in the children's schools, all the loaves given away as out-relief....

And then, for the benefit of the infirm old folk, Crooks persuaded the Guardians to substitute butter for margarine, and fresh meat for the cheap stale stuff so often supplied. He held out for milk that had not been skimmed, and for tea and coffee that had not been adulterated. He even risked his reputation by allowing the aged women to put sugar in their tea themselves, and the old men to smoke an occasional pipe of tobacco.

Rumours of this new way of feeding the workhouse poor reached the austere Local Government Board. First it sent down its inspectors, and then the President himself appeared in person. And Mr. Chaplain saw that it was good and told other Boards to do likewise. He issued a circular to the Guardians of the country recommending all that Poplar had introduced. More, he proposed that for deserving old people over sixty-four years of age 'the supply of tobacco, dry tea, and sugar should be made compulsory'.

This human order of things, you may be sure, did not commend itself to all Guardian Boards; and when later there came further instructions from headquarters that ailing inmates might be allowed 'medical comforts' the revolt materialised. A deputation of Guardians went to Whitehall to try to argue the President into a harder heart. Crooks and Lansbury were there to uphold the new system. Mr. Walter Long had succeeded Mr. Chaplain then. He listened patiently to ingenious speeches in which honourable gentlemen tried to show that it was from no lack of love for the poor that they had not carried out the new dietary scale but—

'Gentlemen', Mr. Long interrupted at last, 'am I to understand you do not desire to feed your poor people properly ?'...

From that day an improved dietary scale was introduced into our workhouses. The man who fed the poor in Poplar saw the workhouse poor of the kingdom better fed in consequence.

22d The Head of the Poor Law Division restates the principles of 1834

Evidence of J.S. Davy to Royal Commission on Poor Laws, *Parliamentary Papers*, 1909, vol. xxxix, p. 125 (29 January 1906).

Q. 2229 (T. Hancock Nunn): I think you said that the fundamental principle of the Poor Law was to relieve destitution, and that it aimed at doing so humanely to the individual pauper, while it safeguarded the community by making the lot of the pauper less eligible than that of the independent labourer ... that is the principle of the poor law understood by the Local Government Board ?—Yes.

Q.2230 ... Does ineligibility consist of these three elements: firstly, of the loss of personal reputation (what is understood by the stigma of pauperism); secondly, the loss of personal freedom which is secured by detention in a workhouse; and thirdly, the loss of political freedom by suffering disenfranchisement. Are those the main elements in ineligibility, or have I left any out ?—I think those would be the main elements.

22e   Two medical views on high infant mortality

Medical Officer of Health Reports, Durham Record Office, CC/H9 pp. 70–1, 108.

Dr Andrew Smith on Whickham:
The infant mortality rate was 138 as compared with 162 in 1906. The improvement was due to the fact that diarrhoea was not prevalent to any extent, and the diminution in the number of fatal cases of diarrhoea more than compensated for the increased number of deaths from measles ....
Dr. Smith points out that an improvement in sanitation alone will not alter this condition of affairs, and that before there can be much further improvement we must have healthy mothers rearing breast-fed children .... 'When called to attend babies for any of these diseases our prognosis depends most largely on whether they are breast-fed or hand fed. We know that their chances of recovery are enormously greater if they are breast-fed.... '

Dr F. Hinton on Sedgefield Rural District. Infant mortality 153 per 1000.
... it will be found that more than half the deaths occurring during the first year of life are practically, so far as the infants themselves are concerned, non-preventible, and are due to sociological causes, such as the marriage of the unfit; the inability to obtain sufficient food in a certain section of the community; the squandering of potential vitality on alcohol; the vitiated taste for stimulating rather than nutritious foods; the consumption of patent medicines, which, frequently taken, lower the vitality, and at times are used undoubtedly for ulterior purposes, and which, while not acting as desired, result in the production of weaklings; and the indifference of the community in general to the science of Eugenics.

22f   The Poor Law Majority Report

Parliamentary Papers, 1909, vol. xxxvii, pp. 596, 643–4.

Leading Defects of the Poor Law System

i)   The inadequacy of existing Poor Law areas to meet the growing needs of administration.

ii)   The excessive size of many Boards of Guardians.

iii)   The absence of any general interest in Poor Law work and Poor Law elections, due in great part to the fact that Poor Law work stands in no organic relation to the rest of local government.

iv)   The lack of intelligent uniformity in the application of principles and in general administration.

v)   The want of proper investigation and discrimination in dealing with applications.

vi)   The tendency in many Boards of Guardians to give outdoor relief without plan or purpose.

vii)   The unsuitability of the general workhouse as a test or deterrent for the able bodied; the aggregation in it of all classes without sufficient classification; and the absence of any system of friendly and restorative work.

viii) The lack of co-operation between Poor Law and charity.

ix)   The tendency of candidates to make lavish promises of out-relief and of Guardians to favour their constituents in its distribution.

x)   General failure to attract capable social workers and leading citizens.

xi)   The general rise in expenditure, not always accompanied by an increase in efficiency in administration.

xii)   The want of sufficient control and continuity of policy on the part of the Central Authority.

Conclusion:

... we feel strongly that the pauperism and distress we have described can never be successfully combated by administration and expenditure. The causes of distress are not only economic and industrial; in their origin and character they are largely moral. Government by itself cannot correct or remove such influences. Something more is required. The co-operation, spontaneous and whole-hearted, of the community at large, and especially of those sections of it which are well-to-do and free from the pressure of poverty, is indispensable. There is evidence from many quarters to show that the weak part of our system is not want of public spirit or benevolence, or lack of funds or of social workers, or of the material out of which these can be made. Its weakness is lack of organisation, of method, and of confidence in those who administer the system. We have so framed the new system as to invite and bring into positions of authority the best talent and experience that the locality can provide. In addition to those vested with such authority we have left a place in the new system for all capable and willing social workers; but they must work in accord, under guidance, and in the sphere allotted to them.

Great Britain is the home of voluntary effort, and its triumphs and successes constitute in themselves much of the history of the country. But voluntary effort when attacking a common and ubiquitous evil must be disciplined and led .... To this end it is organisation we need, and this organisation we now suggest....

Our investigations prove the existence in our midst of a class whose condition and environment are a discredit, and a peril to the whole community. Each and every section of society has a common duty to perform in combating this evil and contracting its area, a duty which can only be performed by united and untiring effort to convert useless and costly inefficients into self-sustaining and respectable members of the community. No country, however rich, can permanently hold its own in the race of international competition, if hampered by an increasing load of this dead weight; or can successfully perform the role of sovereignty beyond the seas, if a portion of its own folk at home are sinking below the civilization and aspirations of its subject races abroad.

22g   The Poor Law Minority Report

Break Up the Poor Law & Abolish the Workhouse, being Part I of the
Minority Report (1909), pp. 516–17, 598–9 and *The Remedy for
Unemployment* being Part II of the Minority Report, pp. 248, 325–8.

We have now to present the scheme of reform to which we ... have been
driven by the facts of the situation. The dominant exigencies of which we
have to take account are:

i) The overlapping, confusion and waste that result from the provision
for each separate class being undertaken, in one and the same district, by
two, three, and sometimes even by four separate Local Authorities, as well
as by voluntary agencies.

ii) The demoralisation of character and the slackening of personal effort
that result from the unnecessary spending of indiscriminate, unconditional
and gratuitous provision, through this unco-ordinated rivalry.

iii) The paramount importance of subordinating mere relief to the
specialised treatment of each separate class, with the object of preventing or
curing its distress.

iv) The expediency of intimately associating this specialised treatment of
each class with the standing machinery for enforcing, both before and after
the period of distress, the fulfilment of personal and family obligations....

The scheme of reform that we recommend involves:

i) The final suppression of the Poor Law Authority by the newer
specialised Authorities already at work.

ii) The appropriate distribution of the remaining functions of the Poor
Law among those existing Authorities.

iii) The establishment of suitable machinery for registering and co-
ordinating all the assistance afforded to any given person or family; and

iv) The more systematic enforcement, by means of this co-ordinating
machinery, of the obligation of able-bodied persons to support themselves
and their families.

Recommendations:

91. That the Boards of Guardians ... should be abolished....

93. That the provision for the various classes of the Non-Able-Bodied should be wholly separated from that to be made for the Able-Bodied, whether these be unemployed workmen, vagrants or able-bodied persons now in receipt of Poor Relief.

94. That the services at present administered by the Destitution Authorities (other than those connected with vagrants or the able-bodied)—that is to say, the provision for:

i) Children of school age

ii) The sick and the permanently incapacitated, the infants under school age, and the aged needing institutional care;

iii) The mentally defective of all grades and all ages; and

iv) The aged to whom pensions are awarded—

should be assumed, under the directions of the County and County Borough Councils, by:

i) The Education Committee;

ii) The Health Committee;

iii) The Asylums Committee; and

iv) The Pension Committee respectively.

Unemployment

The first requisite is the organisation throughout the whole of the United Kingdom of a complete system of public Labour Exchanges on a national basis. This National Labour Exchange, though in itself no adequate remedy, is the foundation of all our proposals....

We ... recommend:

1. That the duty of so organising the National Labour Market as to prevent or to minimise Unemployment should be placed upon a Minister responsible to Parliament, who might be designated the Minister for Labour....

3. That the function of the National Labour Exchange should be, not only (a) to ascertain and report the surplus or shortage of labour of particular kinds, at particular places; and (b) to diminish the time and energy now spent in looking for work ... ; but also (c) so to 'dovetail' casual and seasonal employments as to arrange for practical continuity of work for those now chronically Under-employed....

9. That in order to meet the periodically recurrent general depressions of Trade, the Government should take advantage of there being at these periods as much Unemployment of capital as there is Unemployment of labour; that it should definitely undertake, as far as practicable, the

Regularisation of the National Demand for Labour; and that it should, for this purpose, and to the extent of at least £4,000,000 a year, arrange a portion of the ordinary work required by each Department on a Ten Years' Programme; such £40,000,000 worth of work for the decade being then put in hand, not by equal annual instalments, but exclusively in the lean years of the trade cycle....

13. That for the ultimate residuum of men in distress from want of employment, who may be expected to remain, after the measures now recommended have been put into operation, we recommend that Maintenance should be freely provided, without disfranchisement, on condition that they submit themselves to the physical and mental training that they may prove to require.

23 The emergence of collective security I: Pensions, sickness and national insurance

The establishment of a State pledged to secure minimum standards of welfare for all its citizens was a glittering prize indeed for progressive Liberals. On the one hand, carefully handled, it would give the Liberals a strong political advantage over the Conservatives in the battle for the working-class vote; on the other, and infinitely more important to progressives like W. S. Churchill, it spiked the guns of socialism by effecting real social reform and strengthening the security of the State against revolution born of social distress.

H. H. Asquith (1852–1928) had given the first public Liberal pledge to provide pensions in 1907. Lloyd George, his successor as Chancellor, brought it about a year later. Pensions of 7s. 6d. a week for a married couple and 5s. for single persons over seventy were paid through post-offices (23b), being thus entirely separate from poor law doles. In addition, they were non-contributory and financed by general taxation. The £6,000,000 budget set aside for the purpose was rapidly exceeded and, by 1911, doubled, making further non-contributory benefits unlikely. That Lloyd George's mind was already on these further benefits is indicated by his speech on the second reading of the Pensions Bill (23a). Harold Cox (1859–1936) spoke for the individualist element in the Liberal party in fearing the growth of unproductive dependence because of such State initiatives.

Lloyd George had been much impressed by the range of social service benefits on offer in Germany when he visited that country in August 1908. He returned determined to take similar initiatives in Britain. His original insurance plan included provision not only for sickness but also for widows and orphans, but it fell foul of the powerful and entrenched friendly societies and commercial insurance companies. Both felt their interests threatened by State schemes which would take their best business. Lloyd George was forced to abandon widows' and orphans' benefits and to propitiate the societies by making them agents for administering the State scheme. These compromises, however, failed to ensure the National Insurance Bill an easy ride. The hectoring of the Webbs (23c) only served to make the Chancellor more determined not to follow their didactic paths.

The *Daily Mail* latched on to the inconveniences of administration and launched a campaign against the whole Bill by concentrating on the stamps which the insured must buy and stick on to cards (23d). There was a massive rally of domestic servants in the Albert Hall in November 1911, protesting against the Bill; employers of servants were persuaded that their contributions represented an additional tax from which they derived no benefit, and they vowed not to 'lick stamps for Lloyd George'.

Robert Blatchford's (1851–1943) socialist journal *The Clarion* reprinted a Fabian, Webbite attack on the 'poll-tax' element in the Bill. National Insurance, they claimed, would aid only the better organized and more skilled workers (23e). Philip Snowden (1864–1937) later outlined the dilemma into which the Bill had plunged a Labour party already finding it difficult to retain a separate identity against the tide of progressive legislation (23f). Ramsay MacDonald (1866–1937) saw merit in a contributory scheme, but Keir Hardie (1856–1915) and George Lansbury saw the Bill as a threat to socialism itself, and urged in numerous impassioned speeches that benefits should be non-contributory.

The medical profession, finally, had to be appeased. Doctors were, as ever, extremely wary of State involvement, resented their role *vis-à-vis* the friendly societies and thought the fairly generous rates Lloyd George was prepared to pay for their services inadequate. The British Medical Association was mobilized against the scheme, and Sir James Barr (1849–1938), President of the Association in 1912—an unbending social Darwinist and individualist—encapsulated most of the profession's objections in a ferocious attack published in the *Medical Journal* (23g).

Uncertain compromise though it was, the National Insurance Act represented a massive advance in State intervention. Manual employees between sixteen and seventy years of age or those who earned less than £160 per annum were obliged to join the scheme, paying 4*d*. (3*d*. for women) a week, to which the employer added 3*d*. and the State 2*d*. When ill, and after the third day, employees were entitled to benefits of 10*s*. a week for thirteen weeks and 5*s*. a week for the next thirteen. The self-employed, unemployed and those already covered by health insurance were not included. Doctors, employed by benefit societies, provided 'free' treatment. Subscribers also had a right to sanatorium treatment for the dread tuberculosis, and the government made a grant of £1,500,000 towards the construction of sanatoria. Part II of the Act dealt with unemployment (for which see section 24). The scheme was ambitious, and the government estimated that by 1915–16 no less than £20,000,000 would be paid-out in benefits. It proved very unpopular electorally, however, people perhaps finding the scheme difficult to comprehend and unnecessarily bureaucratic. There was also much truth in the Webbs's criticism that it was directed more to treatment than prevention of illness. This, particularly since National Insurance may be seen as a product of the concern for national efficiency, was a severe drawback. Preventive medicine was still in a primitive state in 1914.

Suggestions for further reading

B. B. Gilbert, *The Evolution of National Insurance* (1966) is, the odd factual blemish notwithstanding, admirable and very full.

23a   Lloyd George introduces old-age pensions legislation

Hansard (4th series), cxc, cols 584–6, 612, 15 June 1908.

I invite the supporters of old-age pensions ... to support the Government not merely on the general principle of the Bill, establishing at the expense of the State provision for old age, but also in the disqualifications which on the face of them may appear harsh and unjust for the moment, and all for the same reason. This is purely an experiment. Every scheme of this kind must be .... We do not say that it deals with all the problems of unmerited destitution in this country. We do not even contend that it deals with the worst part of that problem. It might be held that many an old man dependent on the charity of the parish was better off than many a young man, broken down in health, or who cannot find a market for his labour. The provision which is made for the sick and unemployed is grossly inadequate in this country, and yet the working classes have done their best during fifty years to make provision without the aid of the State. But it is insufficient. The old man has to bear his own burden, while in the case of a young man who is broken down and who has a wife and family to maintain, the suffering is increased and multiplied to that extent. These problems of the sick, of the infirm, of the men who cannot find means of earning a livelihood ... are problems with which it is the business of the State to deal; they are problems which the State has neglected too long. In asking the House to give a Second Reading to this Bill, we ask them to sanction not merely its principle, but also its finance, having regard to the fact that we are anxious to utilise the resources of the State to make provision for undeserved poverty and destitution in all its branches.

Mr. Harold Cox: What he objected to in all these schemes of State charity was that instead of aiming at the abolition of poverty, they tended to perpetuate poverty by treating it as a permanent institution ... the necessary consequence was that they would create a vast number of dependants. The man who earned his living was independent. He could face his master as a man because he gave his work in return for his wages. But if they were going to give a man something in return for nothing they made him a dependant. He ... became dependent on the will of some official or of some committee of elected persons consisting either of superior persons with charitable inclinations or of inferior persons with axes to grind....

23b   The first State pensions are collected

Manchester Guardian, 2 January 1909.

The first payments under the Old-age Pensions Act were made yesterday at post-offices .... Probably about half a million needy old people were made glad yesterday by the first instalment of an allowance which will be continued to them for the rest of their lives, and it is not surprising to read that many of the recipients expressed heartfelt thanks to the willing instruments of the State's bounty—the post-office clerks who handed them their money. The clerks, by the way, seem everywhere to have acted with tact and kindness and to have taken great trouble to make the necessary routine as easy as possible to the old people, very many of whom were infirm, deaf, nearly blind, and otherwise afflicted in body as well as estate.

The majority of the pensioners were women; in some districts the disproportion between the sexes was very marked indeed. Another point about the pensions was the comparatively insignificant number less than the full five shillings. It may be noted that the Birmingham Guardians have decided on a step which will greatly mitigate one of the chief hardships under the Act—the debarring of people who have received Poor Relief from receiving pensions. They have decided to increase to five shillings the amount of out-relief now paid to persons over 70 years of age.

In Manchester and Salford 6,765 claims have been passed by the two Pensions Committees .... Many were waiting at the office doors at eight o'clock, and during the next five hours ... the streets were busy with old people....

[In Knutsford] One old man came up to me [writes a *Manchester Guardian* representative] and said, 'Thank yer' and when I said I hoped he would be coming regularly now for long enough he said 'Aye, I 'ope I will, now it's come.' There was an emphasis on these last three words that gave them a pathetic significance.

23c   The Webbs breakfast with Lloyd George

H. N. Bunbury (ed.), *Lloyd George's Ambulance Wagon: The Memoirs of William J. Braithwaite, 1911–12* (1970 ed.), pp. 115–17.

February 28th, Tuesday. Hurtled off to 11 Downing Street 9.15 to breakfast. The breakfast was Homeric, and deserves to be historic: Mr. and Mrs. Sidney Webb, Chancellor, Bradbury, and self. Fell across Sidney Webb at once myself and his statements that German insurance had greatly increased 'malingering'. Pointed out fallacies in German statistics. Webb very anxious to assure the Chancellor that he knew nothing about the Government scheme, that he is not in any way opposed to it etc. etc. Chancellor duly tempted on, begins to unfold a little bit here and there. Before he can speak, Mr. and Mrs. Webb, singly and in pairs, leap down his throat: 'That's absurd', 'That will never do', 'You should adopt our plan', 'sickness should be prevented, not cured', 'Friendly Societies are quite incapable of dealing with the question'. 'It's criminal to take poor people's money and use it to insure them; if you take it you should give it to the Public Health Authority to prevent their being ill again'!!

The Chancellor was unable to get a word in, and was evidently partly amused and partly annoyed. Sidney became so excited that he quite spoilt his breakfast. Mrs. Webb at intervals was comparatively sane, and apparently wanted to control Sidney; but she pledged her reputation that it would be more popular and practical to take 'the people's' money and give it to the local Health Authority than to let them spend it on themselves by the method of insurance. The Chancellor was coerced into a promise to consult Local Government doctors, and the breakfast broke up with S. Webb at one end of the room explaining to the Chancellor that the true method of national thrift lay in the adoption of the 'dividing-out' principle and Mrs. Webb anxiously asking me, at the other end, how we proposed to deal with venereal disease!

23d 'Daily Mail's' campaign against stamp-licking

'The Householder and his Task of Stamp Licking', *Daily Mail*, 4 November 1911.

The ways of the Bill are dark and devious and, though it meddles in every home, so often has it been altered that it is difficult to say what the householder will have to pay. But he is required every week to stick a certain number of stamps, varying in value from $2^1/_2d$. to $4d$., according to numerous obscure rules, on each of his servants' cards, at his own expense. When this has been done he has to stick a further set of stamps, varying in value from $^1/_2d$. to $3d$., on the cards, and to recover the cost from the servants. Nothing more annoying could be conceived if Mr. Lloyd George had deliberately set out to make mischief. The servants will almost certainly protest against any deduction from their wages .... Take the case of three servants in a house. The employer will have to pay from $7^1/_2d$. to $1s$. in stamps each week from his own share. He will then have to find from $3d$. to $9d$. a week as the servants' share. Finally, he will be taxed to provide the State's 'contribution'. Thus, for him the Bill means three new and separate taxes, two of them levied in the most disagreeable way.

It is not the case that the servant benefits by all this elaborate system of stamp-sticking and this new load of taxation. The money is taken from the servants and their employers to swell the reserves of other classes. The Bill adds a new terror to domestic life, and, if only for this reason, its application in this manner to servants is to be condemned.

23e   Socialist objections to national insurance

'The Fabian Society and the Insurance Bill', *Clarion*, 10 November 1911.

Why the Fabian Society is Opposed to the Bill
First and foremost because it imposes upon the wage-earners what is in effect a poll-tax (i.e. a tax levied irrespective of ability to pay). The total sum to be raised under the Bill is about twenty-five millions sterling. Towards this amount, under the head of 'Sickness Insurance', every working man who is earning not less than 2s. 6d. a day is to contribute 4d. a week, and every woman 3d. a week, which the employer is to deduct from his or her wages before he pays them. The employer himself is in the first instance also to contribute 3d. a week, and the State something like 1½d. In addition to this, every working man in certain trades is to contribute 2½d. per week for insurance against unemployment, whilst the employer pays 2½d. also, and the State 1½d....

To put the case in a nutshell, if Mr. Lloyd George is not prepared to increase the super-tax, then he may as well give up at once all his great schemes of 'social reform', for it is the most elementary of economic truths that you cannot mitigate the evils of poverty at the expense of the poor....

If, as this Bill proposes, you deduct 4d. a week from wages which are at present below the minimum necessary to maintain a family in mere physical efficiency, you are deliberately reducing their already insufficient nourishment, and therefore their power to resist disease.

In its sub-title the Bill is described as a measure for the 'prevention of sickness', but the mere fact that it excludes all non-wage-earning women and children is enough to deprive it of any claim to be taken seriously as a preventive scheme.

The Chancellor claims that he is giving 9*d*. for 4*d*. to every male contributor; but the truth is that the scale of 'minimum' benefits to be provided, although generous enough to the elderly, is only equivalent to what any well-managed friendly society can now offer to any young man or woman for 5*d*....

'But', it may be asked, 'is not this Bill after all better than nothing?' The answer to this question is, that as far as the better-off workers, who are already members of friendly societies or of strong trade unions are concerned, this bill is certainly better than nothing ... it offers them solid financial advantages which the organised section will probably be able to retain. But for the others, the comparatively underpaid, underemployed, and unorganised, the equally emphatic answer is that the Bill is *not* worth having. From their insufficient incomes it will take 4*d*. a week, and in return it will give them no benefits worthy of the name....

If and when ... the Bill comes into force, the problem of low wages will not only remain but will be intensified. Mr. Lloyd George is the first Chancellor of the Exchequer who has conceived the plan of making the working classes themselves finance his measure of social reform. If he is successful, he will not be the last.

23f Lloyd George's scheme splits the Labour party

Philip Snowden, *Autobiography* (2 vols, 1934), vol. i, pp.228–9.

The Bill created disunity in the ranks of the Labour Party. We all welcomed the measure as a recognition of the obligation of the State to deal with the grave problem of disablement and sickness. But a few of us were strongly opposed to some of its main features. For the first time there were serious differences between Mr. MacDonald and his colleagues, the I.L.P. members. The Bill was based upon the contributory principle—the employer and the workmen having to make compulsory weekly contributions, the State supplementing these payments.

The division in our ranks was upon this matter of compulsory contributions. The minority of the Party which favoured a non-contributory scheme consisted of Mr. Keir Hardie, Mr. Will Thorne, Mr. James O'Grady, Mr. F. W. Jowett, Mr. Lansbury and myself. We were opposed to exacting contributions from the workers to finance so-called schemes of social reform, because we held that the cost of such schemes should be spread over the whole community. The contributory principle had been abandoned in our Education system, in Public Health Administration, in Workmen's Compensation, and in the recently passed Old Age Pensions Act. Mr. MacDonald favoured the exaction of contributions from the workers on the grounds that for the State to finance such schemes without calling upon the recipients of the benefits for some direct contribution was not Socialism but State Philanthropy....

Other objections we had against the Bill were that it placed upon the employer a burden which ought to be borne by the community as a whole, and taxed him for this purpose not according to the profits he made but upon the amount of labour he employed.

23g   Medical hostility to the scheme

Sir James Barr, 'Some Reasons why the Public should oppose the Insurance Act', *British Medical Journal*, 30 December 1911.

1. It is a long step in the downward path towards socialism. It will tend to destroy individual effort, and increase that spirit of dependency which is ever found in degenerate races. This spoon-fed race will look more and more to a paternal government to feed and clothe it, and not require it to work more than a few hours daily. They will be further encouraged to multiply their breed at the expense of the healthy and intellectual members of the community.

2. The expense of this huge scheme will be enormous, and will be an ever-growing expense. The cost of administration will be great, and the hard-working, honest man and woman will never get a chance of participating in that barefaced fraud of 'ninepence for fourpence'. The honest working man who has got a family to support cannot afford to be ill for ten shillings a week. It will be the loafers and wastrels who will get the bulk of the ten shillings and enjoy the benefit of free medical service....

3. I have reason to believe that the Act is not actuarially sound. The

meagre facts which have been submitted to the actuaries were from the picked lives of large friendly societies. Consequently, when the Act is applied to a third of the population, it will soon be found that there is not sufficient money to go round, and unless the Act be bounty-fed by the State and county councils it will soon become bankrupt....

4. The provision for medical and surgical attendance, drugs, and appliances, is utterly inadequate for an efficient service—and unless the service be efficient it becomes a fraud—and is calculated to undermine rather than improve the health of the nation....

5. Not only is there no institutional treatment, apart from a few sanatoriums for consumptives, provided in the Act, but the very foundations on which voluntary hospitals have been built up are seriously undermined. Hospital treatment is absolutely essential for the working classes, but the Act will tend to destroy all that fine altruistic feeling which is the highest product of human evolution. Both the employer ... and the labourer are heavily taxed for a very inadequate provision for times of sickness. In times of health they will have to strain every nerve to support an army of officials, to provide means of subsistence for loafers, wastrels and those in chronic ill health, and in times of stress and sickness the honest hard-working man will get a dole on which he and his family can barely subsist, let alone provide medical comforts. Even then he will require to be ill four days before this quack doctor provides him with any refreshing fruit for his parched lips.

6. This Act is supposed to be conceived in the interest of the wage earners; but it will be carried out in such a cumbersome and expensive manner that very few benefits can accrue to those who are the mainstay of the empire. The wage earner is the individual who is best able to take care of himself, and every one who is worthy of his salt does so, and the less unnecessary interference he has with his liberty the better for the State....

7. The supposed benefits of the Act as applied to domestic servants are nothing short of an outrage on humanity. There will be an exaction of 26s. a year on account of each servant for much inferior benefits to those which they now receive for nothing....

8. The sanatorium benefits under the Act apply to the treatment of consumption and not to its prevention....

9. The enormous increase in taxation, the useless and wasteful expenditure which has taken place during the last quarter of a century makes some of us who hold eugenic ideals wonder when this nation is going to cry halt in its rapid descent towards decadence and decay .... Every source of revenue is being tapped for the benefit of the least worthy citizens. Now the medical men are to be sweated in order to

provide gratuitous medical advice for the least worthy of the wage-earning population.

10 .... It may be neccessary for the State to prevent the diseased from becoming a nuisance and a danger to the public, hence the necessity for workhouses, and hospitals for infectious diseases, but the primary duty of the State should be to maintain a high level of health.

I have been one of those who fondly hoped that the future of medicine would be more on preventive lines than it has been in the past.

24 The emergence of collective security II: Unemployment and the labour question

In this period there was much-increased interference by the State in the most basic of economic relationships—that between employer and workman. In 1897, Joseph Chamberlain passed his Workmen's Compensation Act, which made employers liable to pay compensation for most accidents sustained by employees at work. A.V. Dicey (1835–1922) saw this interference with freedom of contract as a decisive turning-point on the road to full collectivism (24a). While this seems now an extreme interpretation, it is true that the State was interfering much more than before to protect the weak from exploitation by the strong. The 'sweated' industries were subject to scrutiny in 1908 (24d) and by the Trade Boards Act, 1909, machinery was established to negotiate minimum wages for 200,000 workers in tailoring, box-making and lace-making. 140,000 of these were women. The Act followed sustained pressure from the National Anti-Sweating League, formed in 1906. The *Spectator* argued that it was self-defeating, since it would only increase unemployment. It did, however, acknowledge that its views were unfashionable in an increasingly collectivist climate (24e). The 1911 Shops Act, introduced by C.F.G. Masterman (1874–1927) protected shop workers from excessive hours, by establishing a 60-hour week and half-day holidays.

Rising prices, which hit most groups of workers hard in the Edwardian period, were the main reason for the campaign to secure a national minimum wage. Few MPs were as well qualified to speak of the miseries of poverty as Will Crooks (1852–1921), a Labour member, and an expert on poverty in the London area (24h). The Liberals were, with some discomfort, able to head off cries for a national minimum, though, to end a damaging six-week strike, they were forced to concede what amounted to a minimum wage for miners in 1912. It is worth noting that miners had already, in 1908, secured for themselves a compulsory maximum eight-hour working day. The radical journalist H.W. Massingham (1860–1924) delivered his views on the labour question towards the end of a period of fierce industrial strife, brought about by falling real wages. In a far-sighted piece, presaging incomes policy, he sought to interpose Government permanently between the warring factions of workers and management, and argued that free collective bargaining, as advocated by the trade union members of the Labour party, was destructive and had already failed to produce the desired results (24i).

Unemployment was the burning issue in labour relations; and in this field there were dramatic developments during the period. The culmination of Chamberlainite public-works schemes, dating from the 1886 Circular, was the Unemployed Workmen's Act, 1905. Though this was a Tory measure, Liberals like Herbert Gladstone (1854–1930) were clearly thinking along the same lines (24b). By the Act, Distress Committees were established in all large centres to provide temporary work for those deemed 'worthy' applicants. John Burns, Liberal President of the Local Government Board, was extremely unsympathetic to a Labour party proposal in 1907–8 for a wider, more permanent scheme. He believed it would distort the free labour market and seduce workers from productive industry (24c).

The seminal work on the subject, produced by William Beveridge (1879–1963) when he was just thirty years of age, appeared in 1909 and altered the entire climate of the debate (24f). It effectively destroyed the individualist case by demonstrating that some degree of unemployment was inseparable from capitalist organization, and turned attention towards the best methods of minimizing unemployment, while providing effective help for those who were out of work. On the recommendation of the Webbs, who had more success in influencing Winston Churchill than Lloyd George at this time, Beveridge was taken into the Board of Trade where he worked on plans for labour exchanges and unemployment insurance. The importance of the Labour Exchanges Act, 1909, can be exaggerated, since the scheme was voluntary and the State merely took over some sixty local authority or private exchanges. Nevertheless, it was the first State scheme. Organized labour was initially suspicious that the enterprise was a ploy to beat down wages and the TUC demanded major changes at its 1910 Conference (24g).

Unemployment insurance, effected by Part II of the National Insurance Act, was compulsory for some $2^1/_4$ million workers, but it was not universal. It applied only to trades regarded as especially vulnerable to seasonal or other greater-than-average fluctuations—building, mechanical engineering, shipbuilding, ironfounding, sawmilling and vehicle construction. Workers and employers each paid $2^1/_2$d. weekly, to which the State added just under 2d. Unemployment benefit of 7s. a week for up to fifteen weeks was provided. The Act was piecemeal and experimental; in practice it aided the skilled man (63 per cent of those insured in 1913 were skilled) and did little for the casual labourer; but it was pregnant with significance. It abandoned all distinctions between worthy and unworthy applicants, so dear to observers in the 1880s and 1890s; it also showed some awareness of the complexity and diversity of the unemployment problem. In a sense, this Act symbolized the final rejection of the individualist tradition.

Suggestions for further reading

J.F. Harris's book (section 12) is central. See also, K.D. Brown, *Labour and Unemployment, 1900–1914* (1971).

24a   Dicey's perception of collectivist legislation

A.V. Dicey, *Lectures on the Relation between Law and Public Opinion in England*, 2nd ed. 1914, pp. 282–4.

In 1897 ... legislation took a completely new turn. The Workmen's Compensation Act of that year ... introduced into the law the new principle that an employer must, subject to certain limitations, insure his workmen against the risks of their employment. At the same time the right of a workman to bargain away his claim to compensation was in reality, though not in form, nullified, since any contract whereby he foregoes the right to compensation secured him by the Workmen's Compensation Acts is effective only where a general scheme for compensation, agreed upon between the employer and the employed, secures to the workmen benefits at least as great as those which they would derive from the Compensation Acts....

This legislation bears all the marked characteristics of collectivism. Workmen are protected against the risks of their employment, not by their own care or foresight, or by contracts made with their employers, but by a system of insurance imposed by law upon employers of labour. The contractual capacity both of workmen and of masters is cut down. Encouragement is given to collective bargaining. The law, lastly, secures for one class of the community an advantage, as regards insurance against accidents, which other classes can obtain only at their own expense ....

The rights of workmen in regard to compensation for accidents have become a matter not of contract, but of status.

24b   A Liberal view of public works programmes

Herbert Gladstone to H.H. Fowler, 1 January 1905, British Library, Department of Manuscripts, Add. MSS. 41217 ff. 164–6.

I believe that large and profitable works can be initiated by the Government, which are barred to private enterprise because there would be no profit for a considerable period.

It is here where I think practical enquiry is urgently required .... West Ham, for example, is absolutely incompetent to deal with the mass of men out of work—men who work in industries to the benefit of the nation. The state of things there is a disgrace to the community and the Poor Law is wholly inefficient to deal with it. Why should charitable people bear the burden of giving relief when it is no concern of theirs? While the vast majority of well-to-do people never lift a finger? Genuine workmen in thousands are demoralised by being forced to depend upon this private charity or the workhouse.

I don't suggest that the Government should bear the whole burden. But the action of Municipal and other public bodies should be organised and co-ordinated, and where the burden is too great for local action, other opportunities for temporary employment ought to be provided by Government which would not tempt men from their ordinary trades but would give them a wage sufficient for the support of themselves and their families, and which would be profitable to the State.

24c John Burns explains the principles of unemployment legislation, and opposes a Labour party plan

Memorandum to Cabinet, Public Record Office CAB 37/91/33

The main features of the present system ... are these:—
1. Persons out of work are entitled to apply to the Distress Committee set up under the Act of 1905 for assistance....
2. Applicants have to submit to investigation, and assistance is limited to cases in which the applicant is honestly desirous of getting work, but is unable to do so from exceptional causes over which he has no control.
3. There is no right given to any one to demand work, and no obligation to supply it.
4. When work is provided, the remuneration offered is less than would be earned by an independent unskilled labourer....
5. Money derived from rates is not available for use by Distress Committees in paying wages.
6. The Distress Committees are limited to the larger centres of population....

The scheme of ... [this] Bill differs very materially from that at present in operation ... its essential outlines are as follows:—
1. Unemployment Committees are to be established throughout the country....
2. Every unemployed person is entitled to be registered, and it is to be the duty of the local committee to provide work for him, or failing this ... to provide maintenance for the man and his dependents.
3. The conditions of labour are not to be lower than those standard to the work in the locality.
4. The work is, so far as practicable, to be suitable to the needs of the individual applicant....
5. There is no limit to the time during which employment may be provided.
6. Refusal on the part of an individual to accept work releases the local

body from its obligations in respect of that person....

7. Cases of deliberate unemployment and habitual disinclination to work may be dealt with by penal methods....

The Bill appears to contemplate that, side by side with independent industry relying upon free contract between capital and labour, there is to grow up an artificial system of industry in which labour is to claim as its right that work is to be executed at the public cost, not because it is wanted or will be remunerative, but as an excuse for paying wages, and the ratepayer or the taxpayer is bound to supply the capital. If the proposal is to work at all it can only be by the artificial system in which labour claims the right to fix the bargain, ousting the independent system of contract, i.e. by the local authority or the State becoming the sole employer of labour.

24d   Report of the Select Committee on Home Work

Cmnd. 246, 1908.

... if 'sweating' is understood to mean that work is paid for at a rate which, in the conditions under which many of the workers do it, yields to them an income which is quite insufficient to enable an adult person to obtain anything like proper food, clothing, and house accommodation, there is no doubt that sweating does prevail extensively. We have had quite sufficient evidence to convince us (indeed it is almost common knowledge) that the earnings of a large number of people—mainly women who work in their homes—are so small as alone to be insufficient to sustain life in the most meagre manner, even when they toil hard for extremely long hours. The consequence is that, when those earnings are their sole source of income, the conditions under which they live are often not only crowded and insanitary, but altogether pitiable and distressing....

Summary of Conclusions

1. That there should be legislation with regard to rates of payment made to Home Workers who are employed in the production or preparation of articles for sale by other workers.

2. That such legislation should at first be tentative and experimental, and be limited in its scope to Home Workers engaged in the tailoring, shirtmaking, underclothing, and baby linen trades, and in the finishing processes of machine-made lace. The Home Secretary should be empowered, after inquiry made, to establish Wages Boards for any other trades.

3. That Wages Boards should be established in selected trades to fix minimum time and piece rates of payment for Home Workers in those trades.

4. That it should be made an offence to pay or offer lower rates of payment, to Home Workers in those trades than the minimum rates which had been fixed for that district by the Wages Board.

24e Opposition to legislation on sweating

'The Sweated Industries Bill', *Spectator*, 29 February 1908.

If a minimum wage is fixed it is certain that a great many people now employed at less than that wage will be thrown out of employment,and thus we shall add to the unemployed, many of whom notoriously are willing to work, but whom the State will not allow to work at the wages at which work can be obtained by them....

In these days he who suggests freedom as a remedy for a social evil must expect to be treated with hatred, ridicule, and contempt, and held up as one who by his nature is half idiot and half tyrant. Nevertheless we venture to say that by an application of the principle of free contract, and by such application alone, will a radical remedy be found for the evils of sweating. Restriction can do no permanent good, partly because it is bound to limit production—and increased production is the only means by which high wages can be obtained—and partly because it is bound to carry with it that State aid which throws more burdens upon the people, and brings more and more of the industrious poor across the line that separates them from the pauper class. If the State forbids a man to take less than a certain wage, and he cannot get that wage, the State has to support him. But the State is, after all, only the working men with an ornamental fringe of capitalists at the top. Therefore what the State is really doing is decreasing the production of the things men desire, with the hope that thereby it will be able to give them more of those things.

24f   Unemployment a necessary concomitant of industrial organization

William Beveridge, *Unemployment, A Problem of Industry* (1930 ed.), pp. 193,235–7.

Unemployment is a question not of the scale of industry, but of its organisation, not of the volume of the demand for labour but of its changes and fluctuations. The changes are of several types; trades decay or are revolutionised by new machines. Through these changes particular parts of the labour supply get displaced. Unemployment arises through their difficulty in getting re-absorbed. The fluctuations, also, are of several types: some co-extensive with the economic life of the nation; some peculiar to certain trades; some purely local or individual. To meet these fluctuations—cyclical, seasonal and casual—there are required reserves of labour power. Unemployment arises as the idleness of these reserves between the epochs when they are called into action. The solution of the problem of unemployment must consist, therefore, partly in smoothing industrial transitions, partly in diminishing the extent of the reserves required for fluctuation or their intervals of idleness, partly, when this plan can go no further, in seeing that the men of the reserve are properly maintained both in action and out of it. The problem is essentially one of business organisation, of meeting without distress the changes and fluctuations without which industry is not and probably could not be carried on. It is not a problem of increasing the mere scale of industry. It is not a problem of securing a general balance between the growth of the demand for labour and the growth of the supply—for this general balance is already secured by economic forces—but one of perfecting the adjustment in detail....

Unemployment is not to be identified as a problem of general over-population. There is no reason for thinking that the industrial system has lost permanently anything of its former power to absorb the growing supply of labour....

Unemployment arises because, while the supply of labour grows steadily, the demand for labour, in growing, varies incessantly in volume, distribution and character. This variation ... flows directly from the control of production by many competing employers. It is obvious that, so long as the industrial world is split up into separate groups of producers—each group with a life of its own, and growing or decaying in ceaseless attrition upon its neighbours—there must be insecurity of employment. It is probable that at least one of the most striking specific factors in the problem—namely, cyclical fluctuation of trade—may be traced ultimately to the same source. Unemployment, in other words, is to some extent at least part of the price of industrial competition—part of the waste without which there could be no competition at all. Socialistic criticism of the existing order has therefore on this side much justification. The theoretic reply to that criticism must take the form, not of a denial, but of a gloss—that there may be worse things in a community than unemployment. The practical reply is to be found in reducing the pain of unemployment to relative insignificance. In this there seems to be no impossibility. If the solution of the problem of unemployment means that every man should have the certainty of continuous work throughout life in the occupation for which he has been trained, then no solution is to be expected, or, indeed, desired. If, however, by a solution is meant that no man able and willing to work should come to degradation or destitution for want of work, then a solution is not indeed within sight but by no means beyond hope .... The demand for labour cannot be stereotyped save in a stagnant industry. The supply of labour may be made immeasurably more capable of following and waiting for the demand.

24g   Organized labour rejects the operation of labour exchanges

Trades Union Congress Report, 1910, Sheffield, pp. 160–4.

Mr. W. Mosses (Patternmakers) moved:—

That in the opinion of this Congress the Labour Exchanges as at present managed are proving prejudicial to the Trade Union Movement, and in order to safeguard the interests of the organised trades the Parliamentary Committee are hereby instructed to take steps to secure the following regulations for the administration of the Exchanges:

1. That a recognised Trade Union official shall, on making application to the superintendent of any Labour Exchange, be supplied with the name and address also the wages paid by any firm offering employment through the medium of the exchange.

2. That under no circumstances shall applicants for situations be sent outside their own district, unless the superintendent of the exchange is first assured that the firm offering employment recognise the Trade Union rates and conditions of the district.

3. ... under no circumstances shall the divisional superintendent ... of any exchange cause to be exhibited any notice ... from firms who may have a dispute with their workpeople, after such dispute has been officially notified by the Trade Union concerned....

The establishment of these institutions was received with considerable misgiving, and ... those misgivings had been fully justified; for they had been found inimical to the best interests of organised labour .... Every trade organisation that was worth the name had its own Labour Exchange, with special facilities for obtaining situations for its members. So far as his society was concerned, the exchanges had been of no use to them. When they were instituted at the beginning of the year, trade was in a worse condition than had ever been known before. From that time to the present, he had calculated that 1,500 persons, over 25 per cent of their number, had obtained employment, and they had not one specific case of a member of their association having obtained employment through the medium of the Labour Exchange. There had been application for labour, but when they had found out who was asking for patternmakers they had discovered some man on the hunt for cheap labour ... Labour exchanges had done a good deal to increase blacklegging....

J. G. Gordon (Sheet Metal Workers), in seconding said ... that the exchanges were becoming positively harmful. They found that men were being sent about the country, from one end to the other, simply to undercut the rates of the particular districts into which they were sent, and that employers were using Labour Exchanges in order to fill up the positions of the men they had locked out.

For the resolution	1,147,000
Against	272,000
Majority	875,000

24h Minimum wage proposals

Hansard 5th series, vol. xxiv, cols 1881–90, 26 April 1911.

Mr. W. Crooks ... moved 'That the right of every family of the country to an income sufficient to enable it to maintain its members in decency and comfort should be recognised; and this House is therefore of opinion that a general minimum wage of 30s. per week for every adult worker should be established by law....'

All we ask is that a man should be treated as a human being, and not as a piece of machinery, with all the loves, the hopes, and desires which make life worth having. I turn to the Government of the day as an employer of labour and I say you, too, have men, and you have contractors who employ men at wages that are not enough to keep the body and soul of two people together, much less any little children, and I do not wonder at all at the Medical Officer of Health for Tottenham declaring that no person there cares to become a mother. They prefer gramophones to babies....

How many times am I going to tell the story of the little boy going home in the night crying all the way. A doctor said, 'Don't cry, if God sends mouths, he sends bread for children.' The little old man looked up in his face and said, 'I know that as well as you. He sends the bread to your house and the mouths to ours.' Think of that. It is a tragedy, it is not a comedy, that these children in their own houses and at their own tables should hear the sorrows poured out. 'Another mouth, God knows how we are going to fill it.' When they get a little older, sixteen or seventeen, go round to the workhouses and infirmaries, and there you will find an abnormal proportion of young girls and young boys, sons and daughters of poor poverty-stricken parents with 30s. a week. They still have to sacrifice. It is not affluence. It is not a day at the Derby once a week, nor a day in the country once a week. It would be everlasting struggle and toil, but you would be saving the boyhood and girlhood of the nation, and the nation wants them. I say to the Government as an employer, as I say to every other employer and the large companies and contractors in the country, 'You are patriotic. You who believe in the defence of the Empire should remember what was said on the floor of this House half a century ago, "The foundations of the British Empire are in the kitchens of the working people." ' And they are too, as you well know. You have to look for the defence of your Empire down there, and not in the middle-class and upper-class homes. I say nothing against them, only I ask you to keep the foundations safe.

24i   A political solution sought for economic discontents

'The Claim for a Share in Life', *Nation*, 28 September 1912.

In the textile trades of the country the actual earnings of male operatives show 48.3 per cent of them earning less than 25s. per week. Among the laborers in each branch of the building trades the percentage is much higher. The most shameful disclosure in the recent railway trouble has been the fact that nearly 100,000 adult employees are receiving less than a pound a week. Of the whole body of adult railway workers, no less than 60 per cent are upon a wage of less than 25s. Far below this reasonable minimum lie whole clusters of trades, some of them involving considerable skill and arduous effort, notably the work of agriculture....

What is to be done? A few thin, scattered voices from the past repeat the old phrases about liberty of individual contract, which always ignored the substance of liberty. A few others have the cunning to dress up their old individualism in the new finery of eugenics, warning us against the subsidisation of the 'unfit'. But the new conception of social health defies such intellectual atavism, demanding the realisation of a living wage, not as an individual right, but as a social security .... The real issue is between collective bargaining and State action, or some combination of the two .... For most of our labor leaders are primarily trade unionists, and would utilise political machinery as a mere accessory to collective bargaining. The steady refusal of the bulk of the Socialists in this country to consider seriously State compulsory arbitration, or any public interference with the liberty of private war between capital and labor in the several trades, is a curious commentary upon their conception of Socialism. Those who take this view—and Mr. Ramsay MacDonald is amongst them—prefer that the living wage shall be obtained, not by Trades Boards or by State intervention, but by the pressure of the workers, organised in their several trades. But the critical form of this pressure is the strike. Now ... there is no evidence of the practical ability of trade unions, either by pacific bargaining or by the strike, to secure a living wage. In numbers trade unionism has never been so strong, but it has not been able to prevent the considerable fall of real wages in recent years....

The workers say they would prefer to settle their quarrels by 'their own powerful right arm'; they do not trust Governments, who always in the last resort take sides with the employer. But this 'own powerful right arm' is seen to be powerless to secure the needed rise of wages .... Why, then, not set themselves to make a Government and a State which they can trust, and which will not 'take sides with the employer'? ... It is idle to say that Governments ought not to and will not interfere in the great conflicts of capital and labor in the future. The public right to industrial peace must be made to overrule the license [sic] of private war. The only really feasible course is to see that this public policy is made consistent with their interests.

Index